Doing Theology in Pandemics

Doing Theology in Pandemics

Facing Viruses, Violence, and Vitriol

Edited by
ZACHARY MOON

Foreword by
Pamela R. Lightsey

☙PICKWICK *Publications* • Eugene, Oregon

DOING THEOLOGY IN PANDEMICS
Facing Viruses, Violence, and Vitriol

Pickwick Publications
An Imprint of Wipf and Stock Publishers
199 W. 8th Ave., Suite 3
Eugene, OR 97401

www.wipfandstock.com

PAPERBACK ISBN: 978-1-6667-0988-9
HARDCOVER ISBN: 978-1-6667-0989-6
EBOOK ISBN: 978-1-6667-0990-2

Cataloguing-in-Publication data:

Names: Moon, Zachary, editor. | Lightsey, Pamela R., foreword

Title: Doing theology in pandemics : facing viruses, violence, and vitriol / edited
by Zachary Moon ; with a foreword by Pamela R. Lightsey.

Description: Eugene, OR : Pickwick Publications, 2022 | Includes bibliographi-
cal references.

Identifiers: ISBN 978-1-6667-0988-9 (paperback) | ISBN 978-1-6667-0989-6
(hardcover) | ISBN 978-1-6667-0990-2 (ebook)

Subjects: LCSH: Diseases—Religious aspects—Christianity. | COVID-19 (Dis-
ease)—Religious aspects—Christianity.

Classification: BV4335 .D62 2022 (print) | BV4335 .D62 (ebook)

03/17/22

For those doing good theology where there is pain

And you have not allowed me to languish alone, but you have lighted the path toward beloved community with the loving witness of the ancestors, elders, and sojourners who have come before me and who stand with me today.

—Dr. Chanequa Walker-Barnes

Contents

Contributors

Dr. Rita Nakashima Brock, PhD, is Senior Vice President and Director of the Shay Moral Injury Center at Volunteers of America. She leads the organization's efforts to deepen understanding about moral injury in the many populations who experience it. Dr. Brock was the Founding Director of the Soul Repair Center at Brite Divinity School, Texas Christian University, where she also was a Research Professor of Theology and Culture. She is co-author of *Soul Repair: Recovering from Moral Injury after War,* Beacon Press, 2012, and *Proverbs of Ashes: Violence, Redemptive Suffering and the Search for What Saves Us,* Beacon Press, 2001.

Rev. Dr. Danielle J. Buhuro, DMin, an ordained clergymember of the United Church of Christ, currently serves as CPE Supervisor at three hospitals in Chicago. As an African American same-gender-loving person, Danielle Buhuro is committed to activism in the areas of race, gender and sexuality. She is currently a Ph.D student at Chicago Theological Seminary where her dissertation focus is social media violence specifically against Black heterosexual women, Black transgender women and Black Muslim women. Danielle Buhuro is the author of two books: *Spiritual Care In An Age of #BlackLivesMatter: Examining the Spiritual and Prophetic Needs of African Americans in* *a Violent America*; and *Is There a Heaven for a "G"?: A Pastoral Care Approach to Gang Violence.*

Rev. Dr. Carrie Doehring, PhD, is a licensed psychologist, a psychotherapist member of the Association of Clinical Pastoral Education, and the Clifford Baldridge Professor of Pastoral Care and Counseling at Iliff School of Theology, where she directs the Master of Arts in Pastoral and Spiritual Care. She is the author of 38 chapters and articles, and three books, including *The Practice of Pastoral Care: A Postmodern Approach.* She recently co-edited the 2019 book *Military Moral Injury and Spiritual Care: A Resource for Religious Leaders and Professional Caregivers.*

Rev. Dr. Danjuma Gibson, PhD, is a professor of pastoral care at Calvin Theological Seminary, and is in private practice as a psychotherapist in Grand Rapids, MI. His most recent book—*Frederick Douglass, A Psychobiography: Rethinking Subjectivity in the Western Experiment of Democracy (2018)*—is an investigation into the formation of Douglass' psychological and religious identity in the context of trauma and the American slavocracy. In addition to psychological trauma, Dr. Gibson's current research includes exploring the intersection of black religious experience and psychoanalytic discourse, and the impact of macroeconomics and microeconomics on urban faith communities.

Rev. Dr. Gabriella Lettini, PhD, is Academic Dean, CAO, and A.H. Reinhardt Professor of Theological Ethics at Starr King School for the Ministry in Berkeley, CA. A native of Torino, Italy, Lettini is an ordained minister of the Waldensian Church. Lettini studied theology at the Facoltà Valdese di Teologia in Rome and received her Ph.D. at Union Theological Seminary in New York. Lettini is the author of *"Omosessualità"* (2000), the co-editor of the Italian version of the *Dictionary of Feminist Theologies* (2010), and co-authored *Soul Repair: Recovering from Moral Injury After War* (2012). As a member of INTERFILM, Lettini was on the Ecumenical Jury at the Cannes, Locarno, Berlin, and Montreal film festivals.

Rev. Dr. Pamela R. Lightsey, PhD, serves as the Vice President of Academic and Student Affairs and Associate Professor of Constructive Theology at Meadville Lombard Theological School. She is the author of numerous publications including the book, *Our Lives Matter: A Womanist Queer Theology* (Wipf and Stock, 2015).

Rabbi Dr. Rachel S. Mikva, PhD, serves as the Herman E. Schaalman Professor in Jewish Studies and Senior Faculty Fellow of the Inter-Religious Institute at Chicago Theological Seminary. The Institute and the Seminary work at the cutting edge of theological education, training religious leaders who can build bridges across cultural and religious difference for the critical work of social transformation. With a passion for justice and academic expertise in the history of scriptural interpretation, Rabbi Mikva's courses and publications address a range of Jewish and comparative studies, with a special interest in the intersections of sacred texts, culture and ethics.

Shelly Rambo, PhD, is Associate Professor of Theology at Boston University School of Theology. Her research and teaching interests focus on religious responses to suffering, trauma, and violence. Her work in providing theological responses to trauma has led to rich partnerships with military, health-care, and higher-education chaplains. She is author of *Spirit and Trauma: A Theology of Remaining* (Westminster John Knox, 2010), *Resurrecting Wounds: Living in the Afterlife of Trauma* (Baylor University Press, 2017), and a co-edited volume with Stephanie Arel, *Post-Traumatic Public Theology* (Palgrave Mac-Millan, 2016).

Christina Amalia Repoley serves as the Senior Director of Experience Design at the Forum for Theological Exploration. Her team works to make spaces for discernment, connection, resourcing, and community building amongst various FTE constituencies including young adults, campus ministries, high school youth theology institutes, denominational organizations, intentional communities and faith-rooted volunteer service organizations. Prior to joining FTE, Christina founded Quaker Voluntary Service and served as its Executive Director for seven years. Before that she served as Peacebuilding Director for the Southeast region of the American Friends Service Committee. She holds an MDiv from Emory University's Candler School of Theology and a BA from Guilford College.

Dr. Patrick B. Reyes, PhD, is the award-winning Chicano author of *The Purpose Gap*, and *Nobody Cries When We Die*. An educator, administrator, and institutional strategist, he is the Senior Director of Learning Design at the Forum for Theological Exploration. He is president-elect of the Religious Education Association and serves on several boards in education and the non-profit sector supporting the next generation of BIPOC leaders and educators. Patrick holds a Doctorate and Master of Arts from Claremont School of Theology, a Master of Divinity from Boston University School of Theology, and is proud to be a graduate of the California State education system, California State University at Sacramento (Sac State). You can learn more about Patrick at patrickbreyes.com.

Rev. Dr. Cody J. Sanders, PhD, is pastor to Old Cambridge Baptist Church in Cambridge, MA, where he also serves as American Baptist Chaplain to Harvard University and Advisor for LGBTQ+ Affairs in the Office of Religious, Spiritual, & Ethical Life at MIT. He is the author, co-author, and editor of several books, including, *A Brief Guide to Ministry with LGBTQIA Youth*, and *Christianity, LGBTQ Suicide, and the Souls of Queer Folk*.

Rev. Dr. Zachary Moon, PhD, is Associate Professor of Theology and Psychology at Chicago Theological Seminary. He has published widely including three books, *Coming Home: Ministry That Matters with Veterans and Military Families* (Chalice Press, 2015), *Warriors between Worlds: Moral Injury and Identities in Crisis* (Lexington Books, 2019), and *Goatwalking: A Quaker Pastoral Theology* (Brill, 2021).

Foreword

Pamela R. Lightsey

Friday, March 13, 2020, I left my office not realizing it would be my last full week of working in that building. Prior to that day, citizens of the United States were frequently assured that the virus known as COVID-19 would disappear. "We're prepared, and we're doing a great job with it. And it will go away. Just stay calm. It will go away." said, then-President Donald Trump.[1] Nearly two years since that remark, the pandemic had not just miraculously gone away nor was the nation calm. By March 13, 2021 over 500,000 persons, in this country alone, had died of the virus and we are currently anticipating that we will reach over one million in 2022. Businesses, schools, entertainment, and so much of life had turned to virtual platforms to continue operating.

The contributors of *Doing Theology in Pandemics: Facing Viruses, Violence, and Vitriol* edited by Rev. Dr. Zachary Moon, recognized—like so many others—that life in the midst of COVID-19 affected humanity in stunningly unforeseeable ways. This would not just go away, and it

1. CNN quote of Presidential remarks made during a meeting with Republican senators. Accessed at https://www.cnn.com/interactive/2020/10/politics/covid-disappearing-trump-comment-tracker/?fbclid=IwAR3B-EaEoc1kwRyW_W8SMHg3JMg-KxDZJSN88LKXLQnROSioYYIURLnGKt8o.

would linger alongside what seems like a repetitive traumatic cycle of mass shootings, white supremacist domestic terrorist behavior and the reemergence of Jim Crow voter suppression public policy making. The authors reflect on these urgent issues reminding the reader of these painful moments in human history. They share their own personal experiences, theological reflections, spiritual and healing practices to help the reader not only remember but also commit to a better future, a better post-pandemic life.

Perhaps what they do best is identify what is meant by *pandemic*. They speak about pandemic from their perspectives as theologians. This book makes clear that a pandemic is a kind of apocalypse—a revealing. One of the authors, Rita Nakashima Brock states that during an apocalypse a "curtain is pulled back on truths that had been denied or hidden by a veneer of things seeming ok" such that the revealing "makes our core institutions suspect."[2]

Having etched out the several pandemics occurring across the nation and the world, the authors guide the reader through the life and death of it all: mourning as a response to trauma in life, mourning as resistance, mourning the loss of lives. What is revealed is the tragedy of structural and individual racism that motivates the killing of one life by the hands of another life, itself already dying inwardly to the true joy of what it means to live and love. The authors motivate the reader to feel life in this time of revealing and uncertainty. They remind the reader to connect with community and the importance of that connection with others in order to be effective in leadership. Their work reminds the reader that even a beloved national theme park like Disney World can become complicit in keeping the country's core beliefs, no matter how detrimental those beliefs may be to a good portion of its citizens. Shelly Rambo leads the reader in the initial portion of her work to consider this reopening as indicative of the nation "keeping its fundamental stories intact, even when the characters in the plot do not reflect their surrounding."[3] She like other authors do the hard work of helping the reader to reflect—even the slow and difficult theological reflection—about traumatized bodies such as Black bodies like George Floyd's.

2. Brock, "Covid-19 and George Floyd: Implications for How We Understand Moral Suffering and Human Nature" YouTube presentation. Accessed at https://www.youtube.com/watch?v=z6D369_esok.

3. Rambo, "Traumatized Bodies and the Slow Work of Theology." Accessed at https://www.youtube.com/watch?v=nZu27kyvTWI.

Pandemics are hard. They are painful. I understand this pain as a Black queer lesbian woman. An entire year in quarantine because my family and love live in different areas of the world. The virus called Covid-19 prevented our gathering. The pandemic of racism against Black bodies on top of the danger of the virus. The cruelty of white supremacist behavior. Murder and torture. The murders of Breonna Taylor and George Floyd. The shooting of Jacob Blake multiple times in the back. Anjanette Young handcuffed and forced to stand naked for nearly an hour until police realize they raided the wrong home. The bigotry of Republican leaders (especially Donald Trump) naming the virus after China and the subsequent rise in attacks against Asian Americans.

How do we do theology as scholars and people of faith when we are subjected to so much pain, as a people and as a nation? *Doing Theology in Pandemics* points to the many pandemics in our society. It helps us recognize the intense malaise that has been so difficult to properly describe. At the same time this work sets before us spiritual practices for healing and self-care. When we are released by the ingenuity of science from Covid-19 the other pandemics will remain. As alluded to in the title of this book, we must face them in order to eradicate them. Theology at its best is always seeking, always clarifying, always facing uninterrogated and even absurd perspectives. Pandemics make that work harder but not impossible. The work continues, as it must.

Introduction

Zachary Moon

How will we remember this time? How will this time impact our lives? Theologians, over generations, have wrestled with the conditions of their times. Substantial historical events, including the Holocaust, the invention of atomic weapons, and the Civil Rights Movement and anti-colonial liberation movements across the globe deeply shaped the theological work of theologians in the Twentieth century. In the first quarter of the Twenty-first century, what demands theological attention? Mass shootings? White supremacist nationalism? Racialized violence by police? The unfolding historical chapter that will be noted for the global pandemic, Covid-19, which in and of itself surfaced a complex matrix of political, social, and economic realities, was further complicated by national governmental leaders who fed toxic misinformation and salacious rumor to a population already overwhelmed by crisis.

Recognizing how trauma impacts our lives is a portal to understanding the experiences of the pandemic. Trauma changes the way you think, cope, behave, and believe. Trauma changes your boundaries in relationships, your perspective on power and agency, and your capability to manage and navigate social spaces. Trauma generates many emotions—sadness, fear, guilt, anger, embarrassment, shame, disgust, weariness—so much so that it's hard to name and claim what the experience is because it expresses in some many different ways. Trauma haunts, thirsty for attention and resistant to engagement all at once. There are no quick fixes or magic bullets.

Trauma recovery is slow work predicated on courage, persistence, and compassion. While some reflection can be done in solitude, much of this work needs the response, care, and accountability of community. There is not a single story of this pandemic, so we need spaces and places to ventilate the rough telling of stories as they need hearing. There is so much that has changed and been lost during this time, so we need space and places to grieve, to ritualize our remembrances and our lamentations. There is so much that demands our attention: fissures in the fabric of a collective common good, systems of government, policing, and education that defy public accountability and necessary transformation, barriers to needed access to healthcare, economic relief, and equal rights. Therefore, we must continue to be dissatisfied with the status quo, continue to be impatient in the face of placations, and continue to be tenacious when confronted with injustice of any kind.

For many of us, our professional and vocational energies and labors were constricted during this time. Many usual habits and familiar patterns were interrupted. But scholars and educators are needed in such times as these. These voices need to contribute substance and stability into the turbulent public discourses that cooler, and more considerate, heads may prevail in the storm. This volume raises some of those voices.

This volume is a compilation of theological leading voices, of different academic disciplines, but of common commitment to addressing and resourcing the urgent issues raised by and during the COVID-19 pandemic.

Rita Nakashima Brock, Senior Vice President and Director of the Shay Moral Injury Center at Volunteers of America, unpacks the intersections of the pandemic and police violence, and how moral injury can be a helpful concept in understanding the suffering generated by these intersecting traumas.

Danjuma Gibson, Professor of Pastoral Care at Calvin Theological Seminary, engages the intersections of public health and ongoing sociopolitical unrest as a matter of cultural trauma that cannot be addressed with clinical mental health models. Instead it requires community investment involving truth-telling and re-storying historical and current narratives that promote and embody recovery and healing, emotional and spiritual flourishing, and the reclaiming of identity.

Danielle Buhuro, an author, teacher, and Clinical Pastoral Education supervisor, recognizes the significance of fear in the interrelated traumas of the pandemic and racialized violence targeting African Americans. Colonial theologies and uses of social media respectively constrict healthy attention and the support of reasonable fear, grief, and anger, and Buhuro articulates spiritual care strategies that can ethically and effectively engage the S.E.L.F., social needs, emotional needs, life meaning and purpose needs, and faith needs of those suffering.

Cody Sanders, pastor of Old Cambridge Baptist Church and campus minister at Harvard and MIT, also attends to the embodied emotional experiences of the pandemic crisis—fear, anger, sadness—and envisions support through transimmanent emotions—wonder, gratitude, and grief—which serve to both transcend and ground human experience during apocalyptic circumstances.

Shelly Rambo, Associate Professor of Theology at Boston University School of Theology, explores collective trauma and meaning making, and the spiritual guidance of Julian of Norwich, Simon Weil, and Howard Thurman to resource an understanding of realignment of internal and external meaning as a pathway for surfacing underlying truths and untruths.

Gabriella Lettini, Academic Dean and Professor of Theological Ethics at Starr King School for the Ministry, reflects on the language used to describe the theological and ethical significance of the pandemic, with particular attention to healthcare workers and international contextual dimensions including the experience of those in Italy and pejorative use of "Chinese-virus."

Rachel Mikva, Professor of Jewish Studies at Chicago Theological Seminary, reflects on the Jewish scriptures of Lamentations, Ruth, and Job as sources of wisdom, sustenance, and inspiration to strengthened resilience during the COVID-19 pandemic and beyond.

Patrick Reyes and Christina Repoley, senior directors at the Forum for Theological Exploration, articulate the challenges to effective leadership during crisis, the task of stepping into moment and knowing what time it is; and how models of shared leadership prove sustainable and life giving during even the most difficult of circumstances.

Carrie Doehring, Professor of Pastoral Care and Counseling at Iliff School of Theology, describes centering practices that address moral stress, clarify values, and enhance spiritual integration.

This volume was made possible through the generosity of the Henry Luce Foundation and the commitment of Chicago Theological Seminary to strengthen the efforts in the public square. Brian Smith, Lisa Zook, and Shea Watts provided necessary pieces to bring this volume to life. The contributors, including Dr. Pamela Lightsey, who wrote the Foreword, gave generously of their time and wisdom, recognizing the urgency and opportunity to engage in publicly significant scholarly work during this time. It has been a privilege to curate these resources for the many communities who will benefit from their insight and encouragement.

1

The Pandemic Paradox

George Floyd, Moral Injury, and the
Sustainability of Social Movements

Rita Nakashima Brock

After months of devastating pandemic news, George Floyd was murdered on May 25, 2020, by police officers in Minneapolis, Minnesota. Witnesses at the scene expressed disbelief, dismay, shock, outrage, horror, and grief, and several tried to save him. There had been many, many more police killings of black men, women, and children before, often with video documentation. Why then, was there such a massive global response to this particular killing?

One reason, I suggest, was the global pandemic itself, which created the conditions for an apocalypse, an unveiling of moral truth in the midst of the collapse of powerful malevolent systems. US media coverage had maintained a steady stream of distressing news about the deep public divide on following guidelines to contain the virus as infection rates climbed, a division sown by an incompetent president supported by White supremacists. Media stories began to use the term "systemic racism" as death rates in Black, Indigenous, Pacific Islander, and Latinx populations rose faster and higher than in White populations.[1] Reports

---

1. APM Research Lab Staff, "The Color of Coronavirus: COVID-19 Deaths by Race and Ethnicity in the U.S."

also began to correlate the president's use of the term "China Virus" with a rise in hate crimes against Asian Americans.[2] By the end of May, racism had already become a major, pandemic-related news story.

During our first one hundred days of solitude, there were no palliative "bread and circuses"[3] to distract a distraught public. Without the collective amusements of live sports events or theater performances, movie premieres or festivals, dinner parties, and holiday celebrations, our one shared experience in real time was pandemic news. The video of the murder of George Floyd buried news of COVID-19 as, in our confinement, his excruciating death unfolded before our collective, unnerved eyes. In the United States, it became the most viewed news story in June, by far, despite both the plague and the crucial political primary season.[4]

The world was able to watch the agony of a nine-minute murder in its entirety because, unlike panic or pursuit shootings with jerky, blurry images and muffled sounds, there was no moment when news reports stopped or blurred the video to avoid showing the graphic taking of a human life. The killing unfolded in real time, as three policemen crushed the air from Mr. Floyd's body and the main killer "took a knee" on his neck—I believe as a deliberate mockery of athletes' protests against police killings of Black lives.[5] As Floyd's murderer proceeded implacably, we became witnesses who shared the anguish of the bystanders desperately trying to save him until he took his last breath.

#BlackLivesMatter protests erupted on all seven continents—in the midst of a global pandemic.[6] In many countries and US cities, protesters included lists of names of people who had been killed by police, and conversations about racism and police violence happened in places where it had never been discussed before.[7] On June 6, hundreds of surfers, a sport not usually associated with social justice movements, held a memorial "Paddle Out" ritual for Mr. Floyd and other Black victims, organized by Black Girls Surf in Santa Monica, California. It took place on a segregated beach that, despite desegregation in 1927, was used by Black surfers for many subsequent decades as the only safe beach. Paddle Outs were also

2. Donaghue, "2,120 hate incidents," and Zhang et al., "Hate Crimes."

3. *Merriam-Webster.com Dictionary*, s.v. "bread and circuses."

4. Berkman, "The Impact of George Floyd's Death."

5. Woodward and Mindock, "Taking a Knee: Why Are NFL Players Protesting and When Did They Start to Kneel?"

6. Mosely, "Mapping Black Lives Matter."

7. Burch et al., "How Black Lives Matter Reached Every Corner of America."

held at many US beaches, in the waters of the Pacific Islands, and along the shores of four-continents.[8]

The US protests were unprecedented. Racism in policing became impossible to deny to the point that some White people, who had never joined a protest before, were shocked enough to organize Black Lives Matter protests. Protests erupted in 40% of all counties and in all fifty states, as well as in five US-occupied territories—even in towns and suburbs that had few, if any, Black residents. Black Lives Matter signs appeared in front of White places of worship, businesses, and people's homes. Eight to ten percent of the population participated in one or more protests, and 93% of them were nonviolent.[9] Demonstrations lasted nearly the entire month of June as the anti-racism protests expanded in focus. Confederate monuments began to be contested and removed; previously published books on racism topped best seller lists; and momentum gathered to declare Juneteenth a national holiday.[10]

According to one social scientist, about three and a half percent of a country's population is required for a nonviolent movement to cause a revolution or change in government, and nonviolent movements are the most effective at making such change.[11] Emerging after the killing of Trayvon Martin, #BlackLivesMatter has become the largest mass movement in US history. As a nonviolent, Black-initiated, anti-racism movement, it is decentralized, attentive to intersectional issues, and has three women founders, of whom two are queer.[12] It is also the most diverse in race, national origin, ethnicity, age, and gender identity.[13] While historically, social change in the US has been accomplished by a small minority of activists, one hopeful sign for political and social change emerging from the current pandemic apocalypse is its sheer size. Public engagement far exceeded the three and a half percent threshold at its height.

George Floyd's murder also resonated with the Christian passion story, which is one reason it touched some people deeply enough to send them outdoors to risk their lives during a plague. Like the crucifixion of Jesus, witnesses, many of them female, watched a man die a slow,

8. Associated Press, "Surfers Honor George Floyd."

9. Chenoweth and Pressman, "This Summer's Black Lives Matter Protests."

10. Aratani, "Calls to Make Juneteenth."

11. Robson, "The 3.5% Rule," and Salzman, "From the Start."

12. Black Lives Matter, "Herstory."

13. Buchanan et al. "Black Lives Matter May Be the Largest Movement."

excruciating death at the hands of official agents of the state. As the spirit was cruelly crushed from his body, he commended his spirit into his deceased mother's hands. His recorded last words were: "I can't breathe" and "mama," which motivated White suburban women in Portland, Oregon, to create a "wall of moms" to stand between the protesters and police forces in several US cities. The group was later disbanded due to its failures to work with Black women, but in its short life, it was another sign of the awakening in White America to the long history of official violence conducted with impunity, to systemic racism, and to White privilege.[14]

The moral outrage that erupted in June 2020 was global, massive, and heartening, as people with privilege awoke to systemic racism and joined the ranks of Black Lives Matter. Moral fury is unsustainable, however, as the energy for a social movement; it can fade quickly or it can deepen into moral injury. The term moral injury was first used in 1994 to describe the demoralization of combat veterans who were betrayed by authorities in power who violated what was right in high stakes situations.[15]

In April 2020, media reports had begun to discuss moral injury in healthcare, using an expanded definition from 2009 that included the collapse of our identity and faith or meaning system because of harm that we cause by our own actions, harm that we witness or fail to stop, or harm that is inflicted on us because people in authority fail to do the right thing.[16] The chaotic working conditions for healthcare staff resembled battlefield medicine, with mass casualties and a mysterious and lethal enemy. Patients often had to die alone as doctors triaged the severest cases to determine who would be left to die, and staff struggled to save others while inadequately equipped with ventilators and personal protective equipment. Improvised morgues had to be created to handle corpses that were biohazards. Beloved co-workers succumbed to the virus, which escalated staff shortages, and many national leaders denied the severity of the pandemic, putting frontline workers and their families at greater risk of infections because they cut programs for dealing with a pandemic and failed to assure access to necessary supplies and equipment.

The most devastating impact of moral injury in frontline workers was first reported at the end of April, when two essential workers in the poorest, hardest hit areas of New York City killed themselves two

14. Blaec, "The Complicated Rise."
15. Shay, *Achilles in Vietnam.*
16. Litz et al. "Moral Injury and Moral Repair."

days apart.[17] The first, the young son of a retired policeman, was a Fire Department emergency medical technician who had started his job as the pandemic began; three months into a job he had loved, he became disheartened, took his father's gun to the river, and shot himself. The second was a mid-career, successful emergency room doctor who survived COVID, returned to an overwhelmed ER, grew despondent, was admitted by her supervisor for a week of psychiatric observation, went home to her family to recover, and took her own life, just as she seemed to be recovering. Empathetic, high-achieving, idealistic, service-oriented people are especially vulnerable to moral injury because they set high standards for themselves and others. When chaos strikes and they cannot see how to do the right thing or doing the right thing is no longer possible, they can be devastated by relentless failure. Our self-understanding and trust in others, our closest relationships, and our faith or meaning systems sustain moral emotions such as love, joy, hope, and compassion, which is why moral injury is so devastating.

Moral injury is marked by a change in character that results from persons or groups being unable to justify, process, and integrate experiences of harm into stable identities and a meaning system that sustains relationships and supports human flourishing. People often cope with it by trying to avoid the excruciating pain of a life unmoored from meaning or purpose. They work beyond exhaustion or leave their careers; use drugs or alcohol to anesthetize their pain; stew in corrosive cynicism or toxic anger and wreck their most important relationships; sink into unrelieved grief and depression; or take their own lives.

Media reports about moral injury often confuse it with post-traumatic stress disorder (PTSD). It is possible, of course, to have both at the same time, but they are distinct. While PTSD involves intense fear emotions that linger from a terrorizing experience, moral injury results instead from a demoralizing experience that challenges our belief in our own goodness and our trust in others. Moral emotions such as outrage, sorrow, shame, guilt, remorse, and despair are conscience-based, not fear-based. Unaddressed moral injury can interfere with treatments for PTSD, while some PTSD treatments, such as exposure therapy, can intensify moral injury. In addition, betrayal has been found to correlate to high rates of PTSD.[18]

17. Weiss, "Two New York City Health Care Workers."

18. Harris et al. "Spiritually Integrated Care for PTSD," and Jordan, et al. "Distinguishing War-related PTSD."

Moral injury is the response of our moral conscience to catastrophic harm when it becomes ungrounded from our pre-catastrophe identities. A return to an earlier meaning system is not possible because new truths about our lives and our world have been revealed and cannot be forgotten. The COVID-19 pandemic, which inflicted death in numbers not seen since the Civil War,[19] and the murder of George Floyd, seen by perhaps a billion people, unveiled devastating truths about state and national government institutions that once could have been masked, ignored, or denied by communities unaffected by those truths. They present us collectively with the question of how we will use this time of unveiling, this moment—the very definition of an apocalypse—as a chance to transform injustice, violence, oppression, and environmental destruction into a just and sustainable society.

Clinicians who study moral injury, such as William Nash and Brett Litz, make the claim that we are born moral. Moral suffering is part of being human, not a mental health disorder or problem. Their claim, which both challenges Christian ideas of original sin and habits of thought that demonize our enemies as evil, is based in knowledge of our brains which are full of nerve cells linked to our entire bodies. Basic physical survival—breathing, digestion, blood circulation, movement, and pain perception—are our most formed skills at birth, but to become a self-conscious human being requires training in love throughout our lives.

Relationships train our bodies to repeat habits through nervous system pathways, solidifying interstitial nerve fibers that transmit brain signals. We become conscious beings related to ourselves and our world, first through essential bodily awareness such as hunger and pain and physical and emotional feelings such as comforting touch; then through habituated, automatic behaviors such as crawling or walking; and finally through our capacities to intuit patterns, learn language, imagine, create, and think, capacities we use to articulate meaning and our core moral foundations. We relate to the world beyond our personal relationships via religion or a philosophy of life, using language and imagination to connect us to transcendent forces through and beyond our sensory perceptions. When Adverse Childhood Experiences (ACE) of abuse, neglect, loss, and difficult household situations such as alcoholism, oppression,

19. Humpreys, *Marrow of Tragedy.*

and poverty, impair this process, the consequences negatively affect mental and physical health and life expectancy.[20]

Relationships are always imperfect, but when they have enough love, we develop a meaning system implanted in our flesh and construct a complex moral identity that has been tested and integrated into an interstitial, relational self. Our habitual behaviors are usually so automatic we rarely think about them, but they are the primary moral ways we relate to other human beings. We only think about what to do or say when habits fail us or when an unusual experience disrupts our behaviors.

The pandemic required us to attend consciously to routine habits we rarely consider as having moral implications. When our ordinary handshakes, hugs, and kisses became life threatening, we were made aware of how much they meant to us because we had to go without them. We got used to wearing masks in public to protect ourselves and others. Such new pandemic habits, however, grew intensely contested and divided people morally, even in families. In opposition to the advice of epidemiologists, the President and his allies ridiculed the measures needed to control the pandemic, encouraged mass gatherings without wearing masks, and repeatedly referred to COVID-19 as the "China" virus. In public spaces, I found myself feeling vaguely suspicious of strangers without masks, not only because of the virus but also because of the rise in anti-Asian hate crimes.

Many still think of ethical behavior as something that reason directs, when we have to think about our moral values because doing the right thing is not obvious. The idea that moral behavior is a conscious choice relates, especially, to hard and fast rules that are, for example, inscribed in a society's customs, commandments, laws, or constitution, and that carry serious penalties for violating them. But in 1982, psychologist Carol Gilligan challenged that limited model by proposing what she called an ethics of care that insisted love and relationship were the basis of being ethical.[21] Philosopher Martha Nussbaum suggested in her 1986 groundbreaking book, *The Fragility of Goodness,*

> Circumstances may force me to a position in which I cannot
> help being false to something or doing something wrong; that
> an event that simply happens to me may, without my consent,
> alter my life; that it is equally problematic to entrust one's good

20. Wade, Roy Jr. et al. "Development and Evaluation."
21. Gilligan, "Carefully Smash the Patriarchy."

> to friends, lovers, or country and to try to have a good life with-
> out them—all these I take to be not just the material of tragedy,
> but everyday facts of practical wisdom.

Nussbaum observes, "It's a form of human love to accept our complicated, messy humanity and not run away from it."[22] In effect, this means we
experience moral values in our flesh and our relationships, and the values
we enact involve both thinking and feeling. Our need to be moral makes
us vulnerable to emotional and physical suffering, which is a testimony to
the moral emotions as embodied phenomena.

Moral identity is continually reinforced by rituals, which are habits
attached to the intentional performance of explicit values. Without them,
meaning systems fade in significance. Rituals do their work in liminal
spaces separated from quotidian, habitual activities. The spaces are either constructed or discovered and either permanent or provisional, but
they create parameters of "inside" and "outside" that contain the ritual
process. Intention is found in the reciting and enacting of narratives and
poetry, the creating of music and visual art, and the choreographing of
body movements, such that an ordinary gesture can take on meaning that
calls forth the emotional power of the entire ritual.[23] A guided mindfulness meditation ritual can take only five minutes, but it's a ritual with
a beginning, such as a chime and welcome; a middle with instructions,
breathing, and silence; and an end with a return to the group and part-
ing words; it has a transcendent purpose designed to calm the body and
spirit and make consciousness focus on present reality.

Rituals have a flow of emotions that is structured in relation to historic events, diurnal patterns, or lunar and solar cycles, and they can confer significant collective meaning to transitions from one state of identity
to another, such as weddings, births, graduations, military boot camps,
and presidential inaugurations. Rituals can delimit the power of harm
to disrupt moral meaning and give our spirits and imagination a chance
to integrate serious life threats such as unexpected deaths or moral injury. They also give us a chance to admit failure, to handle ambiguity and
conflicting moral feelings, to make ourselves vulnerable and integrate
tragedy, and to enact what we aspire to be as our best moral selves.[24]

---

22. Aviv, "The Philosopher of Feelings."

23. Graybiel, "Habits, Rituals, and the Evaluative Brain."

24. Seligman et al. *Rethinking Pluralism.*

We were bereft of many significant rituals during the pandemic, especially in relation to dying. Frontline care workers experienced moral distress from having to leave people to die alone. Families were distraught at being unable to be with dying relatives and having to forfeit funerals. As corpses presented biohazards and overran morgues and mortuaries, workers put the unclaimed dead in numbered pine coffins and sent them to be swallowed anonymously in vast potter's fields.[25] Most people cannot complete a grieving process without a formal farewell ritual, and many of us remain in a state of unresolved grief, complicated by ongoing moral outrage.

To maintain social movements for greater justice and planetary sustainability, we must address two dimensions of moral injury that will linger well into a post-pandemic time. One is its intergenerational transmission among people already traumatized by generations of suffering. Marianne Hirsh, who studies the literature of children of Holocaust survivors, calls this intergenerational transmission "postmemory." She writes:

> To be dominated by narratives that preceded one's birth or one's consciousness is to risk having one's own stories and experiences displaced, even evacuated, by those of a previous generation. It is to be shaped, however indirectly, by traumatic events that still defy narrative reconstruction and exceed comprehension. These events happened in the past, but their effects continue into the present.[26]

Postmemory sanctifies the suffering of victims and the intergenerational transmission of trauma as a basis for moral meaning. When ancestors have experienced devastations such as genocide, theft of their native land, colonization, war, enslavement, lynching, destitution, internment camps, cultural annihilation, or segregation, their descendants may feel as if their own lives are trivial because they haven't suffered in the same way. In the wake of such suffering and through the intense feelings and moral injuries conveyed in fragments of people's recollections, disjointed memories, or emotionally-fraught silences, their children can seek to make their lives feel significant by taking on the trauma of their parents and grandparents. They may even feel guilty for having better lives than their parents or mistrust the opportunities or successes

25. Hennigan, "Lost in the Pandemic."

26. Hirsch developed the concept from writers who were children of Holocaust survivors. Hirsch, "The Generation of Postmemory," 107.

in their own generation, as if happiness were a betrayal of the past. In taking on the traumas of those they love as their own, they shape their identities based on generations of victimization and suffering. The legacies of Asian, Black, Latinx, and Native American communities, women, LGBTQI folk, and religious minorities of all races have been laced with oppression, as have the legacies of landless, indentured White laborers who were pitched White pride as a palliative for poverty.[27]

Postmemories of these long histories can lead us to experience contemporary events with a heightened sense of hopelessness, futility, fury, sorrow, or cynicism that can defeat collective, intersectional solidarity work for the sake of future generations. To enable past oppressions to be held as memories of survival and resistance, emotional trauma bonds must be processed so that the pain of the past does not re-traumatize and smother present life. In feeling trauma as if we lived it, rather than empathetically remembering past trauma about someone else, we can fail to see that our parents and ancestors were far more than victims of the harms visited upon them, as fallible agents of their own lives, which can teach us about fear, failure, internalized oppressions, survival, resistance, and wisdom. We need historical memories of how our peoples survived terror and pain so that they offer us insight and vision for a better future. Just as "each of us is more than the worst thing we have ever done,"[28] each of us is more than the worst thing that ever happened to us. The struggle for justice, grounded in the fullness of historical memories, makes us alert to contemporary injustices and their traumatizing impact and more determined to struggle for justice, while also freeing us to be present to beauty, equanimity, happiness, and love as healing, sustaining powers in our lives.

The second threat to social transformation is the epidemic of moral injury that will follow the pandemic apocalypse and all the devastating truths it has revealed about centuries of systemic inequality still operating in our current society. Powerful institutions betrayed or failed us: a White supremacist national administration and its Justice Department, the Supreme Court, Congress, and many state governors and legislators; White Christian churches; for-profit healthcare and prisons; an economic system built to protect wealth; and law enforcement that kills with impunity. We may have endured profound loss we cannot take in; we may feel devastating guilt, shame, or remorse for things we did or failed

27. Isenberg, *White Trash*.
28. Stevenson, *Just Mercy*.

to prevent; and we may have been crushed by work, exhausted by caring for children or our parents, or swallowed by deep loneliness.

The habits, rituals, and meaning systems of life have been thrown into considerable chaos. We may even feel unworthy to suffer because, in the queasy, isolated sanctuaries of comfort and consumption we inhabit, we have not directly experienced the losses, hates, risks, losses, and constant fears of minoritized and poor communities and the frontline workers who have kept us safe, delivered news of the world beyond our doors and food for our tables, and cared for the sick and dying. We saw a cruel police murder unfold in excruciating detail, and as we have sought to hold some order and purpose to life, we may have felt our humanity or our confidence in the humanity of others slipping away.

Moral injury is a sign of the excruciating remnant of goodness in us that cannot be destroyed. But moral conscience ungrounded from meaningful relationships can become a destructive force that puts self and others at risk. The catharsis of outraged, collective protest releases euphoria in our bodies as a reward for expressing our inner pain and stress but such uprisings flare en masse and then dissipate after people depart, followed by depression or a need to repeat the addicting cycle of outrage and euphoria. Effective social transformation requires moral fury to be annealed into sustained relationships that support strategic thinking and advocacy.

To address the cumulative postmemories and impending moral injury epidemic of the pandemic and all it has revealed, we will need rituals that make compassionate conversations possible among ordinary people, conversations of mutual respect and trust that encourage emotional risk-taking, empathy, trust, respect, and social responsibility. We will need trauma-informed healers and people with the courage to speak of harrowing experiences with honesty, as well as people who can listen to others with open hearts and quiet minds. In training people who can host such conversations in our communities, we can support each other in processing our moral failures without judgment and honor each other as agents of their own lives, not victims to be helped, people to be diagnosed, or enemies to be demonized.

The COVID-19 apocalypse presents us with a paradox of tragedy and hope—of needing to remember what is impossible to forget. We experienced collective moral injury that upended our habits, our rituals, our national myths and illusions, and our ability to trust each other—a level of national division, death, and crisis not seen since Civil War times. But in the devastating moral truths we cannot unsee, we may have the best possibility in our lifetimes for deep social and political change. The pandemic-propelled uprisings that began in May 2020 offered us a focused starting point for listening and healing as we simultaneously remake society and theologies adequate to honoring the moral truths of what we suffered and challenge attempts to restore the past with palliatives about how "we are better than this."

Moral injury is the evidence that the worst harms that human beings can inflict on others is grounded in a fierce war between in-born conscience and trauma, a war driven by insult, violence, fear, frustration, humiliation, failure, and collective fury and hate. The war can be turned outward toward others or end in suicide. Integrating moral injury as a source of theological insight and wisdom can help us construct meaning systems adequate to embrace what we have done and suffered and enable us to live in an interstitial way that reknits our relationships to each other and our world for the flourishing of life. We can discover and create new habits, rituals, and meaning with each other to support spiritual, interstitial identities that can handle ambiguity while sustaining momentum for change through the disappointments and failures that will inevitably come with resistance to our efforts. We will need both a sense of urgency and excruciating patience, coupled with persistence and repeated collective actions to transform our society to support a just, stable, life-sustaining future.

To stay the course for decades to come in the face of inevitable backlash that always comes, we will need spiritual power to ground movements in non-violence and effective rituals to guide collective action, reinforce shared meaning, and sustain life-giving relationships. We must create trustworthy ritual spaces within social movements for people to be received, heard, respected, and reconnected after so long in isolation, fear, and separation. Compassionate listening leads to compassionate reflection, so that we can offer insights and truth to each other as we remake our society. We will also need the strength and wisdom of our ancestors and each other to withstand what is to come. Having survived the pandemic and the truths it exposed, we must build a vision together of the world we want and keep making good trouble for the rest of our lives.

Bibliography

APM Research Lab Staff, "The Color of Coronavirus: COVID-19 Deaths by Race and Ethnicity in the U.S." APM Research Lab, March 5, 2021. https://www.apmresearchlab.org/covid/deaths-by-race.

Aratani, Lauren. "Calls to Make Juneteenth a US Federal Holiday Gain Momentum." *The Guardian,* June 18, 2020. https://www.theguardian.com/us-news/2020/jun/18/calls-grow-to-make-juneteenth-a-federal-us-holiday.

Aviv, Rachel. "The Philosopher of Feelings: Martha Nussbaum's Far-reaching Ideas Illuminate the Often Ignored Elements of Human Life—Aging, Inequality, and Emotion." *The New Yorker,* July 18, 2016. https://www.newyorker.com/magazine/2016/07/25/martha-nussbaums-moral-philosophies.

Associated Press. "Surfers Honor George Floyd in 'Paddle out' Held around World." *Star Advertiser,* June 6, 2020. https://www.staradvertiser.com/2020/06/06/breaking-news/surfers-honor-george-floyd-in-paddle-out-held-around-world/.

Berkman, Fran. "The Impact George Floyd's Death Had on Americans Can't Be Overstated." *Taboola* (blog). July 21, 2020. https://blog.taboola.com/the-impact-george-floyds-death-had-on-americans-cant-be-overstated/.

Black Lives Matter. "Herstory." Accessed April 2, 2021. https://blacklivesmatter.com/herstory/.

Blaec, Jagger. "The Complicated Rise and Swift Fall of Portland's Wall of Moms Protest Group." *Portland Monthly,* August 3, 2020. https://www.pdxmonthly.com/news-and-city-life/2020/08/the-complicated-rise-and-swift-fall-of-portland-s-wall-of-moms-protest-group.

Buchanan, Larry, et al. "Black Lives Matter May Be the Largest Movement in U.S. History." *New York Times,* July 3, 2020. https://www.nytimes.com/interactive/2020/07/03/us/george-floyd-protests-crowd-size.html.

Burch, Audra D. S., Weiyi Cai, Gabriel Gianordoli, Morrigan McCarthy, and Jugal K. Patel. "How Black Lives Matter Reached Every Corner of America." *The New York Times,* June 13, 2020. https://www.nytimes.com/interactive/2020/06/13/us/george-floyd-protests-cities-photos.html.

Chenoweth, Erica, and Jeremy Pressman. "This Summer's Black Lives Matter Protests Were Overwhelmingly Peaceful, Our Report Finds." *The Washington Post,* October 16, 2020. https://www.washingtonpost.com/politics/2020/10/16/this-summers-black-lives-matter-protesters-were-overwhelming-peaceful-our-research-finds/.

Donaghue, Erin. "2,120 Hate Incidents against Asian Americans Reported during Coronavirus Pandemic." *CBS News,* July 2, 2020. https://www.cbsnews.com/news/anti-asian-american-hate-incidents-up-racism/.

Gilligan, Carol. "Carefully Smash the Patriarchy." *The New York Times,* March 18, 2019. https://www.nytimes.com/2019/03/18/style/carol-gilligan.html.

Graybiel, Ann M. "Habits, Rituals, and the Evaluative Brain." *Neuroscience* 31 (2008) 359–87.

Harris, J. Irene, et al. "Spiritually Integrated Care for PTSD: A Randomized Controlled Trial of 'Building Spiritual Strength.'" *Psychiatry Research* 267 (September 2018) 420428. https://doi.org/10.1016/j.psychres.2018.06.045.

Hennigan, W. J. "Lost in the Pandemic: Inside New York City's Mass Graveyard on Hard Island." *Time,* November 18, 2020. https://time.com/5913151/hart-island-covid/.

Hirsch, Marianne. "The Generation of Postmemory." *Poetics Today* 29.1 (Spring 2008) 103–28. http://historiaeaudiovisual.weebly.com/uploads/1/7/7/4/17746215/hirsch_postmemory.pdf.

Humphreys, Margaret. *Marrow of Tragedy: The Health Crisis of the American Civil War.* Baltimore: Johns Hopkins University Press, 2017.

Isenberg, Nancy. *White Trash: The 400-Year Untold History of Class in America.* New York: Penguin, 2017.

Jordan, A. H., et al. "Distinguishing War-related PTSD Resulting from Perpetration- and Betrayal-based Morally Injurious Events." *Psychological Trauma: Theory, Research, Practice, and Policy* 9 (2017) 627–34.

Litz, Brett T., et al. "Moral Injury and Moral Repair in War Veterans: A Preliminary Model and Intervention Strategy." *Clinical Psychology Review* 29, no. 8 (December 2009) 695–706. https://doi.org/10.1016/j.cpr.2009.07.003.

Merriam-Webster.com Dictionary. "Bread and Circuses." Last updated March 26, 2021. https://www.merriam-webster.com/dictionary/bread%20and%20circuses.

Mosley, Tanya. "Mapping Black Lives Matter Protests around The World." Here and Now. WBUR, June 22, 2020. https://www.wbur.org/hereandnow/2020/06/22/mapping-black-lives-matter-protests.

Pollack, Sorcha. "'Frustrated and Angry': Thousands March in Dublin to Protest Death of George Floyd." *The Irish Times*, June 1, 2020. https://www.irishtimes.com/news/ireland/irish-news/frustrated-and-angry-thousands-march-in-dublin-to-protest-death-of-george-floyd-1.4268066.

Press Office. "British Antarctic Survey Supports and Endorses the UKRI Statement on Black Lives Matter." British Antarctic Survey Natural Environment Research Council, June 10, 2020. https://www.bas.ac.uk/media-post/british-antarctic-survey-statement-on-black-lives-matter/.

Robson, David. "The '3.5% Rule': How a Small Minority Can Change the World." *BBC*, May 13, 2019. https://www.bbc.com/future/article/20190513-it-only-takes-35-of-people-to-change-the-world.

Salzman, Sony. "From the Start, Black Lives Matter Has Been about LGBTQ Lives." *ABC News*, June 21, 2020. https://abcnews.go.com/US/start-black-lives-matter-lgbtq-lives/story?id=71320450

Seligman, Adam B., and Robert P. Weller. *Rethinking Pluralism: Ritual, Experience, and Ambiguity.* New York: Oxford University Press, 2012.

Shay, Jonathan. *Achilles in Vietnam: Combat Trauma and the Undoing of Character.* New York: Atheneum, 1994.

Stevenson, Bryan. *Just Mercy: A Story of Justice and Redemption.* New York; One World, 2014.

Wade, Roy Jr., et al. "Development and Evaluation of a Short Adverse Childhood Experiences Measure." *American Journal of Preventive Medicine* 52.2 (2017) 163–172. doi:10.1016/j.amepre.2016.09.033.

Weiss, Clara. "Two New York City Health Care Workers Commit Suicide within 48 Hours." *World Socialist Web Site*, April 28, 2020. https://www.wsws.org/en/articles/2020/04/28/emts-a28.html.

Woodward, Alex and Clark Mindock. "Taking a Knee: Why Are NFL Players Protesting and When Did They Start to Kneel?" *The Independent,* June 9, 2020. https://www.independent.co.uk/news/world/americas/us-politics/taking-knee-national-anthem-nfl-trump-why-meaning-origins-racism-us-colin-kaepernick-a8521741.html.

Zhang, Yan, et al. "Hate Crimes against Asian Americans." *American Journal of Criminal Justice.* Published ahead of print, January 7, 2021. https://doi.org/10.1007/s12103-20-09602-9.

2

Re-Storying and the Joy of Becoming

Healing Cultural Trauma During Social Crisis

Danjuma Gibson

Introduction: Naming Cultural Trauma

THE CURRENT PSYCHOSOCIAL ENVIRONMENT that has been created at the intersection of the COVID-19 global pandemic and the sociopolitical unrest caused by generations of racial inequality and white supremacy is detrimental to the souls of black and brown people. Over the long run, it is corrosive to emotional and mental wellbeing. This risk is especially amplified for those black and brown folk who are further marginalized in terms of economic class, gender, sexuality, or disabilities. Simply put, the ongoing battle to recognize and affirm the value of black and brown life in the collective psychic space of the American imperial democracy can represent a debilitating psychological and spiritual exercise, especially over the long run, unless one is intentional about deconstructing the master narratives that underwrite and sustain the American polis. In this essay, I refer to this debilitating psychological and spiritual exercise as cultural trauma. *I define cultural trauma as an internal melancholy, a manifestation of existential anxiety or stress, or a psychic and soul asphyxiation, that a person or group experiences when over the long run, they are unable to identify life-giving spaces of dignity and self-worth in the controlling narratives that govern the social contract of an institution, culture, or society. The narratives offer no recognition of dignity and truth to the person's history, heritage, or present lived experience. In this essay, the American imperial democracy represents such a culture and society. At its core, cultural trauma reflects the cognitive and spiritual dissonance that is created (over an extended period of time) when the behaviors of an institution or society run counter to its professed ideological commitments and narratives that undergird the collective identity. The lived reality of those who are marginalized or oppressed within the institution, culture, or society are ignored, denied, or minimized. That is to say—those who are marginalized within the institution or culture in question are forced to interact—from behind a veil—with the majority culture who exists within the same system.[1] To this end, the clinical and spiritual intervention for cultural trauma is the creative and artistic re-storying of death-dealing master narratives—that is to say . . . a counterhegemonic move—that recognizes and affirms the fulness and beauty of a person's individual and communal humanity.*

The conversation about cultural trauma has taken on momentum in the last decade. Alexander et al. assert that "the idea of 'cultural trauma' developed over the course of an intensive year-long dialogue among the coauthors."[2] While I do not doubt the integrity of the authors' work in this area, I believe the phenomenon of cultural trauma (by a different name) was recognized at the turn of the 20th century. Alexander defines cultural trauma as trauma that occurs "when members of a collectivity feel they have been subjected to a horrendous event that leaves indelible marks upon their group consciousness, marking their memories forever and changing their future identity in fundamental and irrevocable ways."[3] In that same project, Eyerman defines cultural trauma by contrasting it against the more mainstream understandings of trauma, arguing that "as opposed to psychological or physical trauma, which involves a wound and the experience of great emotional anguish by an individual, cultural trauma refers to a dramatic loss of identity and meaning, a tear in the social fabric, affecting a group of people that has achieved some degree of cohesion."[4]

---

1. DuBois, *The Souls of Black Folk*.
2. Alexander et al., *Cultural Trauma and Collective Identity*, vii.
3. Alexander et al., 1.
4. Alexander et al., *Cultural Trauma and Collective Identity*, 61.

In Dubois' classic work *The Souls of Black Folk*, most are familiar with his observation of the double-consciousness in black people, the "sense of always looking at one's self through the eyes of others." But Du-Bois also talks about the possibility of an internal anxiety that could be detrimental to the black soul if one does not take appropriate care. He describes it as "two souls, two thoughts, two unreconciled strivings; two warring ideals in one dark body, whose dogged strength alone keeps it from being torn asunder." [5] It is this possibility of being *torn asunder*, coupled with the *emotional energy reflected in the dogged strength that keeps the soul from being torn asunder*, that I believe is an early reference to cultural trauma.

In my construction of cultural trauma, I emphasize the clinical and spiritual fall-out of a double-consciousness if one does not take appropriate care to "reconcile" the dissonance that competing internalized narratives can create within the souls of black and brown people. All people, in all cultures, use cultural icons, symbols, narratives, or accepted stories, both consciously or unconsciously, as a part of their emotional, spiritual, and psychological well-being. As it relates to identity formation, the objectivity of a historical truth is secondary to how the narrative has been passed down inter-generationally and used to undergird self-esteem and group identity. Cultural trauma occurs over time, where the master narratives and stories that propel the group identity of the larger culture, lacks the depth and integrity to recognize and affirm the existence of the sub-cultures. If such hegemonic narratives are internalized, over time, the people of the subculture may begin to experience themselves only in-terms of deficiency, suspicion, deficits, shame, or negation. Cultural trauma reflects the dearth of cultural symbols to underwrite self-worth and dignity. The end result is chronic depression, anxiety, or melancholy.

The Context of Cultural Trauma in 2020–2021

The year 2020 has been a period of witnessing the arbitrary brutalization and murder of black and brown bodies across social media. In many cases, it seems as if the killings were just for sport. Especially for those black and brown individuals that work or exist in predominantly white spaces, the experience of witnessing these acts of violence in the media is different from the experience of white colleagues or associates that

5. DuBois, *The Souls of Black Folk*, 9.

witness the same violence. For the former, witnessing such acts of brutalization in the public space represents an existential threat to life itself.
For the latter, seeing stories about the ongoing brutalization of black life
on social media—while disturbing—only represents one of many topics
in a 24-hour news cycle. Even in well-intended anti-racism workshops
or racial reconciliation conferences, the psychological and emotional
toll that black and brown participants experience represents a far greater
emotional toll than that of their majority culture colleagues and friends.

  As a personal example, being the first and only black professor in a
predominantly white institution, to watch the funeral of George Floyd in
the summer of 2020 was just about unbearable because I am too familiar
with the scene. I thought to myself "here we go again . . . the killing of
another black man at the hands of the police, and all for what?" I recall
thinking that his daughter—six years of age at the time of her father's
murder—will have to see the video of his public murder someday, if she
hasn't already seen it. Ahmaud Arbery, on February 23, 2020, was killed
by two white guys while jogging. All for what? Because they thought he
was a threat. Breonna Taylor was shot eight times and killed by Louisville
police on March 13, 2020 as they fired indiscriminately into her apartment building. In the most paternalistic manner, we are later told by the
attorney general of Kentucky that while tragic, no one is responsible for
Breonna Taylor's death, and that the public should be careful not to be
swayed by the outcry of the protesters, but to take his analysis as the one
and only objective truth. We are forced to witness Botham Jean, a black
man in Dallas, killed in his own home in October 2019 by a police officer.
Why? Because a police officer thought she was in her own apartment.
Atatiana Jefferson, a black woman is shot and killed in her own home
in Fort Worth in October 2019. Why? A police officer shot through the
window of her own home because he thought she was a burglar.

  *These images of violence against black and brown bodies, over the long
run, cannot be internalized without psychological and emotional damage.*
The perpetual scenes of brutality and violence send the message that
black bodies are expendable, and *that they indeed do not matter as much
as white bodies* within the psychological caste system of the American
imperial democracy. The significant value of white bodies was put on full
display in the nation's capital on January 6, 2021 when hundreds of white
citizens from far-right terrorist groups stormed the capital in protest
of congress certifying the 2020 electoral votes in favor of President Joe
Biden. That attack resulted in the deaths of five people. Many have since

lamented that even after an abundance of intelligence that warned law enforcement of the inevitability of the attack, even after the U.S. capital building was violently overrun, even after the rioters made it clear that they wanted to harm members of congress, law enforcement seemed to prioritize the preservation of the lives of the white-bodied insurrectionists. This is contrasted against hundreds of police being deployed in preparation for a 2020 BLM peaceful protest in Washington, D.C. Ultimately, the imagery of injustice is nonstop. In due course, in America's democratic experiment, our collective capacity for compassion, empathy, kindness, and moral courage are compromised at best, or stamped out at worst, as the human spirit is slowly ossified by images of brutality. As such, I am concerned about sisters and brothers of good-will, caregivers, and people who are engaged in the fight for justice and freedom (pastors, caregivers, teachers, scholars, activists), but are not preparing for the long-journey, and will ultimately burnout or give up. To this end, my concern here is about individual and communal care in the long run. While the systemic racism and structural injustices we are witnessing now are disheartening, there is nothing new under the sun as it pertains to the present-day inequities. Self-care and self-love are crucial intervention elements in the consideration of cultural trauma.

The American Imperial Democracy

Cultural trauma always occurs within a psychosocial system or container. In order to understand the etiology of cultural trauma and the appropriate care interventions, you must understand the nature of the psychosocial container in which the trauma is created. For the purposes of this essay, the psychosocial system that will be referred to is the *America imperial democracy.*

Referring to the American imperial democracy signals that what we have witnessed in 2020 in terms of the flagrant promotion of white supremacy and racial violence, xenophobia, racial inequality, and the extolling of individualism, self-interest, and state's rights (in relation to the request by health officials for people to wear facemasks for the sake of public health) should not be understood as an aberration in 2020. Instead, it should be understood as the ongoing manifestation of the very nature of the republic, despite the best of efforts to create an illusion of American innocence, progress, and freedom for all. To refer to American imperialism is to point towards the very ontological nature of the republic. Moreover, in order to understand the deleterious impact of cultural trauma and the prospective indigenous communal interventions related to truth-telling and re-storying, we must understand the insidious and seductive nature of the master narratives required to prop up the political ideology of America. That is to stay, it is within the ideological collective psychic container of American imperialism that cultural trauma occurs. As such, you must understand the American empire in order to understand cultural trauma. Remediation from cultural trauma involves deconstructing the master narratives that provide currency to American psychic space, and reconstructing a narrative that recognizes the full humanity and dignity of all people. To this end, the work of Cornell West, Reinhold Niebuhr,[6] Frederick Douglass,[7] and Martin Luther King Jr.,[8] taken together, are useful to understanding American imperialism and the cognitive and spiritual dissonance it creates, all of which are conditions precedent to cultural trauma.

In the thought of Cornell West, the genius of western democracy cannot be separated from the reality of American violence and imperialism without doing significant harm to our relationship with the truth and the integrity of American history.[9] The practice of speaking about the exceptionalism of American democracy with phrases like "this is the best country in the world" without recalling the violent and dark underside of the republic reflects the *narrative tyranny of half-truths* (I will return to this in a moment). For West, the genius of the democratic experiment extends far beyond free and fair election cycles. Informed by the work of Ralph Waldo Emerson, James Baldwin, Herman Melville, and Toni Morrison, West's understanding of democracy reflects a complex constellation of ideas that includes the freedom of individual identity and creativity (not to be confused with self-interest and individualism), the freedom to self-determine, truth-telling and intellectual honesty as a form of resistance to the pressure of internalizing ideological dogma and dishonesty, the rejection of capitalist marketplace principles as a determinant of human value and the quality of life, and social and communal welfare and involvement. It is noteworthy that West does not offer up

---

6. Niebuhr, *The Irony of American History.*

7. Douglass, "What to the Slave is the Fourth of July."

8. King, *A Testament of Hope.*

9. West, *Democracy Matters: Wining the Fight Against Imperialism.*

any one definition or example of democracy. This epistemological fluidity protects the democratic experiment from the dangers of cultural fundamentalism. For West, "all systems set up to enact democracy are subject to corrupt manipulations, and that is why the public commitment to democratic involvement is so vital. Genuine, robust democracy must be brought to life through democratic individuality, democratic society."[10] When it comes to democracy and the confrontation of various structures of oppression, West postulates that democracy reflects the "hearing and heeding of the voices of the victims of hierarchies that have been in place that have dominated and exploited people."[11]

Yet, despite the glorious story of American exceptionalism, and the national propensity to whitewash the record of extreme violence upon which this nation was built, West reminds us that we cannot forget the imperialism of the American democratic experiment:

> The brutal atrocities of white supremacy in the American past and present speak volumes about the harsh limits of our democracy over against our professed democratic ideals. Race is the crucial intersecting point where democratic energies clash with American imperial realities in the very making of the grand American experiment of democracy. The voices and viewpoints of reviled and disempowered Amerindians, Asians, Mexicans, Africans, and immigrant Europeans reveal and remind us of the profoundly racist roots of the first American empire—the old America of expansionist Manifest Destiny. How ironic that this New World outpost of the British empire, which rested upon Amerindian lands and was greatly aided by predominantly African enslaved laborers, would institute a grand anti-imperial revolution and embark on a rich democratic experiment?[12]

But to be clear, this violence is not allocated to some distant past. West outlines three contemporary manifestation of contemporary American imperial violence:

> Democracy matters are frightening in our time precisely because the three dominant dogmas of free-market fundamentalism, aggressive militarism, and escalating authoritarianism are snuffing out the democratic impulses that are so vital for the deepening and spread of democracy in the world. In short,

10. West, *Democracy Matters*, 203.
11. West, *Moments of Interruption*.
12. West, *Democracy Matters*, 14.

we are experiencing the sad American imperial devouring of American democracy. This historic devouring in our time constitutes an unprecedented gangsterization of America—an unbridled grasp at power, wealth, and status. And when the most powerful forces in a society—and an empire—promote a suffocation of democratic energies, the very future of genuine democracy is jeopardized.[13]

In 2021, the dogmas of free-market fundamentalism reflect the ongoing erosion of the middle-class and the continued animus (and apathy) towards the poor. We see aggressive militarism in the ongoing proliferation of the military industrial complex. Lastly, we see escalating authoritarianism when a sitting president along with his congressional cronies attempt to brazenly overthrow a nationwide presidential election that has been decided by the states. There is an unmitigated public and brazen worship of white supremacy, and it seeks to have its way at all costs. The supremacy of whiteness and the worship of Trumpism is the manifestation of West's gangsterization in 2021. Yet when West talks about the gangsterization of America, it is debatable as to whether such egregious acts are a 20th century phenomenon, or if it is better understood as the motif upon which the republic was founded. Nevertheless, it speaks to the spiritual degradation that occurs when we lose our ability to be moral agents. Instead, morality is determined by those in power. Morality is backwards-engineered such that if a person or group has the political, economic, or social power to carry out their lascivious desires, then their preceding actions are deemed moral—either by the proclamations of their followers and constituents, or the silence of the bystanders. Instead of our God-given humanity determining our value and the people that make up the democracy being co-creators of the democratic space, marketplace values and conspicuous consumption, governed by the fundamentals of capitalism and the supremacy of whiteness, determine human value and morality.

But awareness of the imperialist nature of America does not simply reflect contemporary thinking. The contradiction of America's democracy and imperialism was evident in the 19th century as well. In addition to writers like Herman Melville and Ralph Waldo Emerson that informed the thinking of Cornell West, Frederick Douglass was one of the most prolific thinkers and cultural critics of the 19th century. In one of his most well-known orations, Douglass highlights the hypocritical nature

---

13. West, *Democracy Matters*, 7–8.

of the July 4th celebration, as the republic's independence and freedom from Britain was bankrolled on the backs of the enslaved and oppressed. Because of its significance in highlighting the longstanding nature of American imperialism, I quote the speech at length here:

> Fellow Citizens: Pardon me, and allow me to ask, why am I called upon to speak here today? What have I or those I represent to do with your national independence? Are the great principles of political freedom and of natural justice, embodied in that Declaration of Independence, extended to us? And am I, therefore, called upon to bring our humble offering to the national altar, and to confess the benefits, and express devout gratitude for the blessings resulting from your independence to us?
>
> But such is not the state of the case. I say it with a sad sense of disparity between us. I am not included within the pale of this glorious anniversary. Your high independence only reveals the immeasurable distance between us. The blessings in which you this day rejoice are not enjoyed in common. The rich inheritance of justice, liberty, prosperity, and independence bequeathed by your fathers is shared by you, not by me. The sunlight that brought life and healing to you has brought stripes and death to me. This Fourth of July is yours, not mine. You may rejoice, I must mourn. To drag a man in fetters into the grand illuminated temple of liberty, and call upon him to join you in joyous anthems, were inhuman mockery and sacrilegious irony. Do you mean, citizens, to mock me, by asking me to speak today? If so, there is a parallel to your conduct. And let me warn you, that it is dangerous to copy the example of a nation whose crimes, towering up to heaven, were thrown down by the breath of the Almighty, burying that nation in irrecoverable ruin. I can today take up the lament of a peeled and woe-smitten people.[14]

The importance of this historical speech by Frederick Douglass cannot be overstated in the analysis of cultural trauma and its place in the imperial democratic experiment. The words of Douglass ring true today and underscore that *the injustices against black and brown bodies we witnessed in 2020 are not aberrations, but the ongoing attestation of imperialism within the democratic experiment.*

In the last speech before his assassination, Martin Luther King laments the same contradictions that Frederick Douglass raised when he claims "all we say to America is, 'Be true to what you said on paper . . .

---

14. Douglass, "What to the Slave is the Fourth of July?"

if I lived in . . . any totalitarian country, maybe I could understand some of these illegal injunctions . . . maybe I could understand the denial of certain basic First Amendment privileges . . . but somewhere I read of the freedom of assembly . . . the freedom of speech . . . [and] the freedom of press."[15] James Meredith, credited with being the first black person to integrate Mississippi State University, probably exposed the paradox and hypocrisy of America's imperial democracy more than anyone by refusing to be formally labeled as a civil rights activist. For Meredith, the very association of the term civil rights with black people conceded the point to the racists that those who were oppressed were indeed asking for something that was special or beyond the norm. According to Meredith, "if the discussion of any American citizen's rights does not first acknowl-edge that all these rights are eternal, sacred, inviolate, and perfectly equal for every single American citizen, and that the very idea of molesting or negotiating for any of those rights is an obscene process, then it is in my opinion an incomplete, and therefore useless, discussion."[16]

Consequently, I suggest that it is the paradox and contradictions that reside within imperial democracy that causes cultural trauma to fester across generations for those forced to exist at the margin. This form of trauma becomes even more debilitating when the psychic space is infused with religiosity, and for America, this is especially true in its presumption that it is—and has always been—a Christian nation. Rein-hold Niebuhr is especially useful here in observing how Christianity has been coopted in a way that provides currency to the illusion of American innocence and exceptionalism and justifies the abuse of power.[17] In his assessment of America's abuse of power, Niebuhr quotes John Adam's warning to Thomas Jefferson stating that "power always thinks it has a great soul and vast views beyond the comprehension of the weak; and that it is doing God's service when it is violating all His laws."[18] Long before the contemporary scene of the intermingling of Christianity with structures of power in America, Niebuhr observes the dangers of how faith and doctrine can be adopted in a way that blinds societies to it evils. Left unchecked, the difference between faith and culture is blurred such that there is assumed to be no difference between the group identity of

15. King, "I See the Promised Land."

16. Meredith, *A Mission from God: A Memoir and Challenge for America*, 19.

17. Niebuhr, *Irony of American History*.

18. Niebuhr, *Irony of American History*, 21.

the majority culture and Christianity. Said differently, Christianity and whiteness are congealed. That Christianity has provided currency to the America's imperial democracy is undeniable. Niebuhr observes that:

> Whether our nation interprets its spiritual heritage through Massachusetts or Virginia, we came into existence with the sense of being a "separated" nation, which God was using to make a new beginning for mankind. We had renounced the evils of European feudalism. We had escaped from the evils of European religious bigotry . . . our forefathers thought of our "experiment" as primarily the creation of a new and purer church, or, as in the case of Jefferson and his coterie, they thought primarily of a new political community, they believed in either case that we had been called out by God to create a new humanity. We were God's "American Israel." Our pretensions of innocency therefore heightened the whole concept of a virtuous humanity which characterizes the culture of our era . . . We find it almost as difficult as the communists to believe that anyone could think ill of us, since *we are as persuaded as they that our society is so essentially virtuous that only malice could prompt criticism of any of our actions.*[19]

Niebuhr's analysis exposes the fallacy currently being made by some Christian institutions to exclude critical race theory (or the study of structural racism) from their curriculums.[20] Such an erroneous move ignores the historical reality that Christianity has been active and complicit in the erection and justification of the American imperial democracy along with its concomitant violence. That is to say, Christian theology—a temporal project to explain the Divine—is a creation of human beings. As such, Christian doctrine lacks the internal integrity to self-correct. History has shown how Christianity (and it's God-talk) has been complicity in justifying many of the greatest atrocities against humanity. Moreover, in America, much of Christian doctrine is the creation of the powerful.[21] It is only by entering into dialogue with other discourses—and being challenged and critiqued by those discourses—across cultures and disciplines—that Christian theology is able to be held accountable in the formation of its ethics. On this point, Niebuhr is decisive in his

19. Niebuhr, *Irony of American History,* 24–25, emphasis added.

20. Kuruvilla, "White Evangelical Leaders Pledge Seminaries Will Not Teach Key Theory On Systemic Racism."

21. Thurman, *Jesus and the Disinherited.*

observation that "all men are naturally inclined to obscure the morally ambiguous element in their political cause by investing it with religious sanctity. This is why religion is more frequently a source of confusion than of light in the political realm. The tendency to equate our political with our Christian convictions causes politics to generate idolatry."[22]

Religious and Social Fundamentalism:
The Psychology of an Imperial Democracy

The imperial democracy, in part, derives its strength from social and religious fundamentalism. Social and religious fundamentalism is the condition precedent for cultural trauma. Institutions and subcultures within the imperial democracy that adhere to or have internalized its commitments to whiteness, free-market capitalism, authoritarianism, and militarism, risk performances of fundamentalism as well. With this fundamentalism, there is a pre-existing and well-developed cultural framework for in-group/out-group processes such that the communities are very efficient in *implicitly feeling* and *explicitly identifying* individuals that are a part of the out-group. That is—enactments of tribalism seem to be active within the communal life, whereby the unconscious emotional task is the preservation of the tribal-system and the identification of potential outsiders. Secondly, in such constructs, barriers to entry (i.e., acceptance to the community) tend to be relatively high, less permeable, and require assimilation and/or colonization whereby the *telos of membership is to become "like us."* Thirdly, in some cases, the entrenchment of idealized hegemonic masculinity represents a key component to group-identity. That is to say, the community seems organized around idealizing a machismo male figure. Lastly, in each of these instances, the community presents near pathological narcissistic needs. An unhealthy clinical picture depicts the unconscious archaic usage of each other as idealizing and mirroring self-objects. In such a closed system, there is no room for another. To the contrary, the more an institution or subculture adheres to the dictates of the larger narratives of the imperial democracy, the less it has the compacity to be influenced by *another* that is not *like them*. That is to say, those in the out-group have little chance of representing *another*, they instead become *the other*. It is common that the other is

22. Niebuhr, *Love and Justice: Selections from the Shorter Writings of Reinhold Niebuhr*, 59.

often vilified or demonize, and inherently incurs the rage and disdain of the larger group. Such rage is suggestive of projective identification, whereby individual and group identity (in large part) is underwritten by projecting unwanted elements of the group-self onto others. In this way, an out-group is created. The subculture, social system, institution, or organization (religious or secular) then develops a practice of demonizing individuals relegated to the out-group. Ultimately, *imperial democratic identity politics revolve around the capacity to experience oneself as not being like "those people" in the out-group.*

There is no particular subculture or religious tradition that is beholden to the fundamentalism described above. The descriptors of conservative and liberal are inadequate to the task. Yet, any subculture or social system in the democracy where identity is formed around *negation (of acts) and separation (from certain kinds people)* seem to be more susceptible to the mechanisms of the religious and social fundamentalism being outlined here, as well as the imposing cultural trauma on those who live at the margins or are in the out-groups of those subcultures. In my own experience of the Christian faith (and analyzing that experience through the lens of the psychology of religion), I have found that traditions where religious identity is formed around the notion of *"I am a Christian because I do not do . . ."* (you can fill in the blank), or *"because I am a Christian, I do not associate with . . ."* (you can fill in the blank), or *"I am a Christian because I am not like . . ."* (you can fill in the blank) seem to be more susceptible to the mechanics of fundamentalism and imposing cultural trauma on *the other.*

Similar to the master narratives of the American imperial democracy that fears the destruction of its fantasies of virtuosity and grandeur (that prop up its communal ego), for subcultures within the democracy that adhere to the same principles of imperialism (religious institutions, educational systems, for-profit and non-profit organizations, etc.), maintaining the illusions of virtuosity and grandeur—at all costs—becomes the unconscious group goal. Performativity and *being right*—in narrative, spoken word, and script—takes priority over engaging in the wholistic work of *doing right, being well, doing justice, being a moral agent*, and then performing the requisite tasks to *be well*.[23] In the extreme, the capacity

---

23. Performativity requires only engaging cognition to "say" the right thing or offer the politically correct response. To the contrary, I suggest here that the wholistic work of being well and doing good requires the entirety of the human project: body, mind, soul, and spirit.

for reality testing is compromised in the service of crafting and maintaining controlling narratives that underwrite performativity and *being right*. *Suspicion of the other* becomes the dominant relational ethos towards *difference and multiplicity*, or anyone that is not a part of the in-group. *Fear of not being . . .* (you can fill in the blank) or living up to a standard is commonly the governing force that navigates the actions of those beholden to a community governed by scapegoating the other. But in an odd way, the presence of the *profane other* is often necessary for the social or religious identity of subcultures beholden to imperial democracy.

Likewise, subcultures and social systems in the democratic experiment where identity formation is built around affirmation and engagement seem to be less susceptible (but certainly not exempt) to the mechanisms of social and religious fundamentalism and the risks of cultural trauma outlined in this work. Again, in my own experience of the Christian faith (and analyzing it through the lens of the psychology of religion), traditions where religious identity is crafted using a formula like "*I am a Christian because I am . . .*" (you can fill in the blank), or "*because I am a Christian, I engage others and the world like . . .*" (you can fill in the blank), or "*I am a Christian because I do . . .*" (you can fill in the blank) seem to be less susceptible (although not exempt) to the mechanisms of fundamentalism and cultural trauma outlined in this essay. Such communities incur less risk related to the destruction of archaic religious grandiosity. Curiosity *of another* (as opposed to *the other*) becomes the dominant relational ethos towards difference and multiplicity. The presence of a *profane other* in a tangential out-group is not required for identity formation. While the *fear of not being* is an emotion that can haunt any person or group, it doesn't have to be the governing psychologic when social and religious identity are formed around affirmation and engagement.

Theological Ethical Considerations of Social and Religious Fundamentalism

Notwithstanding the psychodynamic implications of unhealthy group narcissistic needs, the theological and ethical implications are relevant as well as it relates to the destructiveness of projective identification and the creation of a *profane other*. The Pauline warning in Galatians is clear that "if anyone thinks they are something when they are not, they deceive themselves. *Each one should test their own actions. Then they can take pride in themselves alone, without comparing themselves to someone else, for each one should carry their own load.*[24] Additionally, in an attempt to answer the famous question put forth by Jesus in his sermon on the mountain "why do you look at the speck of sawdust in your brother's eye and pay no attention to the plank in your own eye," projective-identification seems to be a viable explanation.[25] That is to say, the only conceivable way to know that there is a speck of sawdust in *another's* eye is that you projected the speck of sawdust into *the other's* eye. As previously mentioned, projective identification generally incapacitates a group's ability for reality testing, rendering them incapable of noticing the plank in the group's own eye. Jesus' remedy is simple: attend to the plank in one's own eye or the undesirable elements within the group, then you will see clearly to remove the speck in another's eye—that is, if there was even a speck in the other person's eye to begin with.

Moreover, this entire tribal framework operates, in large part, on the emotion of fear—that is, the fear of falling short of the illusions of exceptionalism, innocence, individual and group chosen-ness, personal and doctrinal purity, or grandeur that props up social or religious identity. Alternatively, practices of radical love—that is, relationality based on the radical acceptance of *the humanity of all as made in the image of the Divine,* and the ornery insistence to apply this to all people—subverts communal identity and relationality predicated on fear. The writer of 1 John 4 is compelling on this point—a point that is worth reemphasizing in the current social crises outlined at the beginning of this essay:

> And so we know and rely on the love God has for us. God is love. Whoever lives in love lives in God, and God in them. This is how love is made complete among us so that we will have confidence on the day of judgment. In this world we are like Jesus. *There is no fear in love. But perfect love drives out fear, because fear has to do with punishment. The one who fears is not made perfect love.*[26]

Albert J. Raboteau captures the essence of Dutch reformed theologian Abraham Johannes Muste on the implications of love (as opposed to fear) being the primary communal ethos. He cites Muste expressing

---

24. Galatians 6:3–5 New International Version (NIV), emphasis added.
25. Matthew 7:1–5 NIV.
26. 1 John 4:16–18 NIV, emphasis added.

that "my own vocation . . . has certainly not been to asceticism as it is usually understood. This is because I have a deep-seated conviction that the aim and the essence of life is love. *And love is in its inmost nature an affirmation, not a negation; an embracing and being embraced, not rejections and withdrawals.*"[27]

Violence and Terror in the Imperial Democracy: The Defense Against Imperialism's Annihilation Anxiety

How do we then account for the violence, terror, indifference, and social animosity accrued towards the black and brown bodies highlighted at the beginning of this essay? The perpetual and ubiquitous nature of this violence suggests a narrative that black life is expendable. These narratives provide currency for cultural trauma when black and brown people are forced to juxtapose this reality against the values of a professed democracy. Recall that the paradigm of the imperial democratic experiment suggests that the terror and violence we have witnessed against black bodied individuals in 2020 is not an aberration, but the norm since the founding of the republic, and continues to this very moment. How then might we account for the immunization of national conscience when it comes to terrorizing black and brown people? In part, it suggests that the role of social and religious fundamentalism plays a key role.

Much has already been written about the psychology of fundamentalism and terrorism, and it is not my goal to extensively rehearse that here. But within the paradigm of imperial democracy, my use of the term tribalism is synonymous with fundamentalism, suggesting that any subculture or group within the democracy can enact fundamentalist tendencies that are injurious to both marginalized individuals within the group, as well as to the larger collective. In many fundamentalist studies, it is my observation that the focus is often limited to fringe religious groups or charismatic Christian cohorts. According to Almond and colleagues, "all fundamentalists . . . intentionally interact with the outside world in some way . . . [and] whatever their patter of relation to the world, [fundamentalist] seek purity, draw sharp ideological boundaries, value mission work, and want to avoid the evils of the fallen world even as they seek to redeem it."[28] For Hood et al. (2005), the essence of funda-

27. Raboteau, *American Prophets*, 56, emphasis added.
28. Almond, *Explaining Fundamentalisms*, 425, 429.

mentalism is its emphasis on an *intratextual* approach to making sense of life and the world, compared to an *intertextual* framework to do the same. The former approach reflects an impermeable meaning-making boundary system where a major text (or personality) is used, exclusively, as the hermeneutical engine to process the data necessary for the task conscious or unconscious meaning making. The authors suggest it is not that fundamentalist are close-minded, but that other texts and interlocutors (outside of the boundary system) are subordinated or thought to be irrelevant to the task of meaning making. The latter approach (intertextuality) reflects a more permeable meaning-making boundary system where alternative texts and conversation partners are introduced (to varying degrees) to the system for the work of meaning making. At its most basic function, the authors locate fundamentalism "as a meaning system . . . [where] it creates a way for them to interpret the world, as well as themselves in relation to the world. This meaning system encompasses all of life and is strongly felt . . . Meaning for fundamentalists, is found wholly within the pages of the sacred text . . . Thus we propose that the primary criterion for understanding fundamentalism is its insistence that all of life be understood in relation to the text."[29]

Interestingly enough, when we think about fundamentalism, we often think of fringe groups (religious or otherwise) that prop up ultra-conservative, classical, or literal interpretations of their tradition; interpretations designed to support a social order that realizes their ideological framework. More often than not, when we consider these fringe groups, it is often through a lens of *us normal people* over and against *those abnormal people or extremist groups of people*; similar to the way some fundamentalist groups may split the world into all good and all bad. And given the amount of violence perpetuated by extremist groups over the last century, a jaded view of fundamentalism is not without merit. *But seldom do we consider the inner workings of the American imperial democracy when we contemplate fundamentalism. I suspect there is a degree of scapegoating in how we understand fundamentalists, who we label as such, and who we experience as weird.* Summers is sound on this observation when he notes that in many respects, the field of psychoanalysis and its respective theories—as an example—mirror the same fundamentalist ideas and practices consistent with that of religious fundamentalist. Summers offers up a compelling conclusion when he postulates "this unwillingness to

---

29. Hood et al., *The Psychology of Religious Fundamentalism*, 5.

acknowledge fallibility in the founder and basis of the school of thought is ultimately what renders the psychoanalytic movement dangerously close to fundamentalist thinking . . . the organization of psychoanalysis into belief systems that assume certain inviolable truths serves a purpose similar to the infallibility of the text in fundamentalist movements."[30]

With this in mind, in what follows, I focus less on religious examples of fundamentalism per se, and more on what tribalism/fundamentalism is psychologically attempting to achieve for any group or subculture existing in the democratic experiment. Here, *I understand fundamentalism or tribalism as the psychosocial processes that any group or institution employs for self-preservation (i.e., to keep things the way they have always been)*, which should not be confused with the healthier organizational or group goal of *survival or continuity for posterity sake*. Understood in this way, I suggest expanding our understanding of fundamentalism. Recognized then as a group resource, a group coping mechanism, or a psychic or emotional defense, practices of fundamentalism can be seen as a response to group annihilation-anxiety. That is to say, practices of tribalism are generally precipitated by the growing threat to a group or institution's long-standing *felt understanding* of collective purpose and identity. The threat is felt when the institution or subculture is faced with the prospect of change, transition, or death that is related to it approaching the final stage(s) of its organizational or group life-cycle, or the growing and encroaching presence of *the other*. Similar to how Summers has understood fundamentalism to be at work in psychodynamic theory and practice, a similar argument could be made for any subculture or group existing within the imperial democracy. When faced with prospective or material change to the master narrative(s) or material situations that have propped up the American imperial democracy, the ensuing annihilation anxiety can cause any subculture or group to engage in the theatrics of fundamentalism or tribalism.

Essential then to the fundamentalism/tribalism framework is the creation of a well-defined *image of people and bodies* that serve as the out-group—the antithesis—of what the in-group aspires not to be. The concept of love tends to be conditional, as it is understood and enacted through a lens of guilt-avoidance whereby adherents to a religious tribalism framework are encouraged to only associate with those who are a part of the in-group, or to only invest in people who desire to be in the

30. Summers, "Fundamentalism, Psychoanalysis, and Psychoanalytic Theories," 349–50.

in-group. Love and affirmation are reserved for the in-group alone. Self-love or interpersonal love tends to be understood through the lens of assimilating into the preset structures and narratives of what is considered *the norm*, compliance with a prescribed set of rules and regulations, and conforming to the group. Love for the sake of love itself, or loving others because of their humanness, or loving difference, is rare, and can be viewed as a compromise of social contract or guilt by association with *the other*. In such tribes or subcultures, there tends to be an elusive suspicion about love-talk, due to the fear that love-talk will lead to compromising standards set by social contract, heritage, and tradition. The notion of *tough love* is touted as the preferred option—a concept that often sets the stage for psychological and emotional brutality against *the other*. In the paradigm of fundamentalism, love is contingent to conforming to a set standard of propositional truths.

The tribalism/fundamentalist framework that I have outlined mirrors the contrast in what Kohut described as the Guilty Man (a conflict-orientation depicting a life centered on avoiding or resolving Freudian oedipal guilt) versus the Tragic Man (a self-orientation where one endeavors to live into the fullness of her life-project or nuclear-program, but recognizes the reality of falling short of such goals).[31] The leap that Kohut is attempting to make from describing the human project through the lens of the Guilty Man to the Tragic Man reflects a pastoral intervention move for those who have experienced cultural trauma, whereby they must ultimately shift their interpretive sensibilities to a more life-giving framework where fear and guilt are not the orienting critical principles by which they organize their worldviews and their individual and collective identities. Yet even for Kohut, such a move was not without due resistance:

> Traditional analysis believes that man's essential nature is comprehensively defined when he is seen as *'Guilty Man'*, as man in hopeless conflict between the drives that spring from the biological bedrock of *homo natura* and the civilizing influences emanating from the social environment as embodied in the superego. Self-psychology believes that man's essence is defined when seen as a self and that homo psychologicus (if you excuse this term that is meant to contrast with *homo natura*) is, on the deepest level, *'Tragic Man'*, attempting, and never quite succeeding, to realize the programme laid down in his depth during the span of his life . . . Why can't we convince our colleagues that

31. Kohut, *The Restoration of the Self*.

the normal state, however rare in pure form, is a joyfully experienced developmental forward move in childhood, including
the step into the oedipal stage, to which the parental generation
responds with pride, with self-expanding empathy, with joyful
mirroring, to the next generation, thus affirming the younger
generation's right to unfold and to be different?[32]

Kohut's rhetorical question of why it was so difficult to convince his colleagues of a psychology whereby the core of man's being was life-aspiring
as opposed to guilt avoidance is symbolic of anyone who desires to de-
tach their self-experience and identity based on the alleged American
dream and a marketplace value system. Mystery, ambiguity, ambivalence,
desire, meaning-making, alterity—concepts that, in part, represent what
it means to be human—are irrelevant in a guilt-laden/guilt-avoidance
anthropological framework. Heritage, history, and the personal narratives that makes every person a distinct being are flattened in an effort
to simplify personhood and commodify what it means to be human.
Kohut's guilty man (or its parallel) seeks to assimilate into predetermined
archetypes and caricatures of faith, religiosity, spirituality, happiness, joy,
love, and ultimately—humanness.

Within the fundamentalism/tribalism framework, the burden and
risks of freedom and meaning making are subsumed under the illusion
that does not require one to wrestle with the issues of life, but to un-
critically submit to a code in which the person or group had no agency
in forming. This sort of interpretive framework is compensatory in nature. Creative and dynamic meaning-making is replaced with the act of
choosing the *right predetermined response* (mentally, emotionally, and
spiritually) to any situation in life, whether positive or negative. Within
the imperial democracy, the group understanding of what it means to
be human reflects a culturally predetermined framework defined by its
recalcitrant nature. The *need to comply* to this commodified theological
anthropology reflects religious tribalism's version of the Kohutian Guilty
Man. As such, when *performances of acting well*, or consumer symbols
of being well, outweigh the authentic self-work or relational work to *do
right, get well, or seek healing*, then violence to self, others, and community tends to be the outcome. In this way, both social, cultural, or religious
symbols do the work of fundamentalism in that it deceives the person or
group into believing its own fantasies of exceptionalism and innocence.

32. Kohut, "Introspection, Empathy, and the Semi-Circle of Mental Health," 402.

In his work on dissociation and the use of religious objects, LaMothe captures this well when he argues:

> What turns the use of religious objects defensive, with regard to dissociation, is when these attributes—omnipotence, sacredness (purity or inviolability), omniscience, and timelessness—are unwittingly used to insure that the group's religious stories and rituals be unassailable, absolute, and unquestionable. The attributes of religious objects, then, contribute to people's beliefs that their formulations are certain and incontrovertible. Because religious beliefs are generally not open to external falsification and verification, the certainty becomes virtually *impossible to breach*.[33]

This begs the question of when a person grows up in fundamentalist framework or subculture, *is the breach that LaMothe speaks of even possible? Such a breach is critical in recovering from cultural trauma.*

James Jones identifies several major themes that appear to surface across religiously motivated terrorist groups.[34] Again, for our purposes here, it is important to emphasize that *fundamentalism is not just beholden to religion but can also represent the master narratives and social contract that govern an imperial democracy such as America.* For Jones, this terrorism involves "the use of violence, often in symbolic but deadly actions, in the service of sacred goals or values."[35] The themes Jones identified as consistent across the fundamentalist groups he studied included: (1) the practice of shaming and humiliating, (2) the experience of being shamed and humiliated, (3) the unconscious individual and communal practice of splitting people and the world into categories of all-good or all-bad, (4) the illusion of the all-good or in-group being, achieving, or maintaining purity, (5) a punitive leader that is idealized, (6) an infatuation with violence, (7) bias against the out-group or anyone who is not a part of the organization and (8) a strong cultural ethos of submission to authority.

When one considers the constant terror and violence against black and brown bodies mentioned at the beginning of this essay, and throughout the history of the republic, *many of the themes Jones identified in religious terrorist groups can also be identified in the American imperial democratic experiment.* While there is much that Jones and others have contributed to understanding religious terrorism, the focus has more

---

33. LaMothe, "I Think of God, in Order not to be Aware," 145, emphasis added.

34. Jones, *Blood That Cries Out from the Earth.*

35. Jones, *Blood That Cries Out from the Earth,* 27

often than not tended to focus on esoteric religious groups forced to exist at the margin. *I have often wondered, in amazement, how it has so often been overlooked as to how religion has played an irreducible role in the violence that America has perpetrated—both within and beyond its borders—for centuries. Is there any religious institution in America (especially Christianity) that can truly argue there are no fundamentalist tendencies evidenced in its lineage and culture?* When we consider the realities of the Native American genocide, the transatlantic slave trade, or American slavery, all of which are paradoxes (to say the least) to democracy, does not the American imperial democracy function within the framework of fundamentalism? Was not each of these events mass atrocities against humanity examples of extremism?

Any subculture, institution, or group within the imperial democracy that has internalized—and uses for its collective identity—the governing narratives that prop up the imperialist nature of the democracy, contains the requisite faculties to harm and precipitate cultural trauma on people who have been subjected to a history of *otherization or thingification* with the democracy. This is the hallmark of social fundamentalism, and it is no different from religious fundamentalism. To speak of religious fundamentalism in America is to also speak of the same social fundamentalism that props up the paradox of imperialism and democracy. While admittedly offering up a somewhat grim reflection on the life-limiting practices of religion, Thomson's warnings about the dark side of religion bear mentioning here:

> Religious moderates wish to avoid submitting to the full implications of their faith, a choice which leads them, in turn, to tolerate the worst irrationalities and violence of their fundamentalist coreligionists. Although it is tempting for Westerners to point the finger at Islam, it behooves us to remember that the cross has accompanied the sword everywhere, including into the Arab world of the Middle Ages. Parts of the Old Testament are blueprints for murder and genocide. Deuteronomy 20:16 instructs those entering the cities promised to them by God to "leave alive nothing that breatheth."[36]

Is it possible to extricate ourselves from a social fundamentalism that defines the imperial democracy? Jones,[37] then building on the work

36. Thomson, "Who are We? Where did We Come From? How Religious Identity Divides and Damns Us All," 37–38.

37. Jones, *Blood That Cries Out from the Earth.*

of Emmanuel Ghent[38] and D.W. Winnicott[39], argues that such a breach would require the individual (or group) surrendering to one's innate desire to experience their *true-self*. Within the Winnicottian framework, most people grow into adulthood with a *false-self*, learning from early childhood to act and behave in ways that appeal to caregivers and other important stakeholders in the immediate environment. Over time, the pain of rejection or the look of disapproval from those we need or that are important to us results in most people becoming crudely efficient and effective in erecting facades designed to protect us from the threat of shame and guilt that comes from the prospect of us revealing *the essence of who we are*. Winnicott's *true-self* reflects who we are at our core, what we desire to live into, but because of the *fear of exposure*, we lack the *requisite practice* at being our *true-self*. In many respects, the true-self/false-self polarity is the orienting framework of Kohut's reference to the Guilty Man and the Tragic Man, with the Tragic Man representing the preferred interpretive lens that represents the essence of what it means to be human; that is to say, living in a way that fulfills the individual or group nuclear-program. According to Jones, Ghent argues that this attraction to the *true-self* reflects a desire to *surrender the false-self* in service to the *true-self*. However, too many obstacles that impede the *desire to surrender* will result in a person engaging in *perverted submission* within their relationships (religious or not) such that the healthy goal of surrendering the *false-self* is replaced with a masochistic orientation; that is to say, *the only way a person knows how to be in relationship is one where they are used, abused, or perverted*. At its worse, abuse and perversion are internalized as love, because *some attention* is the preferred option to being invisible. *The internalization of destructive narratives, just to receive attention or to avoid abuse or emotional brutality, at the expense of neglecting the true-self, is at the heart of cultural trauma.* According to Jones, Ghent believes that "surrendering to experience (especially in a religious milieu) is transformative because the façade of the false selfhood is (at least temporarily) put aside, and the true, free, spontaneous self is reawakened."[40] This leads us then to consider indigenous resources as a possible clinical and spiritual intervention.

---

38. Ghent, "Submission, and Surrender: Masochism as a Perversion of Surrender."
39. Winnicott, *Playing and Reality*.
40. Jones, *Blood That Cries Out from the Earth*, 127.

Indigenous and Community Resources

The intervention for cultural trauma involves both truth-telling, and re-storying the destructive narratives one has internalizing from the imperial democratic experiment. The intervention for cultural trauma involves authentic self-work and introspection. Identity formation and self-worth based on consumerism and marketplace values must be deconstructed. Internalized narratives of racism, misogyny, homophobia, and self-flagellation must be deconstructed in order to heal from cultural trauma. It is a process that will not magically occur over night. The remediation from cultural trauma requires intentional self-care around the narratives that have governed our lived experiences in a life-limiting way.

Hopefully by now, it has become more apparent as to why traditional mental health resources may be limited in the ability to remedy cultural trauma: *in many cases, those same mental health resources have been crafted and shaped in the imperial democracy such that they tend to perpetuate the racism that is at the heart of cultural trauma, and at the same time, fail to recognize the racism that is baked into the mental health system itself.* I make this claim being a fully licensed psychotherapist myself. While cultural trauma is a clear and present danger to the mental and emotional health of black and brown people, its diagnosis is not even recognized in the DSM-V. While the body of psychological literature has made noticeable progress in its recognition of racism and inequity over the past twenty years, that same literature is also replete with testimonies from black and brown patients, clinical students preparing for careers in psychology, and practitioners, who encounter animus, gas-lighting, anger, and even rage from white counterparts when attempting to address issues of race and inequality.[41] Many black psychotherapists have even felt uncomfortable recommending black and brown clientele to white colleagues based on their own personal experiences with those same colleagues.[42] Even within the field of psychology, the resistance to addressing race is only another manifestation of fundamentalism/tribalism within a subculture of the American imperial democracy. As such, put forth several examples of truth-telling and the creativity of re-storying narratives as indigenous and communal interventions for cultural trauma.

Truth-telling and re-storying are built on salient themes in narrative theory which suggests that at our psychological and spiritual core,

41. Winograd, *Black Psychoanalysts Speak.*

42. Del Valle Schorske, "Insights from Black Psychoanalysts Speak."

we are meaning-making individuals that endeavor to craft self and communal identity by the narratives we form in relation to ourself, how we relate to others, how we understand the events of our lives, and how we imagine our future. If we understand how story and narrative impact our very psychological structure, then we understand the deleterious effects of internalizing harmful, death-dealing narratives that objectify our humanity. In his work on narrative theory and family systems theory, Young identifies several key assumptions about the importance of narratives and psychological health and well-being. These themes suggest that: (1) stories are how we understand ourselves, (2) the personal stories we tell ourselves and the public stories we tell others are reciprocal and inform each other, (3) our narratives are formed through the conversations we have with others, and (4) our stories form our behavior and self-experience.[43] Understood in this light then, narrative theory highlights the redemptive nature of re-storying the destructive narratives that have informed how black and brown people have understood their lives and experienced themselves within the imperial democracy, as well as countering hegemonic lies that seek to rationalize the cognitive and spiritual dissonance created by the paradox of American imperialism and democracy.

There is no better example of re-storying than that of Frederick Douglass. In my psychoanalytic analysis of his life, I ask the critical question of why a person would need to write four autobiographies of his life.[44] Simply put, Douglass was engaging in creative journaling. His actions represented a counter-hegemonic move against the American imperial democracy that sought to employ narratives that justified his enslavement while celebrating fantasies of national exceptionalism, innocence, and Divine election. I suggest that "Douglass' ongoing passion to craft a counter-narrative over and against the overarching narrative of white supremacy and black subjugation is clear in his repeated efforts to write down the story of his existence and selfhood."[45] For Douglass, this included journaling his life. *But for others, this could include any practice that creates the liminal space necessary to practice engaging the true-self as opposed to the bewildered false-self we have become accustomed to.*

---

43. Young, "Using Narrative Theory and Self Psychology within a Multigenerational Family Systems Perspective."

44. Gibson, *Frederick Douglass, A Psychobiography: Rethinking Subjectivity in the Western Experiment of Democracy.*

45. Gibson, *Frederick Douglass*, 127.

Truth-telling involves the psychological and emotional exorcism of the myths and lies we have internalized for the sake of the *false-self* that is enslaved to the imperial democracy. In his most recent project, Glaude reflects on the amalgamation of lies that have propped up the fantasy of the American dream, and the illusion of innocence and purity for those who worship the ideology of whiteness, all at the expense of the devolution of black life for over three hundred years. Glaude's work is timely in the age of Trumpism. He refers to the lie as the "value gap." As a matter of mental health awareness, I suggest that it is truth-telling that closes the value gap responsible for cultural trauma:

> If what I have called the "value gap" is the idea that in America white lives have always mattered more than the lives of others, then the lie is a broad and powerful architecture of false assumptions by which the value gap is maintained. *These are the narrative assumptions that support the everyday order of American life, which means we breathe them like air. We count them as truths. We absorb them into our character. One set of lies debases black people; examples stretch from the writings of the Founding Fathers to The Bell Curve. According to these lies, black people are essentially inferior, less human than white people, and therefore deserving of their particular station in American life. We see these lies every day in the stereotypes that black people are lazy, dishonest, sexually promiscuous, prone to criminal behavior, and only seeking a handout from big government.*[46]

Finally, whether we are talking about the act of re-storying one's life for the sake of *finding the true-self*, or truth-telling in order to *surrender the false-self*, both can be achieved through the liberal arts. And this is where indigenous and community resources hold redemptive potential in terms of countering cultural trauma and experiencing emotional healing and wholeness. The liberal arts, whether the focus is on literature, song, dance, cinema, or other forms of media, all have the potential to create liminal spaces where we can practice encountering our true-selves for the sake of truth-telling and re-storying. In many respects, this represented the genius behind the Harlem Renaissance of the early 20th century. While many of the intellectuals and artists that represented this movement in New York didn't use the language of trauma, they recognized all too well that the need to create beauty through the arts, and the power

---

46. Glaude, *Begin Again: James Baldwin's America and Its Urgent Lessons for Our Own*, 7, emphasis added.

of feeling one's beauty through the liberal arts, was a formidable weapon against the lies and dictates of the American imperial democracy, or what Glaude cogently refers to as the value gap. In an on-line article about the importance of self-care for pastors, and community care that I believe represents an effective intervention for cultural trauma, I postulate that:

> similar to how the Harlem Renaissance endeavored to remind us of (and point us towards) the goodness of life in the midst of racial terror, the liberal arts can do the same for pastors today. Indeed, culture and the liberal arts can provide us with resources that reorient us to being lovers, as oppose to life oriented around fear. It can reacquaint us with what it means to love ourselves (as opposed to self-hate), what it means to love another human being (as opposed to being suspicious of the other), what it means to possess courage and dignity (as opposed to cowardice and indecency), what it means to do the work of freedom (as opposed to doing the work of oppression and bondage), and ultimately, what it means to be human.[47]

Bibliography

Alexander, Jeffrey C., Ron Eyerman, Bernhard Giesen, Neil J. Smelser, and Piotr Sztompka. 2010. *Cultural Trauma and Collective Identity*. Berkeley, CA: Univversity of California Press.

Almond, Gabriel A., Emmanuel Sivan, and R. Scott Appleby. "Explaining Fundamentalisms." In *Fundamentalisms Comprehended*, 424–44. Chicago: University of Chicago Press, 2004.

Douglass, Frederick. 1976. "Frederick Douglass: What to the Slave Is the Fourth of July?" *The Black Scholar* 7 (10) 32–37. https://doi.org/10.1080/00064246.1976.11413846.

DuBois, W. E. B. *The Souls of Black Folk*. Chicago: A. C. McClurg, 1903.

Ghent, Emmanuel. "Masochism, Submission, and Surrender: Masochism as a Perversion of Surrender." *Contemporary Psychoanalysis* (1990) 108–36.

Gibson, Danjuma. *Frederick Douglass, a Psychobiography: Rethinking Subjectivity in the Western Experiment of Democracy*. New York: Palgrave Macmillan, 2018.

———. "Self Care and the Liberal Arts." The Thread. February, 2019. https://www.ptsem.edu/news/self-care-and-the-liberal-arts-1.

Glaude Jr., Eddie S. *Begin Again: James Baldwin's America and Its Urgent Lessons for Our Own*. New York: Crown, 2020.

Hood, Ralph W., Peter C. Hill, and W. Paul Williamson. *The Psychology of Religious Fundamentalism*. New York: The Guilford, 2005.

Jones, James W. *Blood That Cries Out from the Earth: The Psychology of Religious Terrorism*. Oxford: Oxford University Press, 2008.

47. Gibson, "Self-Care and the Liberal Arts."

———. *Terror and Transformation: The Ambiguity of Religion in Psychoanalytic Perspective*. London: Routledge, 2002.

Kohut, Heinz. "Introspection, Empathy, and the Semi-Circle of Mental Health." *The International Journal of Psychoanalysis* (1982) 395–407.

———. *The Restoration of the Self*. Chicago: The University of Chicago Press, 1977.

Kuruvilla, Carol. 2020. "White Evangelical Leaders Pledge Seminaries Will Not Teach Key Theory on Systemic Racism." *Huffington Post*, December 4, 2020. Accessed December 4, 2020. https://www.huffpost.com/entry/southern-baptist-critical-race-theory_n_5fc81c12c5b66bc574672b84.

LaMothe, Ryan. "I think of God, In Order Not to Be Aware: Defensive Dissociation and the Use of Religious Objects." *International Journal of Applied Psychoanalytic Studies* (2004) 140–57.

Meredith, James. *A Mission from God: A Memoir and Challenge for America*. New York: Atria, 2012.

Niebuhr, Reinhold. *Love and Justice: Selections from the Shorter Writings of Reinhold Niebuhr*. Louisville: Westminster John Knox, 1957.

———. *The Irony of American History*. Chicago: The University of Chicago Press, 1952.

Raboteau, Albert J. *American Prophets: Seven Religious Radicals & Their Struggle for Social and Political Justice*. Princeton: Princeton University Press, 2016.

Schorske, Del Valle. "Insights from Black Psychoanalysts Speak." *Transition* 115 (2014) 41–50. https://doi.org/10.2979/transition.115.41.

Summers, Frank. "Fundamentalism, Psychoanalysis, and Psychoanalytic Theories." *The Psychoanalytic Review* (2006) 329–52.

Thomson, J. Anderson. "Who Are We? Where Did We Come From? How Religious Identity Divides and Damns Us All." *The American Journal of Psychoanalysis* (2009) 22–42.

Thurman, Howard. *Jesus and the Disinherited*. Boston: Beacon, 1976.

Washington, James Melvin. *A Testament of Hope: The Essential Writings and Speeches of Martin Luther King, Jr.* New York: HarperCollins, 1986.

West, Cornell. *Democracy Matters: Winning the Fight Against Imperialism*. New York: Penguin, 2004.

———. Moments of Interruption. Directed by Noah Stout. Performed by Cornell West. 2020.

Winnicott, D. W. *Playing and Reality*. New York: Routledge, 1971.

———. Black Psychoanalysts Speak. Directed by Basia Winograd. 2014.

Young, Thomas M. "Using Narrative Theory and Self Psychology within a Multigenerational Family Systems Perspective." *Psychoanalytic Social Work* (1996) 137–55.

3

#BlackFearsMatter

Honoring African Americans' Fear and Caring for the African American S.E.L.F. During a Crisis

Danielle J. Buhuro

We are told not to have it. We are told that it can't exist next to our faith. Words chastising us for having it have been converted to popular Facebook memes gone viral. What is it? Fear.

Fear is Not an Alternative Fact, Fear is Real

It is inappropriate and unrealistic to tell African Americans not to be afraid during a crisis. Contrary to what some may say, fear is real. Fear is not something that someone simply creates in their mind. Fear is an authentic, genuine feeling. Fear is a universal feeling experienced by all human beings without regard to race, gender, sexual orientation, class, etc., according to marriage and family therapist Dr. Gloria Willcox.[1] There are six major feelings that all persons experience which Willcox creatively graphed on a Feeling Wheel.[2] Those feelings are "sad," "mad," "scared,"

---

1. Willcox, "The Feeling Wheel," 274–76.
2. Willcox, "The Feeling Wheel."

"peaceful," "joyful," and "powerful." Western civilization suggests that feelings have value. Some feelings are deemed good while other feelings are deemed bad. African-centered psychologist Linda James Myers highlights Western civilization's desire to maintain a dichotomous split between good and bad feelings. Feelings of "sad," "mad," and "scared" are valued as bad or negative whereas feelings of "peaceful," "joyful," and "powerful" are valued as good and positive. On the contrary, Eastern civilization, African traditions in particular, point out that there is no such good or bad value associated with feelings.[3] Feelings are prevalent in various life circumstances and all feelings are real. The only time when feelings are not real is when certain persons use feelings as a manipulation tool to commit crimes, i.e. white racist police officers who murder unharmed Black people then defend their behavior by offering the "get out of jail free card" response: "I feared for my life."

It is hard for one to sit in the space of a "bad" feeling. An example of this can be seen in daily, informal interactions. One person may ask another person, "How are you feeling today?" If the response is anything except a "good" feeling, the questioner may immediately feel the urge to shift the responder to a different, positive feeling. The questioner, without hesitation, may begin to recommend strategies to make the responder feel better. It is as if sitting in the pain of "sad," "mad," and "scared" feelings is at best abnormal and at worse criminal. This desire to shift the other's "negative" emotional state is so common that most persons are unaware of when they are even doing it. This interaction happens within a blink of an eye. This desire to shift one's negative mood harms the profession of spiritual care. Thus, one myth in the practice of spiritual care is that it is the role of the chaplain or spiritual care provider to shift persons from feeling bad to feeling good. It's difficult to sit comfortably in the tension of "uggghhh." Therefore, before spiritual care providers can help others embrace the "ugghhh," spiritual care providers are invited to become self-aware of their own life's "ugghhhs" and learn to sit in those spaces first. Professional board-certified chaplains have learned to rest comfortably in the tension and anxiety of the "ugghhhh, ouch" moment.

The inability to acknowledge and rest comfortably in "sad," "mad," and "scared" feelings has grave consequences. African-centered psychology draws attention to the plight of many spiritual care providers unable to sit in the anxiety-producing feelings of "sad, mad, scared." This results

---

3. Myers, *Understanding an Afrocentric World View.*

in people being inauthentic and superficial in relationships with others.[4] Whenever a married couple happily announces that they've been married for several decades and have never had an argument or fight, this causes wonderment on whether or not the marriage is authentic and genuine. All types of relationships will experience sadness, anger, and scare at various moments.

An inability to acknowledge "sad," "mad," or "scared" feelings fosters a disconnection within the self, causing persons to experience depression, anxiety, and low self-esteem, according to African psychologist Na'im Akbar.[5] Persons will find themselves on a never-ending hamster wheel, forever running and striving to please the other. This gives way to a "never being satisfied or continent" demeanor. For example, this is where perfectionism tendencies are birthed. The unhealthy idealistic desire to remain in "peaceful," "joyful," and "powerful" will eventually lead persons to experiencing an internal implosion.

Equally important, persons must resist pitting feelings against each other. Resist speaking of feelings in "either/or" splits, instead, from an African-centered psychological construct, embrace feelings as "both/and." It is possible for persons to experience feelings of both "scare" and "peace." In the midst of a COVID-19 global pandemic, persons can experience feelings of both "sad" and "joy," "anger," and "power," at the same time. African-centered psychology suggests humans are complex beings capable of holding space for multiple feelings at one time.[6] On the contrary, unhealthy, unethical, and inaccurate theology has gone viral on social media, particularly Facebook, chastising African American online viewers for expressing feelings of scare and seemingly not having enough faith. Many times, these unhealthy messages are birthed from the Black Church. Thus, the Black Church must repent and reclaim its African centeredness of providing nonjudgmental pastoral care *after* listening to the stories, the narratives, the feelings of African bodies feeling afraid in crisis.

Seward Hiltner, one of Euro-America's founding fathers of pastoral theology, proposed the notion that spiritual care can be defined as "shepherding" a people through three caring strategies: healing, sustaining, and guiding. William A. Clebsch and Charles R. Jaekle would later add a fourth caring strategy called "reconciling." African American pastoral

---

4. Myers, *Understanding an Afrocentric World View.*

5. Akbar, *Akbar Papers in African Psychology.*

6. Akbar, *Akbar Papers in African Psychology.*

theologians criticized these surface-level strategies for not taking into consideration systemic sociological oppression's effect on African American persons in the counseling relationship/contract. Thus, the father of African American Pastoral Care, Thomas Pugh, along with the first forefathers of African American pastoral theology, Edward Wimberly and Archie Smith, proposed that pastoral care to the Black body must take into consideration the impact of racism. Wimberly and Smith were the first Black pastoral theologians to highlight that the Black Church is the origin of of where Black pastoral care exists. Emmanuel Lartey would later add that the Black Church provide pastoral care for Black persons that includes "liberation" as a caring strategy.

Wimberly promoted a narrative approach as pivotal to caring for African American persons in the Black Church that would lead to personal and social transformation (Lartey's view of liberation). A key element of this approach is the importance of maintaining a nonjudgemental listening ear to the stories and authentic feelings of the Black persons first. I suggest that this is where the Black Church has deteriorated. In an age of social distancing and relying heavily on quick, snappy, fast-paced social media posts and comments for interaction and connection, the African American clergy no longer has the capabilities to sit face-to-face, in-person, and in long increments of time, and listen to the stories, fears, and pain of parishioners during COVID-19. The act of deep listening through digital technology is possible but many clergy lack the digital/technological skills along with personal patience to provide sufficient "sustaining" pastoral care for long periods of time in digital space. For example, many churches decided to cut the time length of their worship services and church events offered online, fearing that church members could not remain engaged for a long period of time, becoming easily distracted with home vices, or growing weary of physically looking at a screen when online instead of in-person. Providing pastoral care in digital space also requires clergy to enter into an acceptance of re-imagining how pastoral care is called to be in the twenty-first century. In recent years, another contributing factor to bad theology going viral during COVID-19 is the shift of the Black Church, from the three mainline African American Christian denominations of Baptist, AME and Pentecostal/COGIC to nondenominational, charismatic worship centers, embracing conservative principles focused solely on evangelism, discipleship and salvation in the afterlife while ignoring social ills. Thus, quick empty hashtags, like #FaithOverFear, which lack deep empathy and theological accuracy, run rampant during online worship services and church status updates in the midst of our pandemic.

African American clergy, laypersons, social activists, and scholars are encouraged to learn that since it is in fact the case that humans are psychologically complex beings capable of holding more than one feeling at any given time likewise, fear and faith can coexist at the same time during a crisis. I propose African American persons must reclaim their cultural identity, even in digital space, and not be afraid to post, "I'm afraid," during a global health pandemic. With Family Systems Theory in mind, African American online viewers can self-differentiate, from their larger digital family, their own authentic individual identity and feelings. The larger digital family can respond with empathy and empowerment, refraining from shaming and guilting one because he or her acknowledges their own feelings of "sad," "mad," or "scare" on social media.

Social Media Spiritual Care Strategy #1

When one posts "sad, mad, scared" feelings on social media in response to COVID-19 or any other crisis, appropriate spiritual care responses would be:

- Affirm person's openness and vulnerability in sharing their feelings publicly online in digital space:
    - "Thank you for sharing your feelings. That was very brave/ courageous of you."

- Empathize with those feelings:
    - "I can understand why you may feel that way. [Maybe] I've felt that way before to . . ."
    - "How you feel is understandable and normal."

- Affirm persons' steadfast spirituality and, at the same time, their realistic humanity:
    - "I understand that you are a person of deep faith and, at the same time, you are human."
    - "[In Christian contexts] Jesus was both divine and human . . . even Jesus wept."

- Invite further reflection and provide a listening ear:

    - "Would you like to share more (if not publicly, feel free to private message me)?

    - "I am here for you with a nonjudgmental listening ear."

The African American S.E.L.F. Matter—Making Healthy Pastoral Care Go Viral During a Pandemic

Digital space is the new outlet for many African American adults, longing for community, to express authentic feelings, like fear, in a time of social distancing when persons cannot be physically face-to-face with loved ones. Caring for the African American S.E.L.F. in digital space during a pandemic is the new, prophetic methodology of spiritual care. In *Liberating Our Dignity, Saving Our Souls*, theologian and psychologist Lee H. Butler proposes the "theory of African American communal identity formation."[7] Central to Butler's theory is understanding that rage must be transformed to creativity. What can spiritual care practitioners do during a global crisis? With Butler's theory in mind, spiritual care practitioners and the larger digital community are called to transform their own rage, anger, sadness and even fear into creativity in how they care for others in digital space. Instead of shaming and guilting persons who express feelings of scare in digital space about a global pandemic, one is invited to become self-aware of one's own feelings of anger, sadness and scare about a health crisis then transforming those feelings into a spirit of creativity to provide spiritual care to others in digital space.

This writer asserts that a creative online spiritual care methodology of how to care for African Americans is termed "The S.E.L.F. Model." The African American S.E.L.F. Model is an acronym highlighting four specific needs of African Africans in particular:

- S = Social Needs

- E = Emotional Needs

- L = Life Meaning and Purpose Needs

- F = Faith Needs

---

7. Butler, *Liberating Our Dignity, Saving Our Souls*, 161.

These needs arise from particular fears African Americans wrestle with in society.

External Structural Racism Stirs More Fear and Creates Social Needs

First, based on "S" in The S.E.L.F. Model, African Americans have particular social needs. Current social inequalities negatively impact African American's access to affordable health care, causing COVID-19 to become a ticking time bomb stirring greater fear for African Americans. Thus, external social factors cause internal health problems within African American bodies. According to the Centers for Disease Control and Prevention (CDC), four specific external social factors are to blame for African American health disparities:[8]

- Unemployment
- Living in poverty
- No home ownership
- Could not see a medical doctor because of cost

What do these four social factors have in common? Lack of sufficient and sustainable economics is at the core of these factors. What is even more painful yet powerful to note is that the CDC highlights that African Americans wrestle with these social factors through much of adulthood from ages 18 to 64.[9] Examining the effect of unemployment in 2014–2015, the CDC report that African Americans between the ages of 18 and 34 were 7% more likely to not have a job compared to their white counterparts.[10] From ages 35 to 49, African Americans were always unemployed double the rate of white persons.[11] As African American progress to middle age and senior age categories, they continued to maintain higher rates of unemployment compared to white adults in the same age bracket.[12]

8. Center for Disease Control and Prevention (CDC), "African American Health."
9. CDC, "African American Health."
10. CDC, "African American Health."
11. CDC, "African American Health."
12. CDC, "African American Health."

Lack of employment opportunities in 2014–2015 also increased African Americans' probability of living a substantial number of years in poverty. According to the CDC, African American adults were always roughly 10% more poverty-stricken than white adults.[13] Sadly, this percentage increased for African Americans aged 50 to 64.[14] Subsequently, if African Americans were more likely to be unemployed and living in poverty compared to white persons, then African Americans were also more likely to not own their own home. The CDC reports that African Americans were always 20% more likely to be homeless, living with others or renting apartments or house. Lack of employment also negatively impacted African Americans ability to see a medical doctor for care because of cost. In 2014–2015, compared to whites, African Americans had a 4 to 6% more likelihood of not being able to see a doctor.

Another social inequality that negatively impacts African American health is the geographical location of many healthcare institutions. Studies show that in recent years many healthcare institutions are moving out of particular neighborhoods with majority poor persons of color, causing many poor African Americans to be unable to access affordable medical care without reliable transportation to commute to other financially affluent neighborhoods where hospitals are located. According to the Association of Healthcare Journalists, "Hospitals in the U.S. have been abandoning inner cities for years. By 2010, the number of urban hospitals still operating in 52 big cities had fallen to 426, down from 781 in 1970. Meanwhile, hundreds of medical centers built with cathedral-like grandeur have opened for business in affluent suburbs."[15] A research study conducted by the *Pittsburgh Post-Gazette* and *Milwaukee Journal Sentinel* drew attention to how the closures of hospitals since 1991 "left many low-income neighborhoods without an effective safety net, undermined efforts to recruit doctors, and did away with high-wage jobs for local residents."[16]

Even though Medicare and some state Medicaid programs have developed "accountable care organizations" which are intended to be rewarded for esteeming quality and health outcomes over the quantity of procedures

13. CDC, "African American Health."

14. CDC, "African American Health."

15. Rojas-Burke and Bowman, "What Happens When Hospitals Abandon Inner Cities."

16. Rojas-Burke and Bowman, "What Happens When Hospitals Abandon Inner Cities."

given, these healthy systems may still "end up losing money if it applies those processes to fee-for-service patients. In the fee-for-service world, each unnecessary hospital admission, specialty procedure or imaging test that is avoided counts as lost revenue for the hospital and doctors."[17]

When compared to white counterparts, African Americans' high rates of inability to access affordable health care because of unemployment, living in poverty, no home ownership, incapabilities to see a doctor for medical care because of costs and healthcare institutions moving out of poor African American communities slowly and meticulously builds an arduous stone wall named structural racism that inherently affects African American health and further propels African American fear.

More fear amongst African Americans centers on the lack of trust of the COVID-19 vaccine. Many older African Americans lived the experiences of what Harriet A. Washington termed "Medical Apartheid." For younger generations who didn't live these experiences, the narratives of these unethical medical practices have become sacred and passed down through African American lineages via the celebrated oral tradition. Therefore, both old and young alike have forever logged in the communal collective consciousness several narratives of how racism fueled unethical health care practices towards African Americans. The African American community remembers how, in 1619, when their ancestors first arrived on the shores of America, enslaved and kidnapped from the African motherland, white medical doctors partnered with white slave owners to poke, prod, and inspect naked African flesh on auction blocks. The African American community remembers how during this period of African Enslavement (1619–1865), a white male doctor named J. Marion Sims, whom the U.S. would later recognize as the "Father of Gynecology", performed much of his OBGYN research and experiments on enslaved African women against their will and often times without anesthesia. The African American community remembers white psychiatrists creating a fake mental illness diagnosis called "drapetomania" to diagnose runaway slaves and justify psychotropic sedatives to prevent them from running away again.

As many reflect on the COVID-19 vaccine, the story of the Tuskegee Syphilis Study is the incident that weighs the heaviest on many African Americans minds. About 150 poor African American men from Alabama were, unbeknownst to them, injected with a strand of syphilis

17. Rojas-Burke and Bowman, "What Happens When Hospitals Abandon Inner Cities."

to monitor the effects of this disease on the human body. The gentle-
men would later become gravely sick, and many died. What makes this
story sadder was that the nurse who worked with the physician to find
the African American male subjects was an African American woman,
Eunice Evers, who the men trusted as a fellow African American person.
The words of famed Black liberation theologian Jeremiah A. Wright, Jr.
ring true, "Everybody who is your color ain't your kind and everybody
who has your same skin, ain't your kin." Thus, while there has been much
marketing of the COVID-19 vaccine's founder, a Black woman scientist
named Dr. Kizzmekia Corbett, some African Americans are still afraid
because they remember Eunice Evers.

Why is it important to talk about these systemic social issues? How
do these social issues connect with the methodology of pastoral care?
According to the "Multisystems" approach in therapeutic counseling,
psychologists must take into consideration the social needs of persons
and connect or refer counselees to social support systems and agencies:
"Aponte (1994) has made the most significant contribution to the theoretical and clinical development of this model. Building on his foundations as a structural family therapist, he developed the "ecostructural"
model, which examines the role of the family therapist vis-à-vis outside
agencies working with poor families."[18]

African American psychologist Nancy Boyd-Franklin suggests that
therapeutic interventions for African Americans in particular must incorporate a "multisystems" approach because of "the realities of being
Black and poor":

> To be Black and poor is to live in fear. Families are constantly
> afraid for their children and are well aware of the location of
> the local "crack house" or the neighborhood "pusher." Children
> can be enlisted by the "drug culture," first as "runners" and later
> as "pushers" or "users." When disillusionment grows strong,
> drugs and alcohol can often lure youth. The process of educat-
> ing their children is another "minefield" for African American
> parents (BoydFranklin, et al., 2001). Inner-city schools are often
> not responsive to children's needs, and can be viewed by many
> African American parents as just another hostile, overwhelming
> system, one more impossible wall to scale. It is not difficult to
> understand therefore why Black youth have one of the highest
> dropout rates in the nation. There are fears on many other levels

18. Boyd-Franklin, *Black Families in Therapy*, 272.

for African American families living in poverty. Street crime is extremely high in inner-city neighborhoods. The discrepancies between African American inner-city communities and the rest of the nation increase the desperation of these families. The rage that this process causes often erupts in domestic violence, child abuse, and "Black on Black" crime. In many Black inner-city neighborhoods, many African American families are struggling to survive and feel that they have no protection. Experience has taught them not to trust the police or the courts to deliver justice. Thus they avoid these systems at all costs.[19]

Likewise, as psychologists are concerned about the social needs of persons and incorporate the "multisystems" approach in therapeutic interventions, spiritual care practitioners must do likewise in offering spiritual care to African Americans. A social justice, Black/Womanist liberation theological construct supports this thought. From a Christianity-focused perspective, Jesus was always concerned about the social needs of persons first before he said one word about faith or religious concerns. The gospels in the New Testament are engulfed in numerous examples of Jesus demonstrating his life's mission and work to fulfill the prophecy of Isaiah 61: "The Spirit of the Lord is upon me, because he has anointed me to bring good news to the poor. He has sent me to proclaim release to the captives and recovery of sight to the blind, to let the oppressed go free."[20]

Thus, providing digital pastoral care via social media means first addressing online users' social needs. Pastoral care practitioners and the wider digital community are encouraged to share social service referrals online through one's personal and/or institutional social media pages. Sharing these types of resources online provides a wonderful access to a mass group of people. What makes sharing these resources online a powerful engagement is the notion that the distribution of these resources is not limited to waiting and facilitating a physical face-to-face encounter between persons dependent on time and space. An example of this can be seen in the Virtual Poor People's Campaign, organized and facilitated by Rev. Dr. William Barber, to highlight and distribute social service resources for the poor.[21] The digital event, streamed online via Facebook Live, took place on Saturday, June 20, 2020 which ironically drew more attendees virtually then President Donald Trump's physical in-person

19. Boyd-Franklin, *Black Families in Therapy*, 272–73.

20. Luke 4:16–18, NRSV.

21. "Virtual Poor People's Campaign Rally Draws Crowd of More Than a Million."

re-election campaign kick-off rally the same day in Tulsa, Oklahoma.[22] Thus, social media provides an essential medium for circulating much-needed resources in an efficient and wider reaching capacity.

Social Media Spiritual Care Strategy #2

When African American social media users post concerns about economic disparities, appropriate spiritual care responses would be:

- Acknowledge and empathize with the pain and fear that theses disparities cause.
- Ask how and what type of social support services would be helpful to the person during this time (don't assume).
- If the person inquires, (via private message) make referrals to:
  - Unemployment opportunities
  - Resources to address poverty
  - Resources to aid in home ownership
  - Resources to aid in medical care
- Intentionally share posts about economic resources on one's own social media accounts (but don't violate confidentiality by tagging persons in posts or posting on person's wall).
- Participate in social justice advocacy:
  - Support and challenge local/state lawmakers for more economic resources and affordable healthcare institutions in underserved persons of color communities
  - Initiate offering social service resources via faith communities and religious institutions
  - Support service local, state, and national organizations and agencies already doing this meaningful work
  - Post about the importance of social justice advocacy online via social media and hold family and friends accountable to join in the work

22. "Virtual Poor People's Campaign Rally Draws Crowd of More Than a Million."

- Post selfies on social media of yourself receiving the vaccine, encouraging others to also receive the vaccine. Refrain from making online comments about negative side effects that would discourage others or fuel conspiracy theories.

Fear Exists in Adult Stages of Psychosocial Human Development and Creates Emotional/Life Meaning-Purpose Needs

Second, based on "E" and "L" in The S.E.L.F. Model, African Americans have particular emotional and existential (life meaning-purpose) needs. Fear is not simply a feeling experienced by babies and children. Adults become afraid too! Fear is an emotion experienced in the adulthood stages of psychosocial human development, according to psychologist Erik Erikson.[23] In *The Life Cycle Completed*, Erikson suggests that the progression of life from childhood to adulthood is divided in nine stages.[24] There are three specific stages dedicated to adult years: Stage 6 is the young adult stage, Stage 7 is the middle adult stage and Stage 8 is the older adult stage.

According to Erikson, at each stage, persons wrestle with a unique psychosocial crisis or task to accomplish.[25] During Stage 6, the young adult stage, young adults wrestle with the psychosocial crisis of Intimacy versus Isolation. In this stage, Erikson suggests young adults' are primarily afraid and fearful of not being able to gain intimacy with others and therefore remaining isolated.[26] In this stage, young adults struggle to form close relationships and to gain the capacity for intimate love. COVID-19 threatens young African American adults' ability to genuinely establish close relationship and intimacy with others. Government-created "social distancing" and "stay at home" policies become an added barrier. According to Erikson, when young adults are unable to establish close relationship and intimate love with other adults, the young adult wrestles with feelings of isolation and rejection.[27] Thus, young African American adults exhibit fear in response COVID-19 because they don't want to experience feelings of social isolation.

23. Erikson and Erikson, *Life Cycle Completed*.
24. Erikson and Erikson, *Life Cycle Completed*.
25. Erikson and Erikson, *Life Cycle Completed*.
26. Erikson and Erikson, *Life Cycle Completed*.
27. Erikson and Erikson, *Life Cycle Completed*.

On the other hand, young African American adults may seek to demonstrate an external rage against their internal fear by intentionally ignoring "social distancing" and "stay at home" orders by attending large events in mass groups to experience internal feelings of connection and resist internal feelings of isolation. One late Saturday evening on April 25, 2020, *The Washington Post* reported "about 50 young people squeezed into a Northwest Side townhouse in Chicago to dance, drink and chat at a party," Chicago Police Department officials reported.[28] A cell phone video taken by one of the partygoers going "Facebook Live" at the party went viral on social media, eliciting much condemnation from online viewers and political officials. Not only did this gathering violate Illinois' "social distancing" rule, but many of the party attendees stood within inches of dozens of other partygoers without protective face masks. Eventually Chicago police arrived to the town house and evacuated everyone. The mayor of Chicago, Lori Lightfoot took her office Twitter account saying, "What was depicted on the video was reckless and utterly unacceptable," in a tweeted statement.[29] "While most Chicagoans are doing their part to prevent the spread of COVID-19, reckless actions like these threaten our public health and risk erasing the progress we have made."[30] The mayor's comments were similar to other online viewers who, being out of touch, began publicly shaming and guilty the African American young adult party host on social media.

The question many refused to ask however was "why?" Why would so many African American young adults put their lives, and the lives of their loved ones, at risk to physically gather in a face-to-encounter? COVID-19 cast a light on how, *before* this pandemic, certain people were already socially distant and out of touch with other persons—particularly younger people and those of a different economic tax bracket. According to one of the party goers, Ms. Tink Purcell, whose Facebook Live video recording of the gathering went live and subsequently drew both local and national criticism, the gathering was a memorial to honor the lives of two gentleman lost to gun violence in 2018.[31] The gathering pointed to a number of psychological dynamics—one being this idea of people gathering

28. Shepherd, "'Reckless and Utterly Unacceptable' House Party Frustrates Chicago Officials Trying to Fight the Coronavirus."

29. Shepherd, "Reckless and Utterly Unacceptable."

30. Shepherd, "Reckless and Utterly Unacceptable."

31. Harrison, "A West Side House Party Exposes the Disconnect between Young Black Residents."

to celebrate lives lost from two years ago as a method of defusing held on internal grief. This dynamic also highlighted the reoccurring theme of systemic grief (and trauma) in African American communities as a result of gun violence. This gathering, in an effort to pay homage to the two lives ended nearly two years ago, brings to light the notion that grief is complicated, and its effects continue to show up as questionable behavior, pervading the psychological and emotional well-being of young African American adults today. Instead of online viewers chastising the young African American adults for gathering, how can spiritual care providers demonstrate online care through empathizing with the grief these young African American adults experienced after losing friends in their circle?

Purcell highlighted another point that speaks to classism and capitalism during the pandemic:

> I get irritated with these celebrities trying to tell us to stay in the house," said Purcell. "I'll stay in the house if you come build me a basketball court like you got in your house. Come put a zoo in my backyard. These rich people got things to do while they sit in the house. Us people that aren't as rich as them, we don't have nothing to do in the house. Sometimes this can cause you to go into boredom and depression and you have to get out, you have to get some air."[32]

Purcell's comment also inherently spoke to Erik Erikson's theory that young adults look to social interactions and relationships with others for intimacy and the avoidance of social isolation. Thus, instead of shaming party goers in digital space, the online community is called to address feelings of social isolation that these young African American adults face in light of not only COVID-19 and classism/capitalism, but the normal psychosocial crisis they grapple with in their particular age timeframe. Online viewers are called to extend empathy and acknowledge the psychodynamic crisis occurring in this moment, rather than resulting to online shaming, guilting, and condemning the party host and attendees as simply "reckless" or disobedient.

According to Erikson, during Stage 7, the middle-aged stage, middle-aged adults wrestle with the psychosocial crisis of Generativity versus Stagnation.[33] In this stage, Erikson suggests middle-aged adults are pri-

---

32. Harrison, "A West Side House Party Exposes the Disconnect between Young Black Residents."

33. Erikson and Erikson, *Life Cycle Completed.*

marily afraid and fearful of not being able to positively contribute to the world, usually through family and work.[34] COVID-19 threatens middle-aged African American adults' ability to maintain already established relationships with family. I also argue that COVID-19 threatens middle-aged African adults' ability to work and be a positive contributing member to society. According to Erikson, when middle-aged adults are unable to work and contribute to society, the middle-aged adult wrestles with feelings of stagnation and feeling a lack of purpose.[35] Middle-aged African American adults exhibit fear as a defensive mechanism in response to COVID-19 because they don't want to experience lack of purpose in society. Online communities are invited to empower and affirm "Nia" (the Kwanzza term meaning creativity and purpose) in middle-aged African American adults.

According to Erikson, during Stage 8, the older adult stage, older adults wrestle with the psychosocial crisis of Integrity versus Despair.[36] In this stage, Erikson suggests older adults are primarily afraid and fearful of whether their life has been satisfying or a failure.[37] COVID-19 has primarily impacted older senior citizens considered the most vulnerable population health wise in the United States. Thus, the aging population may view the sum of their life as a complete failure if they were to become infected with the virus, leading to feelings of despair.

In light of Erik Erikson's theory of psychosocial human development, young, middle-aged and older African American adults struggle with fears centered on possible lack of intimacy, whether or not a sense of purpose in the world has been fulfilled and whether or not one's living has been in vain. When these "normal" adult fears come in contact with fears surrounding COVID-19, African American adult fears are magnified. Telling young, middle-aged and older adults not to be afraid during a pandemic denies the current adult psychosocial crisis that they experience.

African Americans' emotional needs are also compounded by racism. According to psychologist Monnica T. Williams, racism causes African Americans to experience Post Traumatic Stress Disorder (PTSD).[38] Williams highlights:

34. Erikson and Erikson, *Life Cycle Completed.*
35. Erikson and Erikson, *Life Cycle Completed.*
36. Erikson and Erikson, *Life Cycle Completed.*
37. Erikson and Erikson, *Life Cycle Completed.*
38. Williams, "Can Racism Cause PTSD? Implications for DSM-5."

One major factor in understanding PTSD in ethnoracial minorities is the impact of racism on emotional and psychological
well-being. Racism continues to be a daily part of American
culture, and racial barriers have an overwhelming impact on
the oppressed. Much research has been conducted on the social, economic, and political effects of racism, but little research
recognizes the psychological effects of racism on people of color
(Carter, 2007). Chou, Asnaani, and Hofmann (2012) found that
perceived racial discrimination was associated with increased
mental disorders in African Americans, Hispanic Americans,
and Asian Americans, suggesting that racism may in itself be a
traumatic experience.[39]

African Americans experience what's now being termed as "racial
trauma" as a result of blatant hate crimes as well as subtle racial-based
microaggressions:

Racial microaggressions are subtle, yet pervasive acts of racism;
these can be brief remarks, vague insults, or even non-verbal
exchanges, such as a scowl or refusal to sit next to a Black person
on the subway. When experiencing microaggressions, the target
loses vital mental resources trying figure out the intention of
one committing the act. These events may happen frequently,
making it difficult to mentally manage the sheer volume of racial stressors. The unpredictable and anxiety-provoking nature
of the events, which may be dismissed by others, can lead to
victims feeling as if they are "going crazy." Chronic fear of these
experiences may lead to constant vigilance or even paranoia,
which over time may result in traumatization or contribute to
PTSD when a more stressful event occurs later.[40]

All of this is to say that the provision of spiritual care to African Americans must take into consideration not only meetings African Americans'
social needs, but their emotional and existential (life meaning/purpose)
needs as well.

Social Media Spiritual Care Strategy #3

When a young, middle-aged, or older adult posts about fears centered on
possible lack of intimacy, whether or not a sense of purpose in the world

39. Williams, "Can Racism Cause PTSD? Implications for DSM-5."
40. Williams, "The Link Between Racism and PTSD."

has been fulfilled, whether or not one's living has been in vain, the effects of racism along with who and what persons are called to be and do in light of racism, appropriate spiritual care responses would be:

- Acknowledge the adult psychosocial crisis that many African Americans wrestle with and empathize with how these fears impact persons who must now contend with the scare of COVID-19.

- Ask reflective questions to help adults brainstorm creative responses to their respective psychosocial crisis:

  - Young Adults: "I understand that you wish to be with family and friends right now. This can be a very lonely time. How can you build community with others in different ways? What healthy things (strategies) can you do to address your loneliness?"

  - Middle-aged adults: "I understand that you're feeling like you have no purpose right now. What can you do to be helpful and supportive to someone during this time?"

  - Seniors: "I understand that you're surveying your life right now. What have been your accomplishments thus far? What have you done well before COVID-19 and during COVID-19? How can you continue celebrating these accomplishments?"

- Ask reflective questions to help adults brainstorm creative responses to racism (and other oppressions)?

  - In light of racism, who and what am I called to be and do?

  - How do I transform my rage to creativity?

  - What are my gifts, skills and talents that give a new life meaning/purpose in light of structural racism and oppression?

- Make referrals to African-centered psychologists and counselors who understand the impact of racism and oppression on African American mental health:

  - Black Therapists Rock:
    - www.BlackTherapistsRock.com
  - Therapy for Black Girls:
    - www.TherapyForBlackGirls.com
  - Melanin and Mental Health
    - www.MelaninAndMentalHealth.com

- The Association of Black Psychologists
  - https://www.abpsi.org

In the Midst of COVID-19, African Americans Rage Against Another Deadly Virus Called Police Brutality

In the midst of COVID-19, African Americans rage against another deadly virus called police brutality. The COVID-19 global outbreak had grave consequences for a middle-aged African American gentleman named George Floyd. Relocating to Minneapolis, Minnesota after losing his job in his home state of North Carolina, Minnesota was supposed to be a fresh economic start for Floyd.[41] Minnesota was to be Floyd's escape from Egypt and reward in Canaan. However, Floyd's move to the north turned out to be anything but a new, refreshing promised land. After obtaining a job as a security guard at a restaurant, COVID-19 struck.[42] When Minnesota's governor initiated an executive "state at home" order to decrease the spread of COVID-19 and the numbers of those infected, the restaurant where Floyd recently landed a stable gig closed.[43] The pandemic revealed that simply "staying at home" is not optional for those whose only income is dependent on hourly, minimum-wage jobs. The virus of capitalism saturated American economy and life long before COVID-19, drawing attention to how unless one has salaried-employment with paid-time-off benefits, simply remaining within the comfort of one's home is in fact a luxury which only the upper-class or financially affluent bestowed.

On May 25, 2020, Floyd was allegedly arrested for attempting to purchase items from a small grocer with a counterfeit $20 bill. Arriving officers to the scene of the grocer subdued an intoxicated Floyd, handcuffed his hands behind his back, plummeted him to the ground then partially pinned him under the officer's patrol truck. Officer Derek Chauvin, who had a previous working relationship with Floyd when the two worked together at a nightclub, plunged his knee along with weight of his body into Floyd's neck for 8 minutes and 46 seconds in total, and 2 minutes and 53 seconds after Floyd was unresponsive, according to the medical

---

41. Richmond, "Who Was George Floyd? Unemployed Due to Coronavirus, He'd Moved to Minneapolis for a Fresh Start."

42. Richmond, "Who Was George Floyd?"

43. Richmond, "Who Was George Floyd?"

examiner.[44] As he repeatedly whimpered "I can't breathe," Floyd began to lose consciousness, urinated on the pavement then called out for his deceased mother.[45] Floyd never spoke again. Officer Chauvin would later be charged with third degree manslaughter for the murder of Floyd.[46] Chauvin's police department training included learning how to NOT suffocate persons being restrained.[47] Chauvin kneeing Floyd in the neck for nearly ten minutes was one of the most heinous acts of police brutality caught on videotape by a 17-year-old young lady's cell phone recording.

This type of incident was not Chauvin's first. Chauvin was put on leave in 2011 for an inappropriate police shooting of Alaskan Native American Leroy Martinez.[48] Chauvin shot Ira Latrell Toles, an unarmed Black 21-year-old man in 2008.[49] Chauvin was one of the officers who murdered Wayne Reyes, a Latino man, with 16 bullets forced into him (a total of 42 rounds were shot).[50] Chauvin and another officer were chasing a car in 2005, causing the death of three people according to the Communities United Against Police Brutality.[51] There are 12 police brutality complaints against Chauvin in the Minneapolis Office of Police Conduct complain database which are all listed as "closed," "non-public," and "no discipline."[52] In other words, police brutality against persons of color is a consistent way of life for Office Derek Chauvin as simple as putting on his clothes.

Chauvin's violent and thuggish professional history shines light on how George Floyd was not only the victim of COVID-19, but a virus within a virus called police brutality. According to a research

44. Macaya and Hayes, "Floyd Was 'Non-Responsive' for Nearly 3 Minutes before Officer Took Knee off His Neck, Complaint Says."

45. Hagemann and Neuman, "'I Can't Breathe': Peaceful Demonstrators Continue to Rally Over George Floyd's Death."

46. "Charges Upgraded against Former Minneapolis Officer Derek Chauvin in George Floyd Death."

47. "Floyd's Death Was a 'Murder,' Not about Lack of Training, Minneapolis Police Chief Says."

48. Kim, "What We Know about the Officers Involved in George Floyd's Death."

49. "George Floyd Death Cop Chauvin 'Shot Another Black Man Twice Ten Years Ago.'"

50. Garcia, "Who Is Derek M. Chauvin?"

51. Garcia "Who Is Derek M. Chauvin?"

52. Garcia "Who Is Derek M. Chauvin?"

collaborative, entitled "Mapping Police Violence,"[53] in 2019 police killed 1,098 people.[54] Mapping Police Violence is a research collaborative collecting comprehensive data on police killings nationwide to quantify the impact of police violence in communities.[55] Key finds from their 2019 research includes[56]:

- There were only 27 days in 2019 when police did not kill someone.
- Black people were 24% of those killed despite being only 13% of the population.
- Black people are three times more likely to be killed by police than white people.
- Black people are 1.3 times more likely to be unarmed compared to white people.
- 8 of the 100 largest city police departments kill Black men at higher rates than the US murder rate.
- 99% of killings by police from 2013–2019 have not resulted in officers being charged with a crime.

COVID-19 and police brutality have even more startling consequences for Black women and Black transgender women. In the midst of COVID-19, police brutality against Black women has taken center stage after the brutal killing of an emergency medical technician named Breonna Taylor:

> Just after midnight on March 13, 2020, Breonna Taylor, an EMT in Louisville, Kentucky, was shot and killed by police officers who raided her home. The officers had entered her home without warning as part of a drug raid. The suspect they were seeking was not a resident of the home–and no drugs were ever found. But when they came through the door unexpectedly, and in plain clothes, police officers were met with gunfire from Taylor's boyfriend, who was startled by the presence of intruders. In only a matter of minutes, Taylor was dead—shot eight times by police officers.[57]

53. "Planning Team."
54. "Planning Team."
55. "Planning Team."
56. "Planning Team."
57. Blain, "A Short History of Black Women and Police Violence."

What's most troubling about this case is that Taylor was an essential worker, ruled by the government to be a valued healthcare worker exempt from following executive "stay at home" and "shelter in place" policies. The one tasked with saving lives, ultimately was deemed by Louisville police of being a life not worthy of saving. "Since protests began in late May of 2020, Louisville officials have banned the use of no-knock warrants, which allow the police to forcibly enter people's homes to search them without warning."[58] The irony in this case is that while Louisville officials created the "Breonna Law" named after Taylor, her police officer murderers have yet to be arrested and charged at the time. How does one pass a law named after a person but doesn't arrest the person(s) who killed her? Within one week of his death, the police officer murderer of African American male George Floyd had been arrested and the following week charges were increased to second-degree murder at the time of this writing. This speaks to the sexism, patriarchy, and misogyny that African American women face in the criminal justice system—even in death. According to Kanya Bennett, Senior Legislative Counsel of the ACLU Washington Legislative Office:

> . . . though the Black Lives Matter movement was started by three Black women, we've largely been left out of the national narrative on police violence. Police violence impacts Black women and other women of color just as it does Black men. So sadly, we too need survival tactics for our teen girls attending pool parties and our girlfriends eating at the Waffle House.
> We must also consider other forms of police violence that impact Black women and women of color, like sexual assault. Sexual abuse is the second most reported form of police misconduct after use of excessive force.[59]

According to the "#SayHerName" Project,

> In 2015 alone, at least six Black women have been killed by or after encounters with police. For instance, just before Freddie Gray's case grabbed national attention, police killed unarmed Mya Hall—a Black transgender woman—on the outskirts of Baltimore. Alleged to be driving a stolen car, Hall took a wrong turn onto NSA property and was shot to death by officers after the car crashed into the security gate and a police cruiser. In

---

58. Oppel and Taylor, "Here's What You Need to Know About Breonna Taylor's Death."

59. Bennett, "Say Her Name: Recognizing Police Brutality Against Black Women."

April, police fatally shot Alexia Christian while she was being handcuffed in the back of a police cruiser. And in March, in Ventura, California, police officers shot and killed Megan Hockaday—a young mother of three—within 20 seconds of entering her home in response to a domestic disturbance.[60]

When African Americans highlight feelings of "sad, mad, or scared", it is inappropriate and lacks basic pastoral care skill to respond with derailing statements: "What about Black-on-Black crime?" According to the Southern Poverty Law Center, roughy 80% of white people are killed by other white people.[61] Yet the phrase "White-on-White" crime does not exist. "Black-on-Black" crime is a term that's been coined specifically for Black people to create feelings of self-hatred and disunity within the race. It's a tactic to divide and conquer. This tactic is also psychologically damaging. This tactic stops African Americans from being perceived as victims and reminds all that African Americans are criminals.

To perceive African Americans as violent, subsequently justifies white people being violent towards African Americans as a "necessary evil" to control the stereotyped Black criminal:

> White Americans' unsubstantiated views about the potential of violence from black people was the number one excuse they used to justify slavery, lynching, Jim Crow, and various forms of mass incarceration. Never was Klan violence or the lynching of black people by white people ascribed to an inherent white trait. Without the ability to claim oppression of black people as a form of self-defense, racial segregation and white supremacy would be seen for what they are: rank oppression of other people for financial or other benefit.[62]

The Ku Klux Klan continues to exist today and sometimes wears blue police officer uniforms. Thus, police brutality towards Africans Americans has become a new form of modern-day lynching.

Lynchings and police brutality against African Americans is grounded in a European-crafted scientific belief that African Americans are biologically inferior to white people: "Attempting to address what came to be known as the 'Negro Problem,' American scientists and other intellectuals created a new body of knowledge that they could use to justify white

---

60. Bennett, "Say Her Name: Recognizing Police Brutality Against Black Women."

61. Staff, "The Biggest Lie in the White Supremacist Propaganda Playbook: Unraveling the Truth About 'Black-on-White Crime.'"

62. Staff, "The Biggest Lie in the White Supremacist Propaganda Playbook."

supremacy by scientifically 'proving' black inferiority. Men like Samuel George Morton (1799–1851), who is considered the originator of scientific racism, relied on anecdotal observations and physical measurements."[63]

African Americans not only fear a global health pandemic but also fear the intersection of oppression, grounded in racism, sexism, classism, and transphobia, that continues before, during, and even after the COVID-19 pandemic. This dynamic casts greater fears among African Americans during a health crisis.

Social Media Spiritual Care Strategy #4

When African American social media users post concerns about police brutality, appropriate spiritual care responses would be:

- Empathize with the victims of police brutality, resist judgment of the victim.

- Openly post and comment a stance against police brutality, racism, sexism, homophobia, transphobia, classism, ableism, and body shaming on social media

- Do not respond with "What about Black-on-Black crime?" rhetoric or "All Lives Matter" rhetoric

- Visit www.BlackLivesMatter.com and post helpful facts, advocacy opportunities and social media resources listed on this website

- Visit https://aapf.org/sayhername and post helpful facts, advocacy opportunities and social media resources listed on this website

Bad Theology Kills More Than A Virus and Creates Faith Needs

Finally, based on "F" in The S.E.L.F. Model, healthy, appropriate, pastoral biblical exegesis must be highlighted. I propose that African Americans view illness through the lens of two theological constructs: one becomes sick with an illness because one sinned or one becomes sick with an illness because one is being tested by God. In the first case, many a part of African American religious contexts internalize success and achievement with undying devotion and obedience to God. Often the attainment of

63. Staff, "The Biggest Lie in the White Supremacist Propaganda Playbook."

ample material possessions is the revelation of God's reward to one as a result of one's righteous, humble spiritual attitude and lifestyle. Therefore, when one meets illness, it is believed that one has been disobedient, bad, unholy, unethical, and essentially disconnected from God. The only method for one to receive true and authentic healing from illness is grounded in spirituality and religious rituals. One must acknowledge and denounce sinful behaviors, then repent and no longer continue in the act of these behaviors and finally, through evangelism and proselytizing devote one's life to spread the message with others, ministering to others by ensuring and empowering others to avoid similar sinful behaviors or else others can expect to meet the same ill-stricken fate.

In the second case, many a part of African American religious contexts internalize illness as a test from God. Attention is focused on the story of Job in the Christian bible's Old Testament. The story of Job is interpreted as one in which God has made a wager, gamble or bet with the devil and is dependent on Job to help God win the bet. God is silent with Job never letting on to Job that his wager has occurred. Thus, for God to win the test against the devil, Job must peacefully and joyfully endure the test no matter how painful and tragic the test is towards Job's life. Job can never question the purpose of the test or God's role in the test.

Both of these types of theological constructs are inaccurate, unethical, and extremely dangerous. These types of theological constructs are extremely dangerous because they undergird a psychological construct which suggests that people are separated from, cut off and not connected to the Divine. God is silent because ill people have either been sinful or are currently alone in a quiet test. In Black liberation theology, the invincible Dr. James Cones' plethora of work centers the undeniable, unshakable proposition that God stands on the side of the oppressed African American person in particular against structural racism. In Womanist liberation theology, Dr. Emilie Townes' work centers on promoting a theological construct, particularly in healthcare, which unequivocally asserts that God stands on the side of the Black woman against the intersections of oppression—racism, sexism, classism, *and* homophobia. Black and Womanist liberation theologians agree that during the period of African enslavement in the United States, white slave masters intentionally sought to use the Christian bible to center and interpret bible scriptures that drew a psychological and theological disconnect between God and people of African descent. Thus, Black and Womanist liberation has been courageously called to re-interpret sick, demonstrative Christian white supremacy theological to constructs into liberative, loving, and social justice-oriented meanings for Black people. Carry the courageous call a step forward during COVID-19. During pandemics and police brutality, some African Americans have lost their cultural mind and therefore now reside in the Theological Sunken Place where internalized racism runs rampant. Some African Americans use social media as a weapon of mass destruction to theologically assault other African Americans into believing that African American victims of COVID-19 are either sinners in need of repentance or game show contestants in need of winning a competition.

During times of pandemics and police brutality, persons need connection with the Divine. Persons need to be reminded that God is "Emmanuel," God "with" them. Persons need to be educated to self-differentiate unhealthy, unethical theological constructs passed down from Baptist, Methodist, and Pentecostal religious traditions and embrace a theological and psychological perspective that illness is neither connected to one's shortcomings, growing edges or "sins" or what the other may deem as sinful behaviors in one's life nor is illness connected to some divine, supernatural test, competition, or gamble. During times of pandemics and police brutality, persons need to be reminded of their humanness. Thus, it's healthy to experience feelings of scare. To deny the existence of this feeling is to deny the existence and humanity of the self. Therefore, humans may psychologically separate from their emotions, cutting off their ability to think life-giving, nurturing self thoughts. Bad theology about a virus has the potential to kill more than the virus itself. Bad theology can kill one's spirituality and psychology, causing persons to function in society empty and hopeless as characters on "The Walking Dead."

At the same time, ultimately, some persons may theologize their experience of illness different from the spiritual care provider and therefore, the spiritual care provider must gain peace and contentment with this dynamic as well. According to Susan Nelson, in "Facing Evil: Evil's Many Faces Five Paradigms for Understanding Evil," some persons may make direct connections between illness and their relationship with the Divine, surmising:

> [experiencing suffering and evil] can be God's judgment, it can be the price of the creation in which God delights, but it is also the reality that God judges, resists, suffers, or uses to bring about redemption. It is tempting in conclusion to wrestle these different paradigms into one unified perspective, and the reader may choose to do so. But I will resist that urge, because I have come

to believe that each one of them is necessary to comprehend the vulnerability of the human condition, the human capacity to inflict horrible sufferings upon one another, the resiliency of the human heart to suffer and resist enormous evil, the reality of redemption for both those who hurt and those who harm, and the complexity of God's relationship with creation. They also provide multiple vantage points from which to marvel at the central proclamation of the Christian faith—nothing can separate us from the love of God. I am content to leave it at that.[64]

Social Media Spiritual Care Strategy #5

When African American social media users post theological struggles and concerns in light of COVID-19, appropriate spiritual care responses would be:

- Resist posting and commenting that COVID-19 is a punishment from God in response to sin

- Resist posting and commenting that COVID-19 is a test, or battle that one must overcome because God has made a wager with the Devil on his/her behalf

- Share posts and Christian scriptures drawing attention to God's ultimate, unconditional, and nonjudgmental love for persons impacted by COVID-19.

- Share posts that promote wearing personal protective equipment such as masks and adhering to "social distancing" policies

In conclusion, social media or digital space is the new outlet for many African American adults longing for community to express authentic feelings in a time of social distancing when persons cannot be physically present face-to-face with loved ones. Inaccurate theology has gone viral on social media, particularly Facebook, chastising African American online viewers for expressing feelings of scare and seemingly not having enough faith in God. Clergy, laypersons, social activists, and scholars are invited to learn that because human beings are psychologically complex beings capable of experiencing more than one feeling at any given time, fear and faith often do coexist during a crisis. It is important to practice healthy,

64. Nelson, "Facing Evil," 413.

appropriate, pastoral biblical exegesis. Caring for the African American S.E.L.F. online in digital space during a pandemic is the new prophetic method of spiritual care. We need it now more than ever.

Bibliography

"African American Health." *Centers for Disease Control and Prevention*, 2 May 2017, www.cdc.gov/vitalsigns/aahealth/infographic.html.

Akbar, Na'im. *Akbar Papers in African Psychology*. Mind Productions Associates, 2003.

Bennett, Kanya. "Say Her Name: Recognizing Police Brutality Against Black Women." *American Civil Liberties Union*, American Civil Liberties Union, 14 June 2018, www.aclu.org/blog/criminal-law-reform/reforming-police/say-her-name-recognizing-police-brutality-against-black.

Blain, Keisha. "A Short History of Black Women and Police Violence." *The Conversation*, 12 June 2020, theconversation.com/a-short-history-of-black-women-and-police-violence-139937.

Boyd-Franklin, Nancy. *Black Families in Therapy: Understanding the African American Experience*. New York: Guilford, 2003.

Butler, Lee H. *Liberating Our Dignity, Saving Our Souls*. St. Louis: Chalice, 2006.

"Charges Upgraded against Former Minneapolis Officer Derek Chauvin in George Floyd Death." *POLITICO*, www.politico.com/news/2020/06/03/minnesota-charges-3-more-former-officers-in-george-floyd-death-298949.

Erikson, Erik H., and Joan M. Erikson. *The Life Cycle Completed*. Extended version. New York: Norton, 1998. Kindle.

"George Floyd Death Cop Chauvin 'Shot Another Black Man Twice Ten Years Ago.'" *The US Sun*, 29 May 2020, www.the-sun.com/news/901781/george-floyd-death-cop-derek-chauvin-shoot-another-man-twice/.

Hagemann, Hannah, and Scott Neuman. "'I Can't Breathe': Peaceful Demonstrators Continue To Rally Over George Floyd's Death." *NPR*, 4 June 2020, www.npr.org/2020/06/03/869186653/demonstrations-over-george-floyds-death-and-police-brutality-carry-on.

Harrison, Vee L. "A West Side House Party Exposes the Disconnect between Young Black Residents, Chicago Officials and the News during COVID-19 Pandemic • The TRiiBE." *The TRiiBE*, 4 May 2020, www.thetriibe.com/2020/04/a-west-side-house-party-exposes-the-disconnect-between-young-black-residents-chicago-officials-and-the-news-during-covid-19-pandemic/.

Kim, Catherine. "What We Know about the Officers Involved in George Floyd's Death." *Vox*, Vox, 31 May 2020, www.vox.com/2020/5/31/21276049/derek-chauvin-tou-thao-kueng-lane-officers-george-floyd-what-we-know.

Macaya, Melissa, and Mike Hayes. "Floyd Was 'Non-Responsive' for Nearly 3 Minutes before Officer Took Knee off His Neck, Complaint Says." *CNN*, Cable News Network, 30 May 2020, www.cnn.com/us/live-news/george-floyd-protest-updates-05–28-20/h_d6de512e51a8858a57f93ffa732c2695.

Myers, Linda James. *Understanding an Afrocentric World View: Introduction to an Optimal Psychology*. Dubuque, IA: Kendall/Hunt, 1988.

Oppel, Richard A., and Derrick Bryson Taylor. "Here's What You Need to Know About Breonna Taylor's Death." *The New York Times*, 30 May 2020, www.nytimes.com/article/breonna-taylor-police.html.

"Planning Team." *Mapping Police Violence*, mappingpoliceviolence.org/planning-team.

Richmond, Todd. "Who Was George Floyd? Unemployed Due to Coronavirus, He'd Moved to Minneapolis for a Fresh Start." *ChicagoTribune.com*, Chicago Tribune, 29 May 2020, www.chicagotribune.com/nation-world/ct-nw-george-floyd-biography-20200528-y3l67rrmfnb3dh4x3i5iipneq4-story.html.

Rojas-Burke, Joe, and Robert Bowman July 19. "What Happens When Hospitals Abandon Inner Cities." *Association of Health Care Journalists*, 9 July 2014, healthjournalism.org/blog/2014/07/what-happens-when-hospitals-abandon-inner-cities/.

Shepherd, Katie. "'Reckless and Utterly Unacceptable' House Party Frustrates Chicago Officials Trying to Fight the Coronavirus." *The Washington Post*, 28 April 2020, www.washingtonpost.com/nation/2020/04/28/reckless-utterly-unacceptable-house-party-frustrates-chicago-officials-trying-fight-coronavirus/.

Staff, Hatewatch. "The Biggest Lie in the White Supremacist Propaganda Playbook: Unraveling the Truth About 'Black-on-White Crime.'" *Southern Poverty Law Center*, 14 June 2018, www.splcenter.org/20180614/biggest-lie-white-supremacist-propaganda-playbook-unraveling-truth-about-%E2%80%98black-white-crime.

TribLIVE.com, www.triblive.com/news/world/floyds-death-was-a-murder-not-about-lack-of-training-minneapolis-police-chief-says/.

"Virtual Poor People's Campaign Rally Draws Crowd of More Than a Million." *Institute for Policy Studies*, 22 June 2020, ips-dc.org/virtual-poor-peoples-campaign-rally-draws-crowd-of-more-than-a-million/.

Willcox, Gloria. "The Feeling Wheel." *Transactional Analysis Journal* 12.4 (1982) 274–76. doi:10.1177/036215378201200411.

Williams, Monnica. "Can Racism Cause PTSD? Implications for DSM-5." *Psychology Today*, Sussex Publishers, 20 May 2013, www.psychologytoday.com/us/blog/culturally-speaking/201305/can-racism-cause-ptsd-implications-dsm-5

———. "The Link Between Racism and PTSD." *Psychology Today*, Sussex Publishers, 6 Sept. 2015, www.psychologytoday.com/us/blog/culturally-speaking/201509/the-link-between-racism-and-ptsd.

4

Feeling Our Way through
an Apocalypse

Cody J. Sanders

The Covid-19 worldwide pandemic is undoubtedly the most disruptive global event in recent history. But the pandemic arises out of an even larger context of a planet on the brink.

The pandemic followed quickly on the heels of an ominous announcement from the Bulletin of the Atomic Scientists—keepers of the "Doomsday Clock" since 1947. The Bulletin moved the hand on the clock from its 2018 position of two minutes till midnight to just 100 seconds till midnight, indicating our proximity to a catastrophic human-made threat to our very existence. In this case, the Bulletin's Science and Security Board are most concerned by the simultaneous existential threats of nuclear war and climate change, both now compounded by "cyber-enabled information warfare" that "undercuts society's ability to respond."[1]

This followed just over a year after the warning of the Intergovernmental Panel on Climate Change (IPCC) that the world has only until 2030 to take drastic action to reduce CO_2 levels by 45% to avert

---

1. "Closer Than Ever."

irreversible climate-driven disaster. With over 6,000 scientific references, the 2018 IPCC report warned of catastrophic consequences if the global net CO2 levels do not quickly fall by that drastic measure. This is a feat that would "require rapid, far-reaching and unprecedented changes in all aspects of society."[2]

While the dire warning of looming climate catastrophe settled into our collective consciousness, evoking very little response (especially by the United States), we watched wildfires swiftly burn through the continent of Australia. Record-breaking temperatures, windy conditions, and severe drought throughout the country brought about the fires. These were the very environmental circumstances warned of by scientists, now becoming increasingly severe and frequent the world over. The Australia bushfires burned more than 27.2 million acres of bush, forest, and parks before they came under control.[3] Months later in Siberia, one of the earth's coldest regions, fires raged across a landscape normally frozen.[4]

The novel coronavirus that would become a global pandemic first became a public concern in January 2020. By March, the U.S. declared Covid-19 a national emergency. Sates began issuing stay-at-home orders, schools and businesses shuttered, legislation was signed into law providing $2 trillion in aid to hospitals, small businesses, and local governments to buffer against the pandemic's ravages. Early on, it became clear how the faltering of an industrial sector in one part of the world could affect the supply chain and the availability of resources in every other region of the globe, from electronics to medicine. For weeks, grocery store shelves were bare and food bank lines became ever longer. Hospital morgues filled to the brim and mass graves were dug on New York City's Hart Island.

Racial disparities became determinative of the communities most adversely affected by the coronavirus, unsurprising in a country accustomed to such inequality.[5] Meanwhile, top doctors at the CDC and NIH recommended that Americans wear face coverings in public to prevent the spread of the virus, while the recommendation was ridiculed by the White House and hotly politicized among the president's base. By October, President Trump was infected along with numerous others in his administration. Many U.S. states quickly attempted to reopen for business

2. "Summary for Policymakers."

3. "Australia Fires."

4. Stone, "A Heat Wave Thawed Siberia's Tundra."

5. Godoy, "What Do Coronavirus Racial Disparities Look Like State By State?"

in order to boost the faltering economy. Lt. Governor Dan Patrick of Texas stated the push for economic rebound clearly from the perspective of many of the president's supporters in government: "There are more important things than living and that's saving this country."[6] All the while, the worldwide death toll soared into the millions.

Then, in the very midst of the pandemic's grip, the Minneapolis police killed an unarmed black man named George Floyd in front of rolling cellphone cameras. Police knelt on his back and neck, pressing him into the pavement for 8 minutes and 46 seconds as Floyd cried, "I can't breathe!," and residents of the neighborhood surrounded him, pleading for police to relent. Floyd's lynching at the hands of the police occurred in front of the entire world already on a precipitous brink.

The country erupted in protest and riots. From coast to coast citizens gathered in the streets with signs reading "Black Lives Matter" and "Defund the Police." White supremacists, aided by social media, infiltrated the protests in many cities, turning some of them violent and destructive.[7]

Many cities took action to bring down monuments to the Confederacy and its prominent figures in response to the demands of protesters. Yet while hospitals across the country struggled to maintain stocks of personal protective equipment for healthcare personnel serving the Covid affected, the country's police departments had a seemingly unending stock of tear gas, rubber bullets, and riot gear, using tactics against protesters in the streets of the U.S. that are prohibited on the battlefield.[8] Some of these protests lasted late into summer, when federal agents from the Department of Homeland Security, clad in camouflage and driving unmarked vans, began arresting people on the streets of Portland, OR. It eventually came to light, after official DHS denial, that the department collected and analyzed information from the electronic devices and social medial accounts of protesters for an intelligence report disseminated to federal law enforcement agencies, including the FBI.[9]

On the precipice of the inauguration of Joseph Biden as the 46th President of the United States, Washington D.C. erupted in turmoil as a January 6th rally led by the soon-to-be former President Trump continued to sew doubt about the results of the election, falsely characterized

---

6. Samuels, "Dan Patrick Says."

7. Bauman and Brooks, "The Origins of the Extremist 'Boogaloo' Movement."

8. Field, "Why Is Tear Gas Banned."

9. Harris, "DHS Analyzed Protester Communications."

as stolen and fraudulent, even as the results of the electoral college were being certified by the U.S. Senate. Insurrectionists from the rally stormed the U.S. Capital, breaking windows and breaching police lines. Carrying Confederate flags and wearing insignia of white supremacy and anti-Semitism, they roamed and ransacked the halls of Congress for hours leaving four dead before law enforcement secured the Capitol again.

The world continues to edge toward to the brink. All of the old divisions remain alive—racism, nationalism, classism, etc. But rifts are opening wider between Americans, as well as between the U.S. and its sibling nations. Everything from the wearing of face coverings during a pandemic to a brand of beans[10] can be politicized to intensify the rifting. Old and venerated institutions become precarious, historic social wounds become raw once again, and democracy's future is continually called into question by the actions of politicians and the failures of governance. Religious institutions are not above the fray in the national melee. The fault lines run through our very pews. To say that emotions run high during these times would be an understatement.

The End of the World (As We Know It)

"There is no doubt about this point: the West has landed on all other civilizations like an Apocalypse that has put an end to their existence."

—BRUNO LATOUR, *FACING GAIA*[11]

While none of this necessarily portends the impending "end of the world," these circumstances do suggest *the end of the world as we know it.* It isn't the first ending the world has faced, and there are many endings yet to come.

Many cry foul at first mention of an era being "apocalyptic." Charges of being "alarmist" or "overly dramatic" or "catastrophist" abound. And, of course, a more conservative Christian millenarian eschatology has made the term "apocalypse" anathema to mainline or progressive expressions of Christian theological praxis.

But as Latour notes, we can only deny the continual arrival of apocalyptic conditions from a historically comfortable (white) Western

10. Stockman, Kelly, and Medina, "How Buying Beans Became a Political Statement."

11. Latour, *Facing Gaia*, 205.

position in which we have become complicit in the existence-ending conditions of so many others the world over. European colonization, the transatlantic slave trade, the genocide of Native Americans, the rampant extraction of resources from the world's poorest regions, the destruction of entire ecosystems, the end of myriad species, neocolonial domination, predatory capitalism, globalization, neoliberalism—all land like an apocalypse upon someone, ending their world or, at very least, the world as they knew it.

Now the apocalyptic horsemen that the West has unleashed upon the world have come home to us. When the world as we know is pushed to the brink—either beginning to slip away off a cliff of our own making, or violently stripped from us by force of power—our grasping for safety, security, and survival becomes palpable. And that grasping arises with the *affects* of apocalypse—the *feelings* brought about by an *ending*.

Feelings need critical attention in an apocalyptic era. Emotions "constitute the primary motivational system for human beings" affecting cognitive and behavioral aspects of our lives, including, "attention, inferences, learning, memory, goal choice, motivational priorities, communication of intention," as well as how and with whom we form community.[12] Emotions serve the critical evolutionary function of helping humans to adapt to our surroundings and work toward the preservation of our well-being.

It is impossible to separate emotions from cognitive thought. Emotions are integrated with reason and intuition in helping us navigate our way through the world, integral to making decisions, directing action, and ascribing meaning and value to all that we encounter.[13] Emotion is a part of our sacred embodiment and our evolutionary inheritance. Without attending to emotional experiences, we cannot understand why we behave the way we do, how to engage others who interpret the world very differently from us, or how to shape thinking and acting toward the reduction of violence and promotion of flourishing.

Living on a planet on the edge, at the brink, disappearing, our sense of security eroding as we come face to face with our various endings, powerful emotional experiences call for great care. Three major affective dimensions of apocalypse are *anger*, *fear*, and *sadness*. They aren't the *only* emotions triggered by the many endings we face, but they are pervasive.

12. Fuller, *Spirituality in the Flesh*, 33.
13. Lester, *The Angry Christian*, 24.

These are affects of survival that must be attended to with care, valued for the messages they hold that direct attention and prompt action. Yet, unattended, they are also emotions that can devolve into harmful experiences that work against our ability to survive and flourish in community.

Those practicing leadership within communities of faith and spiritual praxis in apocalyptic times must practice care in relation to the apocalyptic emotions in order to strengthen lasting bonds between humans, while also attending to relationships between humans and the more-than-human.[14] Beyond this, practices of care amid apocalyptic emotions should move us toward promoting adaptation and flourishing—even on the brink—through cultivating transimmanent emotional experiences of wonder, gratitude, and grief.

Whatever else we do, we must learn to *feel our way* through an apocalypse.

Apocalyptic Emotions

"Ah, my love. An apocalypse is a relative thing, isn't it?"

—N. K. JEMISIN, *THE STONE SKY*[15]

Speaking of an *emotion* means addressing a feeling state that is brought about by an immediate stimulus and only lasts a few seconds or minutes. Emotions originate in the subcortical region of the brain (*below* the neocortex, or the higher-order *reasoning* area of the brain). Emotions are aroused by a person's perception and immediate interpretation of their environment.[16] Generally, these responses to *immediate* stimuli in our environment are not the focus of this chapter. These are only the beginnings of an emotional experience of apocalypse.

---

14. By this term, coined by David Abram, I mean to indicate a shift toward a non-hierarchical understanding of humanity's relation to other beings in a universe. This is a shift in which, as Andras Weber describes, "human subjects are no longer separated from other organisms but instead form a mesh of existential relationships—a quite real 'web of life.'" Thus, rather than thinking in human/non-human dichotomies, the "more-than-human" invites imaging human life within a larger web of biospheric relation that doesn't privilege the supremacy of humans. Weber, *Enlivenment*, 46. See also Abram, *The Spell of the Sensuous*.

15. Jemison, *The Stone Sky*, 6.

16. Lester, *The Angry Christian*, 30–31.

Momentary emotional experiences can be elongated into *moods* that last for days or weeks and influence our motivation, perception, and cognition for longer periods.[17] Moods are shaped by the "larger background of one's life, which feel either troubled or trouble free" and reference the "larger, pervasive, existential issues of one's life."[18] You can begin to see here how apocalyptic emotions are, as Jemisin suggests above, experienced relative to our social location in an apocalyptic context.

Like the behavior shaping power of emotions *in the moment*, moods also shape our behavior, narrowing our alternatives, and forming our cognitions for longer periods of time.[19] Moods get us *closer* to the subject of the chapter, but there is potential for moods to become something yet more.

Emotions-turned-moods can, over time, morph into a *pervasive outlook on life*, an *orientation toward the world*, a *temperament* or *general disposition* that shapes one's everyday experience. It is the emergence of the emotional experiences of fear, anger, and sadness into pervasive outlooks or general dispositions that is the central focus here. This is when emotions can become truly apocalyptic in their scope and orientation.

We experience emotions like fear, anger, and sadness frequently in apocalyptic times, and for good reason. We sense our life and wellbeing placed at risk, and we witness the destruction of people, places, values, institutions, and ways of life that we deeply love. But fear, anger, and sadness also *exacerbate* the apocalyptic circumstances if left unattended. These emotions are evolutionary gifts that have equipped us to effectively respond to threatening experiences and preserve our wellbeing. But they can also become the go-to emotional lenses that color our interpretation of events, direct our actions, shape our motivations, and out of which we form community, or withdraw from it.

When these emotional experiences are triggered with frequency and become longer lasting dispositions, a cycle develops through which we evaluate what is happening around us in ways consistent with our emotional experience. This evaluation justifies and maintains the emotion and sustains our ways of responding in relation to that emotional experience.[20] Thus we can get caught up in—*stuck*, even—in apocalyp-

---

17. Fuller, *Spirituality in the Flesh*, 30.

18. Lazarus, *Emotion & Adaptation*, 48.

19. Ekman, *Emotions Revealed*, 51.

20. Ekman, *Emotions Revealed*, 63.

tic emotional cycles of fear, anger, and sadness and the interpretations, motivations, and behaviors they invite. In this way, apocalyptic emotions can become exacerbating of the apocalyptic circumstances.

Andrew Lester explains this with a narrative framework, saying, "Over time, after being intentionally changed, a new story becomes so rooted in one's character—and therefore within the neurology of our brains, particularly the neocortex—that we respond differently to a particular stimulus without being conscious of our decision."[21] For good and ill, emotional experiences can be shaped over time into pervasive orientations toward life. At no time is this more possible than when these emotions are constantly triggered by circumstances we might rightly call apocalyptic—a continual cycle of endings.

Importantly, emotional triggers also become embedded in our neurology by the formation of new connections through cell assemblies in our brain. As Ekman notes, "Our nervous system doesn't make it easy to change what makes us emotional, to unlearn either the connection between an emotional cell assembly and a response, or between a trigger and an emotional cell assembly."[22] Apocalyptic emotions become recursive, with the frequent triggering of emotions shaping the cellular connections formed in our brains, and our brain's cell assemblies affecting how easily and frequently those same emotions can become triggered.

All emotions have an evolutionary, a social, and a personal history.[23] It is the role of those with responsibilities of caregiving and community leadership in an apocalyptic situation to attend to the complexity of these emotional histories and to cultivate responses that diminish suffering and promote flourishing of life, even at the end of the world as we know it.

Fear

Fear is an evolutionary gift to humanity. Without the capacity to experience and respond to fear, we would not have survived as a species. That's why I'd rather not term these emotions—fear, anger, and sadness—"negative" emotions. While they may be uncomfortable emotions, I don't want to give the impression that the discomfort is something to simply be avoided. We must cultivate the capacity to listen to these emotions for

21. Lester, *The Angry Christian*, 102.
22. Ekman, *Emotions Revealed*, 43.
23. Svendsen, *A Philosophy of Fear*, 24.

the messages they carry, and attended to them with care so that they don't become overwhelming of our experience of the world.

We speak of "fear" and "anger" and "sadness" as specific, singular emotions, but emotions are not as singular and discrete as we often assume. More accurately, they are each a part of a larger family of emotional experiences. While fear is my focus, emotions like anxiety and worry are also part of the emotional family of fear.

Fear arises from confrontation with a concrete threat that likely holds potential for physical harm in the immediate present.[24] This emotion has a specific objective: to protect us from threat of harm in our immediate environment. Anxiety is an emotional state aroused in relation to a less specific, more ambiguous perception of possible danger.[25] Anxiety responds to a threat, but it is a threat of *future* harm, not immediate injury.

In an apocalyptic context, anxiety may be very palpable, but we have no shortage of *specific objects* of fear arousal, be they the calamitous outcomes of climate collapse that are now at our doorstep, or parents sending their Black children out into a world where the police may kill them. All of these can arouse the feeling of *fear*, while a generalized sense of anxiety likely lingers in the emotional background.

The danger posed to Black bodies by police is not ambiguous. The threat of police killing is very real and is being played out in front of our eyes. The racialized body we move about with in the world affects just how relative that fear becomes to us. A white body may never experience the palpable immediacy of fear from watching the Floyd killing on video or have the memory of that fear brought immediately back to us when we encounter a police officer on the street. Apocalyptic emotions are relativized by our racial embodiment, and empathic exploration is required to understand how emotions are triggered differently in our different embodiments.

Climate change poses genuine, immediate, and growing threats to our lives and wellbeing that are playing out day-to-day. The threat is no longer in the far future. We wake up to the scenes of climate-driven disaster every day—if not in our own backyards, then as portrayed on the news. Our geographic locations have often buffered our feeling the

24. Lazarus, *Emotion & Adaptation*, 235, 238. Yet, Svendsen also notes that fear contains a future projection concerning pain, injury, or death as well. *A Philosophy of Fear*, 38.

25. Svendsen, *A Philosophy of Fear*, 35.

immediacy of these fears that are now becoming more palpable through extreme weather events all over the world.

As the pandemic devolves economies into the worst recession since World War II, fear of layoffs, eviction, homelessness, and loss of health insurance are immediate and unambiguous.[26] Our economic positions make us more or less susceptible to the immediacy of fear in relation to economic collapse—the stock market dipping may cause some a sense of anxiety, while a sudden layoff, loss of insurance, and impending eviction may stimulate immediate fear in relation to one's wellbeing.

Our racial privilege, our sense of national security, or our class status may create buffers for us against experiencing the frequent and immediate provocation of fear. Some may now only feel an ambiguous anxiety. But the immediate and very real threats that prompt the emotional experience of fear are not difficult to pinpoint. Those for whom the threat has felt ambiguous or delayed up to this point will increasingly feel the palpability of fear.

Fear operates as a subcortical signal to us, occurring outside of the rational thought processes of the neocortex. When activated, fear calls forth "avoidance behaviors" that elevate the preservation of our safety to a top priority in shaping our goals and gathering information from our surroundings.[27] When the emotion of fear informs, or overtakes, our thinking processes, the result is a type of tunnel vision that is fixed on the threatening object, and communication patterns that are intent on alerting others to the danger we perceive in our environment.[28] Thus, it's easy to see how functioning in many areas of one's life becomes more challenging when in the midst of the above named fearful situations.

It is not difficult to see why fear is an evolutionary gift to us. Fear helps us flee from dangerous situations without having to think too much about our response—a snake on the hiking trail, an oncoming car barreling toward us, etc. But fear can also take a harmful turn when elongated into a pervasive orientation and outlook on life.

26. "COVID-19 to Plunge Global Economy."

27. Fuller, *Spirituality in the Flesh*, 30.

28. Fuller, *Spirituality in the Flesh*, 34.

Fear as a Pervasive Outlook

Fear can, and perhaps *has*, become a general, unifying perspective on life, and is a basic characteristic of our culture.[29] We can come to interpret our environment from a perspective of fear, or experience what Lars Svendsen terms, "the colonization of our life-world by fear."[30] He goes on to say, "a world you fear is a place where you can never feel completely at home."[31]

In a context that feels apocalyptic, with life as we know it coming to an end in so many different ways, a world that continually provokes our experience of fear may begin to feel like a world to which we no longer belong. Especially when fear and anger comingle, these apocalyptic emotions may motivate persons for whom fear has become a pervasive outlook either to seek another world through escapist eschatological fantasies, or to radically alter this world in response to the perceived fear stimuli.

We are all too familiar with fear used as political resource, a trump card, a way of undermining the partisan opposition and their leadership.[32] This has become a primary theme in political campaigns at all levels of government and across party lines. It is a central feature of the Trump presidency, for example, in disparaging immigrants from Mexico as violent criminals, as well as by continually portraying the coronavirus as the "Chinese virus." Fear mobilized as a political tool shapes political behavior.

In an era of high connectivity via social media, fear is trafficked through digital emotional contagion. Emotional contagion describes the phenomena through which our emotions, either consciously or unconsciously, become more similar to the emotions we perceive in others as we are exposed to their emotions.[33] Digitally, this takes place through the spread of our emotions on the Internet, especially through social media. Constant exposure to others' fear, anger, and sadness—whether in person or in the digital realm—can lead us to experience many of the stresses associated with these emotions, even if we "caught" those emotions from others.[34] Beyond simple memes, "deep fakes" portend an era

---

29. Svendsen, *A Philosophy of Fear*, 19.

30. Svendsen, *A Philosophy of Fear*, 7.

31. Svendsen, *A Philosophy of Fear*, 43.

32. Svendsen, *A Philosophy of Fear*, 16.

33. Goldenberg and Gross, "Digital Emotional Contagion," 317.

34. Rempala, "Cognitive Strategies for Controlling Emotional Contagion," 1529.

in which emotional experiences can be cultivated and curated for cyber warfare that will further increase social/political rifting.[35]

When we cannot do anything in relation to the threatening circumstance, we are likely to experience fear as an overwhelming emotional state.[36] When the originating fear stimulus itself is *invented* for political or ideological purposes, this becomes especially problematic! When the fear is rooted in the lives of people who have become the *objects* of those invented fears, the situation portends violence.

Often, in response to fear, our attempts to reduce danger actually increase it. Svendsen argues, "The more precautionary we are, the more frequently will we introduce measures to prevent harm that would never have materialized. All these measures make a demand on resources that result in less resources being available."[37] When our attempts are aimed at reducing the "danger" of supposedly dangerous others, the threats to life and flourishing for those others increases precipitously. Immigrant children end up separated from parents and warehoused in cages at the border, for example.

It is easy to see how fear operated helpfully for the survival of small tribal bonds in the face of immediate threats present in the surrounding environment. It is also easy to see how these same patterns of attention, memory, behavior, and communication can create adverse circumstances when the fear stimulus is *cultural* in nature, rather than *environmental*. Perceiving threats to our "cultural boundaries" can provoke fear responses that are widely communicated and serve to "heighten loyalty and conformity" in order to protect one's culture, way of life, or most notably, privilege.[38]

But when fear becomes a general orientation toward life, it erodes trust in other human beings and leads to a decreasing sense of security when we are with others, ultimately contributing to social disintegration, avoidance of those we fear based on racial, religious, or national difference, and an increase of isolation throughout society.[39] Fear as a long-lasting disposition can inculcate a sense of helplessness, a giving in to apathy, and immobilization in the face of very real dangers that we've become too fearful to address.

35. See "Tackling the Misinformation Epidemic."

36. Ekman, *Emotions Revealed*, 156.

37. Svendsen, *A Philosophy of Fear*, 69.

38. Fuller, *Spirituality in the Flesh*, 31.

39. Svendsen, *A Philosophy of Fear*, 94.

Treating Fear with Care

Throughout the biblical text there are admonitions about fear, almost always inviting those in a frightful situation to lessen their fearful response. Words like "be not afraid" show up again and again in the Hebrew Bible and the New Testament. Since fear is an evolutionary gift, we can hear all of those passages in the Bible encouraging us to "fear not" as messages with a fuller intention behind them. They're not messages that denigrate the necessity of fear as an emotion of survival, but as admonitions against fear becoming the dominant orientation of one's life.

"Do not fear" might be understood as a message like, "Do not let the fear you feel consume you. Do not let the fearful experiences of life sever your connection to others and the world around you. Do not let fear immobilize you."

To treat fear with care, we must attend to the ways that some fears are invented for political purposes (e.g., political fear mongering in relation to immigrants), while some fears are felt in direct proportion to very critical threats in our surrounding environment (e.g., Black people fearing being harassed, attacked, or killed while taking a jog in a white neighborhood). In both cases, situations real or imagined, the *feeling* of threat and danger are stimuli that influence our behavior.

The question when addressing fear is not whether the fear is rational. Remember that fear responses initially occur outside of the rational oversight of the neocortex. Our fear response may even contradict what we rationally *think* or *believe*. Fear is an embodied response and, as Resmaa Menakem reminds us, "our bodies don't care about logic, truth, or cognitive experience. They care about safety and survival. They care about responding to a perceived threat, even when that threat is not real."[40]

Significantly, fear also "redirects memory to retrieve similar threatening patterns" and prompts communication patterns that alert others to the perceived danger to mobilize them to strengthen their communal bonds of solidarity.[41] We might interpret the public tactics of Black Lives Matter or Extinction Rebellion as attempts to strengthen communal bonds by alerting others to the dangers of increasing police militarization and perpetual violence against black lives, or the threats to survival posed by climate collapse, respectively. We might also see those drawn into the morass of conspiracy theory communities like QAnon as motivated by a

40. Menakem, *My Grandmother's Hands*, 28.
41. Fuller, *Spirituality in the Flesh*, 30.

contagious spread of fearful orientations toward life that perceive dangers that do not exist, but feel palpably threatening to particular ways of life in the world, and increasingly motivated to do something about these perceived threats.

Central questions for caregivers when addressing fear's arousal for individuals or within communities are these:

How do I perceive my wellbeing, or that of my wider world of concern, being put in danger?

From what harms do we sense the need to protect ourselves and those we love?

How is fear inviting me to respond to others and to the world around me? Does this accord with how I want to be in community with others?

If fear had a voice, what would it be saying to me in those times it arises?

In what ways is fear motivating me toward behavior that seems life preserving?

In what ways is fear motivating me toward behavior that seems exacerbating of adverse circumstances?

Anger

Fear and anger are related, interdependent emotions.[42] Both emotions have the primary objective of *survival*.[43] They also have very similar biochemical components.[44] Thus, much of what is explored above in relation to fear is also applicable to an exploration of anger.

In U.S. society, anger is a racialized emotion that is experienced and expressed differently with different consequences depending on one's racial embodiment. As bell hooks contends, "To perpetuate and maintain white supremacy, white folks have colonized black Americans, and a part of that colonizing process has been teaching us to repress our rage, to never make them the targets of any anger we feel about racism."[45] Buddhist Lama Rod Owens in his book on anger attests to this, saying, "As

42. Lazarus, *Emotion & Adaptation*, 225.

43. Lester, *The Angry Christian*, 82.

44. Reddy, *The Navigation of Feeling*, 12, quoted in Svendsen, *A Philosophy of Fear*, 25.

45. hooks, *Killing Rage: Ending Racism*, 14.

a Black man, I was conditioned to believe my anger was dangerous—if I channeled anger and expressed anger, then I would be punished. I would be killed, I would be put in jail, I would be silenced. I would be erased."[46] To discuss anger in the U.S. without recognizing this colonization of emotions would be naïve and, for BIPOC, potentially dangerous.

For example, months before the insurrection at the U.S. Capitol, dozens of primarily white men armed with semi-automatic weapons showed up at the Michigan State Capitol in early May 2020 protesting the state's shutdown in attempt to contain the coronavirus pandemic. After being denied entry to the House chamber by police, some armed protesters went into the Senate gallery and shouted down at lawmakers below while they were in session.[47] Police took no forceful action against these white protesters of the state's shutdown policy. Weeks later when Black Lives Matter protests erupted over the police killing of George Floyd all over the country, unarmed protesters—many Black—were met with police in riot gear firing rubber bullets and tear gas into the crowds. In both instances, anger was a motivating factor for the protesters. In each instance, that anger was met with a markedly different response by the state.

Lazarus proposes a simple description for the provocation of anger in adults: "a *demeaning offense against me and mine*."[48] Lester adds that the arousal pattern of anger is physical, mental, and emotional and is characterized by a desire to either attack or defend.[49] Our subcortical brain is well primed to arouse anger in relation to *physical threats* to our wellbeing (e.g., when confronted by an armed person posing a threat to our family). But the neocortex and its higher order thought processes come into play when more "complicated threats" to our values, meanings, worldviews, future plans, and personal identity are threatened.[50]

In the realm of cultural traditions, values, and identity, is easy to see how anger becomes a tool of both political and religious mobilization, holding the physiological promise of sustaining high levels of energy among those experiencing the emotional state, as well as the potential to direct

---

46. Owens, *Love and Rage*, 15.

47. Rahal and Mauger, "Armed Protesters in Michigan Capitol."

48. Lazarus, *Emotion & Adaptation*, 222, emphasis added.

49. Lester, *The Angry Christian*, 4.

50. Lester, *The Angry Christian*, 79.

that anger against a common enemy in ways that promote communal solidarity.[51] Anger is a key affective tool in modern political campaigns.[52]

Anger as a Pervasive Outlook

Ekman warns, "One of the most dangerous features of anger is that anger calls forth anger, and the cycle can rapidly escalate."[53] As with fear, anger is a highly contagious emotion, spreading faster than other emotions on social media through digital emotional contagion.[54] This points to what Achille Mbembe calls "microfascism" via digital technology intent on formatting our minds, shaping our desires, and colonizing the unconscious. Through these processes of computational media and digital technology, our symbolic world is reshaped, "blurring distinction between reality and fiction."[55] No matter the fictional status of the stimuli—memes decrying the loss of cultural values, deep fakes portraying political "enemies" making anger-inducing speeches that were never actually given, or other political propaganda—the emotional response that the stimuli cultivates is all too real. And that emotional reality holds the power to shape our motivations and our community-building practices.

When anger becomes chronic it can lead to a host of other emotional experiences that can become more pervasive as a mood or even an interpretative orientation toward life in the world. Some of these more complex and long-lasting emotional experiences are resentment, bitterness, hostility, or hatred.[56] As an orientation toward life, anger as a pervasive outlook holds the potential to cultivate resentment, cynicism, us/them thinking, contempt, and vengefulness. Relationally, these longer-term emotional dispositions are disastrous. While focused on couples, John Gottman identifies criticism, contempt, defensiveness, and stonewalling as the "four horsemen of the apocalypse" for

51. Fuller, *Spirituality in the Flesh*, 31.

52. One of the key shifts in how fear-anger-inducing campaign elements developed such modern electoral sway is the racially charged attack ad used by George H.W. Bush in 1988 in his campaign against Michael Dukakis featuring the story of a Black man named Willie Horton. See Baker, "Bush Made Willie Horton an Issue in 1988."

53. Ekman, *Emotions Revealed*, 111.

54. Goldenberg and Gross, "Digital Emotional Contagion," 320.

55. Mbembe, *Necropolitics*, 113.

56. Lester, *The Angry Christian*, 5.

relational communication,[57] which I believe to be true for relationships beyond romantic couples. Once these anger-related patterns show up with frequency, it is very difficult to recover healthy relationality, as parties move increasingly toward irreparable rifts. Clearly, these horsemen are standard features of our political landscape and fundamental to our inability to come together amidst a national crisis like the Covid-19 pandemic in order to institute even the simplest measures to prevent transmission.

Treating Anger with Care

Trying to rationally "talk one out of" being fearful of a stimuli does not take into account the subcortical regions of the brain that are triggered by these stimuli. Neural pathways develop as a result of traumatic experience. Memories that are connected to the hippocampus and the amygdala record, store, and recall painful and traumatic events, and the entire limbic system can be immediately alerted to danger if the brain interprets a new stimulus as similar to a past traumatic event. The body is mobilized for action before our rational brain can begin re-interpreting the situation.[58]

And yet, Lester posits, anger is a "hermeneutical event," rooted in our naming and describing of events in our environment that construct the meanings we assign to these experiences.[59] This is especially the case when we are dealing with anger-inducing stimuli that touch on cultural values, meanings, worldviews, future plans, and personal identity, rather than the immediate threat of bodily harm. Here, it is the consistent inducement of anger stimuli targeting meaning and values that I am most concerned about becoming an orientation toward life that pervades our interpretation of the world and our ability to cultivate community with others across myriad lines of difference.

In situations of physical trauma, violence, and abuse that have elevated one's activation of fear and anger responses, it is helpful to seek a trauma-informed, somatically aware clinician who can help one work through the ways that the fear and anger inducing trauma is lodged in

57. See Lisitsa, "The Four Hosemen."
58. Lester, *The Angry Christian*, 78–82.
59. Lester, *The Angry Christian*, 85, 94.

one's body.[60] But for the pervasive fear-shaped orientations toward life that have become common in our socio-political landscape, practitioners of care should develop the competency to address fear-orientations openly in order to bring them into the light of a caring exploration.

Central questions when beginning to address fear's arousal for individuals or within communities are these:

> *How do I perceive my values being threatened? These may be values of justice, survival, wellbeing, flourishing, wellbeing of "my" community, etc.*

> *Against what threats do we sense the need to react in order protect ourselves and those we love?*

> *How is anger inviting me to respond to others and to the world around me? Are these the ways I most wish to respond to others in my life?*

> *If anger had a voice, what would it be saying to me in those times?*

> *In what ways is anger motivating me toward behavior that seems life preserving?*

> *In what ways is anger motivating me toward behavior that seems exacerbating of adverse circumstances?*

Sadness

Emotions are rarely experienced as singular events. While the ravages of climate change or the killing of unarmed Black people by the police or an ill-prepared governmental response to a pandemic are apt to provoke fear and anger, any of these circumstances are likely to create an emotional experience of sadness as well.

While a clinically informed diagnosis of "depression" may, at times, be appropriate for some, the term "depression" is too clinical to describe the emotional experience of sadness we are all prone to have in times that feel apocalyptic—an emotional experience that is as cultural as it is psychological. The notion of "impacted grief"[61] holds some promise, but it doesn't account for the fact that the sadness I'm describing is not about one specific loss alone, but about many sadness-inducing stimuli occurring simultaneously or at a rapid rate of succession.

---

60. This type of therapeutic trauma work is further described in Menakem, *My Grandmother's Hands*, and van der Kolk, *The Body Keeps the Score.*

61. Lazarus, *Emotion & Adaptation*, 248.

Whereas fear and anger promote engagement and activity in relation to threatening stimuli (e.g., fleeing, fighting), sadness moves us toward *resignation* rather than toward struggle.[62] Lazarus says that the "core relational theme" of sadness is irrevocable loss that holds a sense of helplessness about any potential for restoration. He argues that if the loss is not considered irrevocable, then anger, among other emotions, can be activated to direct behavior toward possibilities of *restoring* the loss.[63] Sadness can also transcend focus on a single encounter or stimuli and merges with the "existential quality of life in reflecting in general relationships with the world."[64] This is the case when sadness becomes an apocalyptic emotion.

Sadness as a Pervasive Outlook

Sadness is already one of the longer lasting of our emotions. In response to a sadness inducing stimuli, there is often a period of "protesting agony," after which a longer period of sadness sets in, inviting a feeling of helplessness.[65] When sadness develops into a pervasive outlook on life, longer lasting experiences of despair, loss of meaning, emotional numbness, extreme fatigue, and withdrawal from others can soon develop.

There are clearly important racial considerations in the experience of sadness, too. Claudia Rankine asked a friend what it is like being the mother of a Black son. Rankine's friend replied, "The condition of black life is one of mourning." Liberal white people, Rankine says, can feel temporarily bad about Black suffering, but "no mode of empathy . . . can replicate the daily strain of knowing that as a black person you can be killed for simply being black."[66] While white people may feel sadness in relation to ongoing racial injustice and violence, this weight of sadness, or condition of mourning, is not experienced equally across racial embodiments.

In addressing sadness on a planetary scale, Australian environmental philosopher Glenn Albrecht developed a new vocabulary for what he terms "earth emotions." These are emotional responses that humans have to the current scale and pace of environmental change. Key among

---

62. Lazarus, *Emotion & Adaptation*, 247.
63. Lazarus, *Emotion & Adaptation*, 248.
64. Lazarus, *Emotion & Adaptation*, 251.
65. Ekman, *Emotions Revealed*, 84.
66. Rankine, "The Condition of Black Life Is One of Mourning," 145–46.

these is the emotion of "solastalgia," described as "the lived experience of distressing, negative environmental change."[67] Albrecht sees solastalgia causing pain, distress, and ongoing loss of solace that is rooted in one's sense of desolation and a pervasive negative environmental change within a landscape or territory that one feels as "home." In addition to a sadness-inducing sense of loss, this eco-change can also feel like an anger-inducing *attack* on one's sense of place in the world—one's "home."[68]

On an economic and political level, womanist theologian and ethicist Keri Day names loss of meaning, despair, and helplessness as feelings associated with neoliberalism, arguing that our current political and economic climate "attempts to render us cynical and apathetic about our ability to be different from the calculating, radically self-interested individual that neoliberal capitalism presumes as given."[69] On the levels of racial injustice, environmental degradation, and political and economic systems, sadness-inducing stimuli are constant and systemic.

Treating Sadness with Care

There are no thoughts that are not colored by feelings, no feeling that do not eventually come into the interpretive sway of cognition, and no feeling state that doesn't resonate throughout the whole of one's body. Sadness as a long-lasting temperament can become immobilizing of our bodies, coloring our thoughts and curtailing our activity in the world. The real danger of sadness becoming the emotional valance that colors our outlook, directing our behavior in relation to our environment, is that sadness's orientation is toward *resignation* rather than toward struggle, of a learned sense of *helplessness* and *despair*, rather than active engagement with the problems we face together.

Central questions when caregivers begin addressing sadness's arousal for individuals or within communities are these:

> *What important parts of my world feel like they are being lost or irreparably damaged?*

> *How does my wellbeing, or that of my wider world of concern, feel like it is being taken away?*

67. Albrecht, *Earth Emotions*, x.

68. Albrecht, *Earth Emotions*, 38.

69. Day, *Religious Resistance to Neoliberalism*, 14, 17.

From what stimuli do we sense the need to withdraw, and what stimuli feel too overwhelming for us to handle?

How is sadness inviting me to respond to others and to the world around me? Are these the ways I most want to respond to others in my life?

If sadness had a voice, what would it be saying to me in those times?

In what ways is sadness motivating me toward behavior that seems life preserving?

In what ways is sadness motivating me toward behavior that seems exacerbating of adverse circumstances?

Not only can our individual lives become overtaken by the apocalyptic emotions of fear and sadness and anger, but our practice of faith can also become consumed by these powerful emotions and their ability to direct our attention and shape our action. We can get so mired in the constant and pervasive triggering of these important primary emotions that we begin to do the work of ministry out of fear, as if we are constantly under threat. The experience of sadness becomes the pervasive mood of our worshipping life so that celebration never has the opportunity to emerge and energize us. We begin to undertake all of our work of justice from a place of anger, motivated to *counter* other's agendas rather than to cultivate a way of being in the world. The relational aim of all three emotions is corrosive to communal bonds, should they become pervasive orientations toward life.

While there are many helpful tools, such as mindfulness and other meditative techniques, that can aid us in approaching our emotional experiences of fear, anger, and sadness with care, we must also move beyond emotion regulation techniques to the active cultivation of more adaptive emotional experiences for our apocalyptic context. We must increase our capacity to *feel our way through* an apocalypse.

Transimmanent Emotions

"If the world is torn to pieces, I want to see what story I can find in the fragmentation . . . When everything feels like it is coming apart, the art of assemblage feels like a worthy pastime."

—Terry Tempest Williams, *Erosion*[70]

70. Williams, *Erosion*, xi.

The powerful emotions of fear, anger, and sadness are embodied experiences, occurring first in the subcortical regions of the brain. Thus, we cannot *think our way* out of their influence and potentially adverse effects (as white liberals are especially wont to do). We must cultivate alternative emotional experiences that we can develop within the context of community. These emotional experiences aren't *antidotes* to fear, anger, and sadness, but they hold potential to subvert the tendency for fear, anger, and sadness to become *overpowering orientations* toward life in the world, exacerbating the apocalyptic sense of the world's many endings.

The aim is *not* to cut us off from the signals that fear, anger, and sadness hold. But whereas the apocalyptic emotions promote cognitive, motivational, communicative, and communal actions of withdrawal, aggression, and resignation, apocalyptic times call for intentional communal responses that cultivate emotional experiences opening us toward community, promoting generosity, compassion, and love, and helping us to engage fully in the world around us through struggle toward justice and flourishing.

The three complex emotional experiences I suggest here are *wonder*, *gratitude*, and *grief*. I call these emotional experiences "transimmanent" because I see them serving both the functions of transcendence—opening us to the world beyond our individual "selves," even to an ultimate context, or God—as well as immanence, helping us to relate differently to the human and more-than-human world immediately present to us in our context or environment, as well as to our sense of "self" within that context.[71]

Lester says, "Our mental processes look for a plot line or a story line to explain information . . . Each new sensation, stimulus, and interpersonal transaction is shaped by our mental processes into a story, by which our experiences are given their individual distinctiveness as *our* story."[72] The aim of cultivating transimmanent emotional experiences is to help us subvert the potential for our dominant story line to become one of fear, anger, and sadness, instead shaping our mental processes and communal practices with emotional plot lines of wonder, gratitude, and grief. These transimmanent emotions hold the potential to shape our lives and communities toward flourishing and livability, even in a world on the brink.

---

71. Philosopher Jean-Luc Nancy has developed a theory of "transimmanence," but I am not using the term here in exactly the same ways that he develops it.

72. Lester, *The Angry Christian*, 95.

Wonder

In a precautionary world where fear becomes a general orientation toward life and future musings are always dominated by dangers rather than possibilities, Svendsen says that we begin living with "a *telos* that is constantly directed toward catastrophe."[73] We might imagine that a similar telos exists for a life lived from a pervasive outlook colored by anger with its *telos* of vengeance, or a general disposition of sadness with a *telos* of resignation. But toward what *telos* would we be directed by developing a disposition of wonder?

While wonder doesn't make it onto the list of "primary emotions" for many modern Western psychologists, a third century B.C.E. Indian Sanskrit text about the nature of consciousness does name wonder as one of the nine basic emotions. This text links wonder with the ritual act of "seeing divinely." Robert Fuller explains,

> Whether occasioned by a temple icon or a sacred place in nature, "religious seeing" is thought to disclose the life and consciousness that pulsates throughout the whole of creation . . . Religious seeing entails actually participating in the essence and nature of the person or object that elicited this perception (including participating in the essence and nature of the divine ground of this person or object).[74]

Similarly Rabbi Abraham Joshua Heschel sees wonder, or what he terms "radical amazement," as a chief characteristic of a religious orientation to the world: "perpetual surprise at the fact that there are facts at all."[75] Heschel views wonder both as a form of *thinking* and a constant *attitude* that never ceases and must be continually cultivated. Wonder is the origin of one's awareness of the divine and resistance to the sin of indifference to the sublime, according to Heschel.

Here are some ways Fuller sees wonder operating at the heart of our search for the Divine, as well as in cultivating community with the human and more-than-human in our environment: Wonder helps us suspend our habitual ways of looking at the world. Wonder lures us into creative engagement with our surroundings. Wonder induces receptivity and openness and connection to our environment. Wonder prompts us

73. Svendsen, *A Philosophy of Fear*, 71.

74. Fuller, *Wonder*, 11.

75. Heschel, *God in Search of Man*, 45. I am grateful to my colleague Dan Smith for making this connection to Heschel's "radical amazement."

to consider life from new perspectives. Wonder entices us into relational aspects of reality, giving us a vision of our relatedness to the world, to other beings, and to sources of ultimacy, or the Divine.[76]

In addition to a religious/transcendent orientation, Martha Nussbaum links wonder with the immanent capacity to move beyond self-interest into acts of love, empathy, compassion, and the preservation of life, even when there's no immediate benefit to us personally.[77] As an emotional orientation informing our ethical praxis, wonder may even serve as a radical antidote to neoliberalism's reduction of all *life* to its value on an economic scale, of *worth* to productivity and earning potential, of the *web of life* to a ledger of natural "resources." Wonder can feel like having the whole of your attention caught somewhere between the immanent and the transcendent in deep connection and receptivity to the world around you, awestruck by curiosity and compassion.

While wonder may have little evolutionary adaptive significance for the individual in any immediate context, experiences of wonder prompt the development of moods and attitudes over time that serve adaptive needs of a wider community and aid in cultivating religious and philosophical orientations toward life that serve the long-term survival of humanity.[78] Wonder is also an emotional experience that motivates us to "venture outward into increased rapport with the environment,"[79] in contrast to the withdrawal invited by fear and sadness, and the hostility and aggression provoked by anger. Wonder won't help us survive an immediate threat to our physical wellbeing, but it can promote long-term communal health and survival by drawing us outward in compassion, curiosity, and connection toward human others, the wider web of life, and toward a sense of an ultimate context.

In an apocalyptic era characterized by rapid change, wonder also aids in the creation of expansive categories of understanding in increasingly novel, uncertain, and even chaotic circumstances. Wonder is, as Fuller argues, "a principal source of humanity's creative adaptation."[80] A community cultivated through wonder becomes ever more curious, creative, compassionate, and connected as emotional experiences of

---

76. Fuller, *Wonder*, 12.

77. Nussbaum, *Upheavals of Thought*, quoted in Fuller, *Wonder*, 20.

78. Fuller, *Wonder*, 54–55.

79. Fuller, *Wonder*, 60.

80. Fuller, *Wonder*, 63.

wonder evoke a sense of awe, curiosity, engagement, and deep interest in the world around us. Each of these wonder-induced characteristics of community can promote problem solving that subverts the tendency to separate from those on the other side of the fear/anger divide. Each orients us toward possibilities, even in the face of perils. Wonder is a characteristic of human flourishing, without which we may be unable to survive in ways we would deem desirable.

Gratitude

Gratitude holds a strong connection to wonder. Dianna Butler Bass defines gratitude at its deepest and most transformative levels as "the emotional response to the surprise of our very existence, to sensing that inner light and realizing the astonishing sacred, social, and scientific events that brought each one of us into being."[81] Gratitude could even be conceived as a *response* to wonder. But it is not a response inculcated by our dominant cultural influences.

Bass notes the Western historic propensity to define gratitude as a transactional "commodity of exchange," which organizes gratitude around ideals of wealth and power. Mary Jo Leddy adds to this, "ingratitude is ingrained in our economic system," having shaped our worldview and imaginations for more than two centuries, shaping the dominant values of our culture in the U.S., rooted in a sense of perpetual *dissatisfaction* that propels the desires and cravings of consumers.[82]

In contrast to the traditional Western economic-informed definition of gratitude, Bass proposes a spiritual and ethical orientation toward gratitude as a structure of "*gift and response.*" Through an ethical lens of gratitude, we begin seeing that everything we need is present in the world. Freely responding to these gifts means cultivating a life of mutual care.[83] She continues, "When we share gifts, we become benefactors toward the well-being of all. Ultimately, the new structure [of gift and response] is a way of being."[84]

Gratitude experienced and expressed outside the commodity model of transactional exchange pairs the emotions we feel in response to life's

81. Bass, *Grateful*, 43.

82. Leddy, *Radical Gratitude*, 4, 6.

83. Bass, *Grateful*, xxiv.

84. Bass, *Grateful*, xxv.

gifts with ethical responses to those gifts. The implications function on both personal and public/communal levels.[85] Bass argues that gratefulness is "ultimately about connection,"[86] an outward-focusing emotion, positioning one toward that which is transcendent—in one's human community, in communion with the more-than-human others in one's ecological setting, or toward the gifts of the Divine. Clearly, gratitude that departs from the commodity-transactional model and enters into a gift-and-response mode becomes a counter cultural witness against the enclosed self-sufficiency, radical independence, and atomized individualism of capitalism and neoliberalism.

"Consumerism works only as long as we are even slightly dissatisfied with what we have," Leddy argues.[87] If we play by the rules of capitalism and consumerism, we are seduced by the belief that a bit more material gain might assuage our dissatisfaction, thus lulling us into complicacy with the status quo and stripping us of impulses toward reform or revolution. Bass adds that in addition to ideals of capitalism, racial privilege also renders white people less capable of experiencing gratitude: "After all, we deserved good things and success. The American dream was ours. God gave it to us. Saying thank you was polite recognition of that fact. Maybe saying thank you too profusely, however, made us feel humiliated that we were not as in control as we thought."[88] Gratitude as an emotional experience that, over time, becomes a pervasive outlook on life is both a counter to white supremacist attitudes and to capitalist, neoliberal hegemony.

Psychologist of gratitude Robert Emmons describes gratitude as a "social emotion." In addition to all of the physical and psychological benefits demonstrated by his research (e.g., stronger immune systems, lower blood pressure, greater experiences of alertness and pleasure, etc.), Emmons has also found that gratitude cultivates an individual's sense of generosity, compassion, and forgiveness and leads to decreased feelings of loneliness and isolation. He argues that gratitude is "a relationship-strengthening emotion because it requires us to see how we've been supported and affirmed by other people." In addition to the immanent focus on the support of others and the web of life for our sustenance, gratitude promotes a transcendent focus on "figuring out where that goodness

---

85. Bass, *Grateful*, xxvi.

86. Bass, *Grateful*, 53.

87. Leddy, *Radical Gratitude*, 23.

88. Bass, *Grateful*, 34.

comes from . . . recognizing the sources of this goodness as being outside of ourselves."[89]

In the midst of apocalyptic circumstances when the situations we face are ones of very genuine threat to survival, we may need to search for what feels like a *gift* in our lives, eliciting our openness toward the world and the people around us. Whether cultivating a radical awareness of life's gifts and graces through practices like journaling or through communal ritual like singing, gratitude developed into a pervasive orientation or temperament holds ethical import. Our ministries of justice-seeking can move away from the motivational resource of anger to take shape as radical responses of gratitude for the gifts of life and our deepest desires to preserve and protect them: the lives of our fellow humans against systems of racism, the lives of our more-than-human companions in the web of life from rampant destruction, etc.

There is much in our lives in an apocalyptic age for which we simply cannot be grateful. This makes each possible experience and expression of gratitude even more important. But for quite a bit else we experience at the end of the world as we know it, gratitude must give way to grief.

Grief

While gratitude opens us toward a transcendent reach outward in response to the gifts of community, the ecological web of life, and the Divine, grief moves us toward others in response to profound loss of these gifts. Gratitude and grief are intimate partners in our emotional response toward a world on the brink of many endings.

"Lament" is a grief resource familiar in the biblical tradition. Fred Craddock describes well how the practice of lament is connected to all that provokes within us a feeling of gratitude and wonder: "A lament is a voice of love and profound caring, a vision of what could have been and of grief over its loss, of tough hope painfully releasing the object of its hope, of personal responsibility and frustration, of sorrow and anger mixed, of accepted loss but with energy enough to go on."[90] One can see in this description how the emotional cultivation of grief draws together primary emotions of sadness, anger, and fear.

---

89. Emmons, "Why Gratitude Is Good."
90. Craddock, "Luke," 229.

The practice of grief as a complex emotional experience is one that stays present with the sadness and anger we are experiencing over the loss of what we hold dear, and the fear of impending losses. But it is an emotional experience that moves from solitude and passivity induced by pervasive feelings of sadness into expressions of community and activity in response to pain and loss. While grief stays with the discomfort and pain, it doesn't necessitate reliving it in ways that exacerbate the trauma that may be associated with those losses.[91]

Lazarus argues that "grieving is the process of coming to terms with a loss, especially the loss of meaning." He continues, "When grieving is successful, old and cherished meanings are retained and integrated with more serviceable new ones, which are more appropriate for the new life conditions."[92] Whereas sadness is a passive emotion, often leading to a sense of helplessness and resignation if it becomes a long-lasting temperament, grief, on the other hand, is an active emotional process seeking to cope with a loss.[93]

In addition to exploring what losses we need to intentionally mourn and lament, communally oriented grieving invites us to ask with whom we can share in this important work of grief and lament. We have many practices that place us in community for the complex emotional work of grieving beloved losses: funerals and memorials for loved ones lost to death, silent vigils in the wake of tragedy when words are not enough, protests taking on an emotional tenor of grief and lament when we place our bodies alongside one another in the streets to voice a mixture of sorrow and anger that energizes us enough to go on in our striving toward justice. Thus grief is a complex emotional experience that holds potential to shape active motivation and communal engagement in the face of pervasive emotional orientations of fear, anger, and sadness that might otherwise serve to pull us apart, invite us into intractable adversarial positions, or quiet us into resignation.

---

91. Menakem provides a similar description of working through the pain and discomfort of trauma, but the same can be true for our sadness over losses that may be less traumatic, but nevertheless distressing. *My Grandmother's Hands*, 14.

92. Lazarus, *Emotion & Adaptation*, 247–48.

93. Lazarus, *Emotion & Adaptation*, 249.

Practicing Care in an Apocalypse

"Our bodies have a form of knowledge that is different from our cognitive brains . . . Often this knowledge is stored in our bodies as wordless stories about what is safe and what is dangerous."

—Resmaa Menakem, *My Grandmother's Hands*[94]

"Care" may seem futile in times that feel apocalyptic. Achille Mbembe pointedly says that the spirit of the current times is about cultivating a renewed "will to kill" rather than a "will to care" by repairing ties that have been broken.[95] We are at a critical stage in the midst of the many endings we face and the potential beginnings they portend. Repairing ties that have been broken, rewriting the wordless stories held within our bodies, shifting our societal will to kill toward a will to care are all acts that require us to fully engage our emotional experiences of life in apocalyptic times.

We are apt to talk about the transimmanent emotional experiences of wonder, gratitude, and grief as if they are emotions we need to nurture simply so that we don't burn our in our work of justice. We are likely to treat them as though they are emotional experiences we need in order to sustain ourselves in the "real" work. But in many ways, practicing care in relation to apocalyptic emotions so that they don't exacerbate the apocalyptic context *is* as much the "real work" as anything else we do. I want to invite you to treat the transimmanent emotions with curiosity enough to wonder how they might actually become *central* to our sense of what it means to open outward toward the world around us in a posture of compassion, and to undertake the deeply connected ministry of peace and justice.

Transimmanent emotions like wonder, gratitude, and grief cannot simply be thought into existence. They are embodied experiences as much as fear, anger, and sadness. Only the more complex emotional experiences of wonder, gratitude, and grief, are unlikely to be provoked with immediacy through subcortical neural processes. They involve higher order interpretive processing and, to reach a sustained orientation toward a life shaped by these transimmanent emotions, a communal element is involved. This is emotional work we must perform *with* others. As *embodied* work, paying attention to the sensory elements of these

---

94. Menakem, *My Grandmother's Hands*, 5.
95. Mbembe, *Necropolitics*, 107.

emotional experiences gives us clues as to how to nurture these transimmanent emotions for ourselves and within community. For example:

What does (wonder / gratitude / grief) *taste* **like?** Grief can taste like the presence of a dead relative resurrected to gustatory life by preparing an old recipe scrawled on a tattered notecard. Gratitude may taste like the first ripe peaches of the season. Wonder might come to taste like a combination of spices in a dish from a culture entirely unknown to our taste buds.

What does (wonder / gratitude / grief) *feel like in my body* **or in a** *tactile way?* Gratitude might feel like the first cool breeze felt after a blistering hot summer, portending the change of seasons soon to come. Wonder can feel like the intensity of intimate touch. Grief may be felt in the weight of a deceased loved one's article of clothing worn against our skin.

What does (wonder / gratitude / grief) *look* **like?** Wonder can look like a full moon in a clear night sky, inviting you to feel your relationship to every human and animal whose eyes have gazed at that bright orb in every generation that has ever existed and that ever will exist into the far, far future. Grief might look like an old growth forest razed to stumps, or gratitude like the green of new growth resurrecting.

What does (wonder / gratitude / grief) *smell* **like?** Grief may smell like the perfume of a deceased loved one whose presence-in-absence lingers like the sweet smell, triggering olfactory memories we had almost forgotten. Wonder might smell like a dog curled up close to our body on the couch—the ineffability of interspecies companionship. Gratitude can come rushing to us in the old smell of a church building where early memories of faith were formed.

What does (wonder / gratitude / grief) *sound* **like?** Gratitude may sound like the singing of a multitude whose voices are joining in harmony. Wonder might sound like escaping the city's familiar buzz into the novel sounds of a forest. Grief can sound like silence—the absence of a voice once as familiar to us as one's own.

What *connection to* **others—human and more-than-human— does (wonder / gratitude / grief) invite?**[96] The feeling of intimacy with others in a street demonstration calling in unity for a more just future can connect us to others in grief as much as any funeral. Wonder can lead us into unexpected relationships of curiosity and exploration of problems

96. This is what Keri Day terms the "erotic" that is "about deep-shared feelings, sensation, and connection with and for each other that wake us up to love, freedom, and pleasure." *Religious Resistance to Neoliberalism*, 77.

yet unsolved. Cleaning up and rebuilding a nearby community after a disaster can become a communal undertaking of gratitude for gifts of life that we know through the power of nature are not ours to possess with clenched fists.

Though not "antidotes" to apocalyptic emotions, the transimmanent emotions can be "responses" to times that are filled with painful endings. And these three—wonder, gratitude, and grief—are certainly not the only possibilities for powerful emotional approaches to our many impending endings. They are just starting places in our search for transimmanent emotional experiences to cultivate within caring community.

Wonder, gratitude, and grief won't save us from the endings we face. The questions become: What difference will it make to our communal strivings toward justice if we undertake them out of a sense of wonder for the interconnected web of life in which we live, rather than out of a pervasive sense of anger? What would it mean to form community with well-developed practices of grief and lament to attenuate the resignation-inducing power of sadness as a pervasive outlook on life? How would our entirely necessary adversarial and agonistic struggles against the powers of violence and oppression be strengthened by an ethic of gratitude for the gifts of life and community, rather than simply being fueled by lingering temperaments and communal orientations of anger?

For leaders in communities of faith and spiritual practice, the task of care amid apocalyptic emotions is twofold:

First, we must honor the role that fear, anger, and sadness play as evolutionary gifts of our embodied experience. These are a vital part of our creation in the *imago Dei*. Helping individuals and communities listen to the embodied voices of these apocalyptic emotions and learn what they tell us about our deepest values and most intimate connections honors their role in our lives while keeping them from *overtaking* our experience of life in the world in ways that operate outside of our conscious awareness. Feeling fear, anger, and sadness in relation to the many endings we face at this moment in our common human experience is normal, to be expected, and necessary. But allowing fear, anger, and sadness to develop into long-lasting temperaments and orientations towards life exacerbates our experience of endings and cuts us off from adaptive movement toward flourishing, even at the end of the world as we know it.

Second, caregivers in our communities must turn toward developing multisensory, embodied ways to cultivate the transimmanent emotional experiences. We cannot simply explore the emotions of anger, fear, and sadness ad nauseam, nor can we meet the affects of apocalypse with *thinking* about apocalypse alone. We must engage in the cultivation of more complex, communally oriented transimmanent emotions like wonder, gratitude, and grief. When we come to the task of creating liturgy or ritual, we should be attentive to the affective dimensions that they aim to cultivate in participants as much as the theological content they bear. When we gather in community, we can gather in ways that aim toward collective emotional engagement in wonder or gratitude or grief, as much as we focus on the content of our discussions and deliberations. When we verbally process our experiences of life in the midst of so many endings, facilitators can help participants attend to the embodiment of their emotional experiences as much as the rational deliberations by inviting reflection on experiences of wonder, gratitude, and grief. In an apocalyptic era, the task of leading people into experiences of transimmanence must always remain central.

Life as we've known it is coming to an end. It isn't the first ending the world has faced, and there are many endings yet to come. With all there is to think about and all that calls upon us to do, we must also learn to feel our way through this apocalypse.

Bibliography

Abram, David. *The Spell of the Sensuous: Perception and Language in a More-Than-Human World*. New York: Vintage, 1996.

Albrecht, Glenn A. *Earth Emotions: New Words for a New World*. Ithaca, NY: Cornell University Press, 2019.

"Australia Fires: A Visual Guide to the Bushfire Crisis." BBC News. Accessed August 2, 2020. https://www.bbc.com/news/world-australia-50951043.

Baker, Peter. "Bush Made Willie Horton an Issue in 1988, and the Racial Scars Are Still Fresh," The New York Times. December 3, 2018. https://www.nytimes.com/2018/12/03/us/politics/bush-willie-horton.html.

Bass, Dianna Butler. *Grateful: The Transformative Power of Giving Thanks*. New York: HarperOne, 2018.

Bauman, Anna, and Anthony Brooks. "The Origins of the Extremist 'Boogaloo' Movement." On Point. July 20, 2020. https://www.wbur.org/onpoint/2020/07/10/the-origins-of-the-extremist-boogaloo-movement.

"Closer Than Ever: It's 100 Seconds to Midnight." Bulletin of the Atomic Scientists. Accessed January 23, 2020. https://thebulletin.org/doomsday-clock/current-time/.

"COVID-19 to Plunge Global Economy into Worst Recession since World War II." The World Bank. June 8, 2020. https://www.worldbank.org/en/news/press-release/2020/06/08/covid-19-to-plunge-global-economy-into-worst-recession-since-world-war-ii.

Craddock, Fred. "Luke," *Interpretation: A Bible Commentary for Teaching and Preaching*. Edited by James L. Mays. Louisville: Westminster John Knox, 2009.

Day, Keri. *Religious Resistance to Neoliberalism: Womanist and Black Feminist Perspectives*. New York: Palgrave Macmillan, 2016.

Ekman, Paul. *Emotions Revealed: Recognizing Faces and Feelings to Improve Communication and Emotional Life*. Revised edition. New York: Owl, 2003.

Emmons, Robert. "Why Gratitude Is Good," Greater Good Magazine. November 16, 2010. https://greatergood.berkeley.edu/article/item/why_gratitude_is_good.

Field, Matt. "Why Is Tear Gas Banned in War but Not from Peaceful Protests?" Bulletin of the Atomic Scientists. June 4, 2020. https://thebulletin.org/2020/06/why-is-tear-gas-banned-in-war-but-not-from-peaceful-protests/

Fuller, Robert C. *Spirituality in the Flesh: Bodily Sources of Religious Experience*. New York: Oxford University Press, 2008.

Fuller, Robert C. *Wonder: From Emotion to Spirituality*. Chapel Hill, NY: University of North Carolina Press, 2006.

Godoy, Maria. "What Do Coronavirus Racial Disparities Look Like State By State?" NPR. May 30, 2020. https://www.npr.org/sections/health-shots/2020/05/30/865413079/what-do-coronavirus-racial-disparities-look-like-state-by-state.

Goldenberg, Amit, and James J. Gross. "Digital Emotional Contagion." *Trends in Cognitive Science* 24, no. 4 (2020): 316–28.

Harris, Shane. "DHS Analyzed Protester Communications, Raising Questions About Previous Statements." The Washington Post. July 31, 2020. https://www.washingtonpost.com/national-security/dhs-analyzed-protester-communications-raising-questions-about-previous-statements-by-senior-department-official/2020/07/31/313163c6-d359-11ea-9038-af089b63ac21_story.html?itid=lk_inline_manual_25.

Heschel, Abraham Joshua. *God in Search of Man: A Philosophy of Judaism*. New York: Farrar, Straus and Giroux, 1955.

hooks, bell. *Killing Rage: Ending Racism*. New York: Henry Holt and Company, 1995.

Jemison, N. K. *The Stone Sky*. New York: Orbit, 2017.

Latour, Bruno. *Facing Gaia: Eight Lectures on the New Climatic Regime*. Translated by Catherine Porter. Medford, MA: Polity, 2017.

Lazarus, Richard S. *Emotion & Adaptation*. New York: Oxford University Press, 1991.

Leddy, Mary Jo. *Radical Gratitude*. Maryknoll, NY: Orbis, 2002.

Lester, Andrew D. *The Angry Christian: A Theology for Care and Counseling*. Louisville, KY: Westminster John Knox, 2003.

Lisitsa, Ellie. "The Four Horsemen: Criticism, Contempt, Defensiveness, and Stonewalling," The Gottman Institute. April 23, 2013. https://www.gottman.com/blog/the-four-horsemen-recognizing-criticism-contempt-defensiveness-and-stonewalling/.

Mbembe, Achille. *Necropolitics*. Translated by Steven Corcoran. Durham: Duke University Press, 2019.

Menakem, Resmaa. *My Grandmother's Hands: Racialized Trauma and the Pathway to Mending our Hearts and Bodies*. Las Vegas: Central Recovery, 2017.

Nussbaum, Martha. *Upheavals of Thought: The Intelligence of Emotions*. Cambridge, England: Cambridge University Press, 2001.

Owens, Lama Rod. *Love and Rage: The Path of Liberation Through Anger*. Berkeley: North Atlantic, 2020.

Rahal, Sarah and Craig Mauger. "Armed Protesters in Michigan Capitol Have Lawmakers Questioning Policy." The Detroit News. May 2, 2020. https://www. detroitnews.com/story/news/local/michigan/2020/05/02/armed-protesters-michigan-capitol-have-lawmakers-questioning-policy/3071928001/.

Rankine, Claudia. "The Condition of Black Life Is One of Mourning" In *The Fire This Time: A New Generation Speaks about Race*, edited by Jesmyn Ward, 145–55. New York: Scribner: 2016.

Reddy, William M. *The Navigation of Feeling: A Framework for the History of Emotion* (Cambridge: Cambridge University Press, 2001), 12.

Rempala, Daniel M. "Cognitive Strategies for Controlling Emotional Contagion." *Journal of Applied Social Psychology* 43 (2013): 1529–1537.

Samuels, Alex. "Dan Patrick says 'there are more important things than living and that's saving this country." The Texas Tribune. April 21, 2020. https://www.texastribune. org/2020/04/21/texas-dan-patrick-economy-coronavirus/

Stockman, Fara, Kate Kelly, and Jennifer Medina. "How Buying Beans Became a Political Statement." The New York Times. July 19, 2020. https://www.nytimes. com/2020/07/19/us/goya-trump-hispanic-vote.html.

Stone, Madeleine. "A Heat Wave Thawed Siberia's Tundra. Now It's On Fire." National Geographic. July 6, 2020. https://www.nationalgeographic.com/science/2020/07/ heat-wave-thawed-siberia-now-on-fire/.

"Summary for Policymakers of IPCC Special Report on Global Warming of 1.5°C approved by governments." IPCC. Accessed January 21, 2020. https://www.ipcc. ch/2018/10/08/summary-for-policymakers-of-ipcc-special-report-on-global-warming-of-1-5c-approved-by-governments/.

Svendsen, Lars. *A Philosophy of Fear*. London: Reaktion Books, 2008.

"Tackling the Misinformation Epidemic with 'In Event of Moon Disaster,'" MIT News. July 20, 2020. http://news.mit.edu/2020/mit-tackles-misinformation-in-event-of-moon-disaster-0720.

van der Kolk, Bessel. *The Body Keeps the Score: Brain, Mind, and Body in the Healing of Trauma*. New York: Penguin, 2014.

Weber, Andras. *Enlivenment: Toward a Poetics for the Anthropocene*. Cambridge: The MIT Press, 2019.

Williams, Terry Tempest. *Erosion: Essays of Undoing*. New York: Sarah Crichton, 2019.

5

Traumatized Bodies and the
Slow Work of Theology

Shelly Rambo

The Carousel of Progress

Those of you who have been to Disney World may remember a ride called the Carousel of Progress. It is hard to forget, because the tune is branded into your memory—in just 21 minutes: "Now is the time. Now is the best time. Now is the best time of your life."[1] For those of you who have never been to the Magic Kingdom, let me usher you into Tomorrowland, and to the moving theater that has been in operation at Disney since 1973. The Carousel is a stage production, featuring auto-animatronic characters who narrate the story of twentieth-century American innovation. Father John, beginning on stage one in 1890, welcomes the audience into the home of an American family. In a deep broadcaster voice with the right mixture of warmth and humor, he tells the American story, inviting us to take the journey of progress from the late nineteenth century and the invention of electricity through the 1920s, 1950s, 1980s

---

1. Sherman and Sherman, "The Best Time of Your Life," 17–18.

to the family's wireless living room. John's family—wife, daughter, son, parents, dog—are experiencing the wonders of technology—from telephones to toasters, sewing machines to microwaves.

This Disney production was first introduced at the 1964 World's Fair. Walt Disney's brainchild, it narrated American progress through its development, displaying the innovative leaps in energy and invention that sets America apart. When he was asked to submit a proposal to the World's Fair committee, he reached out to General Electric to sponsor the production. This marriage of industry and entertainment is the longest-running stage show in the history of American theater. Walt considered Carousel of Progress a vehicle for his philosophy. It contained the right mixture of nostalgia and promise. The American dream rooted in a the "sparkle and glean" of yesterday's memories and its forward glance to a bigger brighter future.[2] Walt wanted to make the drive for innovation infectious. Walt commissioned the Sherman Brothers to produce a theme song "A Great Big Beautiful Tomorrow."[3] With the move to Orlando, the theme song switched to "The Best Time of Your Life." Both songs, with their over-the-top optimism, transition the audience from stage to stage.

The Carousel is a sensory onslaught of American tropes and apple-pie idioms. The striking thing about the ride is that audience members are not just watching the decades pass before their eyes. The stage isn't revolving around the audience. The theater and its spectators are revolving around the stage. I imagine Walt having an 'ah-ha' moment. American progress is not something you passively witness. It is something you participate in. The movement of the audience, rather than the stage, fortifies the message: that everything is moving forward, and you will not be left behind. You are part of it. You *are* on the carousel of progress.

After two revolutions, my body began to anticipate the turn to the next frame, skipping to the next decade. With the upswing in Father John's inviting words, there was just enough pause, that we knew the music would start. We are "forward marching and we are in the parade."[4] It was already braced for the journey. In fact, after exiting the theater, we were immediately placed on the moving walkway—the People-Mover—through the City of Tomorrow.

2. Sherman, "The Best Time of Your Life," compact disc.

3. Sherman and Sherman, "Great Big Beautiful Tomorrow," 198.

4. Sherman, "The Best Time of Your Life," compact disc.

Let me be clear. I *loved* this ride. From the tingle of the tune to the anticipation of seeing the gadgets of the future, I loved how it made me feel. It was part of my own journey south each summer to visit my mother's family, all of whom moved to Orlando, one uncle following another to leave western Pennsylvania because business ventures were more promising in Florida. My family looked a lot like Father John and the aspirations were similar. My family was the born-again Christian version, products of the Second Great Awakening, who, up through the 1980's, were mostly working-class. But the promise of making new creatures out of the old—of becoming new, kneeling at the altars of America's outdoor tent revivals, this revolution of the Carousel aligned with the evangelical spirit. American revival preachers quickly learned how to take the conversion message and tailor it to the energy of this promised land.

I thought of this ride as the news broke of Disney's reopening of the Magic Kingdom amidst a COVID surge in Florida. Of all of the reopening plans, this made sense to me; but not because it was a sensible plan. Rather, the drive to reopen Disney World seemed like a fundamental American reflex. Disney was the dispenser and disseminator of dreams. No other figure ushered children into the dream of America better than Walt Disney. He provided a full sensorial orchestra for the stories that we have told about ourselves over decades. America needed Disney—and all of its supporting mechanisms—to keep the carousel moving.

Disney's reopening signaled how important it is for the country to keep its fundamental stories intact, even when the characters and plot do not reflect their surroundings. The carousel's popularity and survival—with only modest updates—testifies to the work that it does. It not only stories American core beliefs; it sustains these beliefs through *muscle memory*. Forty-some years later, I can recite every line of the Carousel theme song. The muscle memories, formed early and attached to people and places that I loved, still move to the rhythms of the Sherman Brothers. As a child, the script of American dreams was already taking root in me. As a child, I did not think about whether the workers at General Electric were offered fair wages, whether they had protections in place to ensure a safe work environment. I did not consider that the family featured in the carousel had white bodies or that the vision of the future was narrated by a white American father. I did not consider it.

* * *

In this moment, truths about the impact of the longstanding stories America tells about itself are rising to the surface. And they are surfacing as wounds that have always been there but whose temporary bandages have been ripped off, exposing them to the open air. The current crises have surfaced truths about the mechanisms that keep the Carousel of Progress in operation. The support systems for buoying this narrative rely disproportionally on the labor of Black and brown workers, of vulnerable economic communities. Anti-Black racism, workplace inequalities, redlining, gerrymandering, and alarming health disparities are not momentary problems that we can trace back to March 2020. They are all components that keep the carousel moving into that great big beautiful tomorrow. They have been deep in the collective body of the United States.

Studies in trauma have turned us to embodied truths, truths that live as body memories that do not always register in language or in conscious awareness. These somatic insights lead us to think differently about current events. The notion that we may, collectively, be operating more in line with our fight/flight/free part of our brain than with our reasoning/language part of the brain is shifting how we think about addressing the vexing political and social problems that are glaring in this time. Trauma teaches us that bodies hold truths. Some truths are too painful to speak. Some are unlanguageable. Right now, images of traumatized bodies are everywhere. And it is important to provide an account for what remains unconsidered and yet is registered at another level. If we hope to heal trauma, we need to better understand how we 'know not what we do' and yet are still accountable for the harm that it produces.

I began with my white eight-year-old body, because it is my task to figure out how the strong cultural messages about worth and value came to live inside me. It is a task that requires a significant spiritual realignment and spiritual conditioning. If our bodies have developed ways of moving that live deep, at the level of muscle memory, how do we loosen these muscles? How do we release the hold of longstanding narratives that have worked their way into the DNA of our faith? Christian theologies must rethink themselves through the traumatized body, a figure used more and more frequently, to name our current societal moment. Doing theology in this time requires working at the level of reflex and muscle memory. This is slow work. It requires, for many of us, a change of pace. As I think about the important contributions by theologians on the significance of *place* in the doing of theology (contextual theologies) I am mindful during this pandemic time that we need to rethink our *pace*.

In this chapter, I invite us to think about the *slow work of theology*. Beginning with the figure of America as a traumatized body, particularly in connection to racial trauma, I underscore the challenge to Christian theology and imagine what it might look like for theology to work at the level of reflex and muscle memory. In response, I present three spiritual teachers who guide us in re-pacing our theologies in order to attend to the texture of wounds surfacing in the present moment.

America as a Traumatized Body

The language of trauma and moral injury offers a public vocabulary for naming the current moment. Cycles of harm perpetuated in and through core institutions are being captured, in real time, on camera. The moral injury of these institutions becomes apparent, as lower-wage workers are required to enter buildings, sacrificing their safety to perform tasks that keep the economy moving forward. Traumatized bodies, both individual and collective, have become literal and figurative metaphors for the moment. The double pandemics have also surfaced questions about whether this is a time of racial reckoning in America that will result in real substantive change. There are public declarations of change. But will they take hold? Black scholars and cultural critics call into question the conditions in which real change can happen. Is white America really up to the task? The answer: No. Pause. Not unless.

In *Between the World and Me,* Ta-Nahisi Coates teaches his son about what it means to live and move in the United States with a Black body. As a reader, you notice really quickly that Coates shifts from the language of Black man to almost exclusively referencing Black bodies— his body, his son's body, and other bodies. Coates shifts our language and, in doing so, insists that we, as readers, consider bodies and the experience of living in a body that others have raced. Black man is a raced term. Race is the designation placed on bodies that signal or indicate that certain things can and cannot be done to them. Some bodies are more protected; others are not.[5]

Ibram Kendi in "Is This the Beginning of the End of American Racism?" says that what distinguishes this current moment is that the

---

5. Coates writes: "To be Black in the Baltimore of my youth was to be naked before the elements of the world, before all the guns, first, knives, crack, rape, and disease." Coates, *Between the World and Me,* 17.

reflexes of white America have been exposed. The American President, Kendi writes, "has held up a mirror to American society, and it has reflected back a grotesque image that many people had until now refused to see: an image not just of the racism still coursing through the country, but also of the reflex to deny that reality."[6] What they saw was not simply their reflection but the reflex to turn away from what they are seeing. It is not the reflection alone that was exposed. It was the reflex to turn away that immediately follows. Maybe this time, the reflex to *turn away,* or, in keeping with the carousel, to project the future without considering the trauma of past actions, may be intercepted.

Similarly, Kimberlé Williams Crenshaw writes about this moment of national reckoning on race by speaking about the nation as a *traumatized body*. In a piece in *The New Republic* titled, "Fear of a Black Uprising," she writes that the work of addressing racial injustice requires body work:

> In order to prevent yet another reversion to the status quo of white moral panic, we need to prod the emerging new discourse around racial justice and policing to engage the deeper question of how we might reckon with, and finally dislodge, this toxic muscle memory that continually disfigures our body politic.[7]

The deeper questions require working in a different register—targeting the patterns of behaviors and movements that keep the body movement, without consideration.

In *My Grandmother's Hands: Racialized Trauma and the Pathway to Mending our Heart and Bodies,* Resmaa Menakem organizes his analysis of racial trauma around traumatized bodies.[8] As a psychiatrist, he uniquely takes the wisdom of body-centered therapies and considers how we all carry trauma in our bodies, albeit differently. White bodies. Black bodies. Police bodies. It is trauma rooted in the myth of race. According to Menakem, I, as a young white girl riding the Carousel of Progress, was taking in messages about race, not just in my thinking brain, but in and through my senses. He writes: "White-body supremacy doesn't live just

6. Kendi, "Is This the Beginning of the End of American Racism?".

7. Crenshaw, "Fear of a Black Uprising: Confronting the White Pathologies that Shape Racist Policing."

8. Menakem notes this lineage of referring to bodies as sites of harm, rather than abstractly talking about the 'problem of race,' by listing a host of writers: George Yancy, Kelly Brown Douglass, James Baldwin, Richard Wright, bell hooks, Teju Cole, and ending with Coates. Menakem, *My Grandmother's Hands,* 17.

in our thinking brains. It lives and breathes in our bodies."[9] If we are going to heal, we need to work trauma out of our bodies. Note, as well, that he inserts *body* into the term white supremacy.

Working from the figure of traumatized bodies, certain things stand out. You cannot talk trauma out of the body. If, and when, wounds surface, watch the reflexes. Healing and truth-telling are not linear. Although those who work in the area of trauma have a great deal to say about each of these, they point not just to rethinking of the content of our theologies but to a reorienting how we approach theological reflection. Theological education privileges words. Systematic theology often operates like a logic problem. Theologian Jürgen Moltmann writes: "Every consistent theological summing up, every theological system lays claim to totality, perfect organization, and entire competence for the whole area under survey. All the statements must fit in with one another without contradiction, and the whole architecture must be harmonious, an integrated whole."[10] He warns of the drive of systematics to achieve a view of totality. In response, he concludes: "For that reason, I have resisted the temptation to develop a theological system, even an 'open' one. The common, tried and tested view of what dogmatics is also made me hesitate."[11]

The mirror has been placed in front of Christian theology; but it is *the reflexes and gestures of denial so deeply embedded within us* that are more difficult to name and acknowledge. Production of theological knowledge operates with its own practices of looking away. Christian theologians writing about race are noting the absence of reflection on these reflexes operating within theological education itself. Recent works by Willie Jennings consider the raced origins of modern Christian theology in respect to the reflexes and muscle memory of its educational practices.[12] The reflexes are subtle, and they often go unnoticed. How do students with Black bodies in classrooms come to know that the privileged writings of Christian theology require them to either erase or perform their racial identities? How do white professorial bodies, like my own, signal that, without ever speaking it? How do students from Korea, Africa, and Columbia comes to know that their mother tongue has to be

9. Menakem, *My Grandmother's Hands*, 25.

10. Moltmann, *The Trinity and the Kingdom*, xi.

11. Moltmann, *The Trinity and the Kingdom*, xi.

12. He writes: "I watched a complex process of dissociation and dislocation that was connected to the prescribed habits of mind for those who do scholarly theological work," in Jennings, *The Christian Imagination*, 7. See also, Jennings, *After Whiteness*.

translated to be accepted and acceptable? While theological degree programs emphasize formation as one of its primary learning outcomes for students, these scholars note the absence of reflection on the formational practices that constitute theological education.[13]

The figure of the traumatized body is generative, given that Christian theology centers itself around a traumatized body. James Cone's theology is prescient when, in *The Cross and the Lynching Tree,* he asks how it is possible for Reinhold Niebuhr to have a brilliant theology of the cross and yet be unable to see Black suffering.[14] Cone probes: "How could Niebuhr make the tragedy of the cross the central theme in his theology while ignoring the obvious tragedies of slavery, segregation, and lynching in the United States?"[15] How is it that he is not moved by Black suffering? This disconnect or dissonance confounded Cone. But Black theologians a generation later are responding. It is the unchecked reflexes that make up the corpus of Christian theology.

Right now, there seems to be a sharpness, a clear voice around naming the problem of racism, and anti-Black racism in particular. The acknowledgment of white supremacy within our institutional spaces is happening. But the acknowledgement of white *body* supremacy is different. Thinking differently is not enough. The question is whether muscles can release, whether the nerve centers can shift, and whether the neural pathways that have channeled 'truth' can be rerouted. Is theology up to the task? The evidence is right in front of our faces. But studies in trauma teach us how trauma, when brought into public view, can quickly be made invisible again. It is what Judith Herman called the central dialectic of trauma: both the "will to deny horrible events and the will to proclaim them aloud."[16] These studies also teach us that no *logic* is sufficient to work out the toxic muscle memory of white supremacy. You cannot

13. The Association of Theological Schools Commission on Accrediting, "Degree Program Standards," 3.

14. Cone writes, "Niebuhr could have explored this story with theological imagination, seeing Blacks as crucified like Jesus and forced like Simon to carry the crosses of slavery, segregation, and lynching. But he did not." Cone, *The Cross and the Lynching Tree,* 48

15. Cone, *The Cross and the Lynching Tree,* 63.

16. Herman, *Trauma and Recovery,* 1. Herman also describes how the dialectic is experienced by the survivor: "She finds herself caught between the extremes of amnesia or of reliving the trauma, between floods of intense, overwhelming feeling and arid states of no feeling at all, between irritable, impulsive action and complete inhibition of action." Herman, *Trauma and Recovery,* 47.

simply talk it out of the body. What it requires is change at a somatic level. If we consider the traumatized body, we need to learn how to work at the level of reflex and muscle memory. But to work with reflexes of denial and toxic muscle memory is work of a different kind, requiring intentional postures and re-pacing. The traumatized body operates on a different timeline—non-linear and easily triggered. This is where body-centered approaches to trauma can help us. If we are going to work trauma out of this collective body without being caught up in ongoing cycles of trauma, we need to re-pace the work.

There is incredible potential here to address the toxic muscle memory. But not if we rush past difficult truths or cover them over. Christian theologians, recognizing the implication of theologies in the problems of this time, deliver calls to action. Quoting Martin Luther King Jr., they underscore that there is the urgency of now. The reflex to action is a good one. And yet Resmaa Menakem might stop and ask a few questions. He would remind us that we are dealing with traumatized bodies—not just the bodies out there but the bodies that we bring to the work. *Our* bodies. He asks whether we are operating from clean or dirty pain. Slow down. Notice. Consider. Breathe. Quick action needs a set of practices for *staying with* and *attending to pain*—what Rev. Cristina Rathbone calls "muscular stillness."[17]

I want us to pause. The "us" is directed to those with white bodies who are used to determining the agenda for Christian theology. How do we know, especially as white theologians, that we aren't enacting the longstanding reflexes? We may, referring to Kendi, be staring at the ugly image only for a split second before quickly turning away. Think of Cone's question: Why did Niebuhr have the logic right and yet fail to be moved by Black suffering? Keeping with the metaphor, Niebuhr did not sustain the stare. His reflex was to look away.

We need *spiritual guides for this slow work*. I invite us to consider three spiritual teachers who lived in different times but can teach us something about what it means to do theology in this time. They provide wisdom for a slow theology. Each extends an invitation. Julian of Norwich models how to work with messages that come to live in us over time. Simone Weil urges us to practice towards what we do not know. Howard Thurman invites us to have a long conversation with ourselves.

17. Rathbone, Boston University School of Theology 2020 Distinguished Alumni Panel.

First Guide: Julian of Norwich

At the age of six, Julian of Norwich witnessed the death toll in Norwich. One-third of the city's residents died as a result of the Black Plague. The year was 1348. She later took vows to live a life of solitary prayer and devotion. As an anchoress, she inhabited a room attached to the sanctuary of the church in Norwich. Her vows required that she cross the threshold from the outside world to the enclosed space and never leave. She spent her days in the rhythm of prayer, sacraments, and counsel.

We know through the writings of Margery Kempe that Julian was a spiritual director. She advised villagers who were seeking spiritual wisdom in the midst of the pandemic.[18] We also know of her, because she left behind some writings, which began with a series of mystical visions and ended in reflections that have since been studied by Christian theologians. In *Revelations of Divine Love*, Julian reports receiving fifteen visions under what we might consider hospice conditions.[19] She prayed for God to bring her suffering and to show her the meaning in it. And in her pain, she experienced the crucified Christ speaking to her in his agonized state.

She spent the next thirty years unpacking these visions, meditating on them, and grappling with their meaning. The "short version" contains the visions (the showings), and the "long version" is the extended reflection. The visions she received did not align with the teachings that Julian had received through more formal channels. One of the central teachings of Holy Church was about how God accounts for sin.

For years, Julian had been shaped by *this* account: Human beings stand guilty in judgment before God and are punishable (blameworthy) for their sins. Julian found this account hard to accept. How can human sin be so great that it overwhelms God's love? "O wretched sin," she asks, "what are you?"[20] I see God in *everything*, she goes on to say, and I do not see you there. She can't find sin anywhere, because God is everywhere.

18. One way we know of Julian's work as a spiritual counselor is that she was recommended to Margery Kempe as a source of wise advice. Kempe, *The Book of Margery Kempe*, 77.

19. Julian, *Showings*, 5.

20. Julian writes: "O wretched sin, what are you? For I saw that God is in everything; I did not see you. And when I say that God has made everything, I did not see you. And when I saw that God is in everything, I did not see you. And when I saw that God does everything that is done, the less and the greater, I still did not see you." Julian, *Showings*, 166.

And yet, she knows, the Holy Church describes human sin as an obstacle to God's love. And she *feels the blame* for sin within her. She writes:

> Good Lord, I see in you that you are very truth, and I know truly that we sin grievously all day and are very blameworthy; and I can neither reject my knowledge of this truth, nor see that any kind of blame is shown to us. How can this be? For I know *by the ordinary teaching of Holy Church and by my own feeling that the blame of our sins continually hangs upon us,* from the first man until the time that we come into heaven. This, then, was my astonishment, that I saw our Lord God showing no more blame to us than if we were as pure and as holy as the angels in heaven.[21]

She asks for knowledge and for relief in the midst of her spiritual struggles. The suffering Christ on the cross positions Julian in a particular way to the suffering, transporting her from her sickbed to the cross, offering a view from the angle of the suffering Christ himself. This transport offered in the vision results in Julian calling into question whether the church's account of human fault/blameworthiness/God's wrath is a truthful account. She asked Christ to see sin as God sees it.[22]

A response comes to her with such directness that she cannot shake it. The series of visions from the cross are later illustrated through a parable, which she identifies as a "wonderful example" given to her.[23] The parable provides a response to her spiritual struggles. At the center is the parable of the lord and the servant—the servant runs off with eagerness to do the will of the lord, falls into a dell and cannot get out. She insists on certain things. First, the servant gladly leaves to do the lord's bidding; the servant is neither defiant nor disobedient. Second, the servant is not at fault for falling. Third, the fall into the ditch is a real problem. The servant cannot get out. And they lose sight of the lord, even as the lord continues to gaze in the servant's direction. The gaze of the lord *remains constant,* and it *is always loving.* The servant, however, does not see or feel this gaze upon them. The servant is stuck in the dell and cannot on their own efforts

---

21. Julian, *Showings,* 266. Emphasis added.

22. Julian, *Showings,* 266–67.

23. In chapter 45 she writes, "And to all this I never had any other answer than a wonderful example of a lord and servant, as I shall tell later, and that was very mysteriously revealed," Julian, *Showings,* 257. In Chapter 51 she writes, "And then our courteous Lord answered very mysteriously, by revealing a wonderful example of a lord who has a servant and gave me sight for the understanding of them both," Julian, *Showings,* 267.

get out. But the parable emphasized this part: The servant's suffering is increased by the perception of the lord's absence. The lord has been waiting, looking on the whole time. But the servant, deep in the ditch, loses sight of the gaze. They experience the fall as real separation. They feel fully cut off. And when they look up, they can only feel the weight of their fault, their blameworthiness. And with years of dell-dwelling, cut off from the loving gaze, I imagine that the load of blameworthiness only increases.

The parable, Julian reports, comes like a flash. But she feels its lingering effects. She writes: "The wonder of the example never left me."[24] The suffering Christ delivers a message. But it is only later—through inward instruction—that she reconciles the question of God's relationship to suffering. Julian's writings refer to both external and internal work. *External work* is demonstrated in her engagement with church teachings. Julian demonstrates what it looks like to work with messages that have been longstanding. She displays the process of moving between exterior teachings and inward instruction. First she states the teachings of Holy Church. Then she states who she knows God to be. Moving between the two, she is loosening the hold of the teachings of Holy Church and their accompanying reflexes. And what happens, as we witness the unfolding of her insights, is that she creates space for a different meaning to take root. The parable makes room for Julian's questions. It operates like a wedge that you prop in a window to keep it open. It provides a portal through which the outdoor air can come into the room.

A lot has been made about her reading of the parable of the lord and servant for what it contributes to atonement theology. It *is* a profound meditation, theologians note, on theological anthropology, soteriology, Christology—and all of the categories of systematic theology.[25] And yet this focus cuts short the fuller guidance of Julian. It is the *internal work*—"the inward instruction"—that is important here.[26] It takes time for the meaning to sink in. Scholars have focused extensively on external struggle with church teachings. But Church teachings are not the focus of the Long Version.

Julian's work, over years, is to release the hold of blame that has come to live in her. This is reflected in the second half of the sentence: "For I know *by the ordinary teaching of Holy Church and by my own feeling that*

24. Julian, *Showings*, 269.

25. For an excellent examination of these contributions, see Grace Jantzen, *Julian of Norwich: Mystic and Theologian*.

26. Julian, *Showings*, 270.

the blame of our sins continually hangs upon us, from the first man until the time that we come into heaven." I know *by my own feeling*. Julian has been dell-dwelling, feeling the weight of judgment within her. The blameworthiness was not simply an external teaching; it had worked its way into her body. The internal work of addressing the *feeling* of blame is work of a different kind. And it is this feeling that requires a different set of practices. For Julian, these were a combination of ongoing practices of prayer, counsel, and writing. In the vision, the suffering Christ removes the barrier that keeps Julian from seeing herself as beloved by God. He reveals to her that the gaze of God upon her has never wavered. But this insight alone is not enough to remove the feeling of blame. Releasing the hold of blameworthiness is the slow work.

Church teachings can often hover above the dell, rendering judgment; and yet Julian's message comes to us down in the dell. The message comes from someone sitting there, who stumbled there, not because she was willful but because there are a lot of dells out there. The primary spiritual work is to lift the weight of blame. This is life-line theology needed when you are unable to *feel* goodness.

The spiritual work for Julian over the thirty years is to come to feel her goodness. And to emerge in such a way that the blameworthiness was *worked out of her muscles*. Blame no longer had a hold on her. Instead, we witness in the progression of her writings a kind of spiritual release, a growing sense of joy. And note that she does it over a long period of time. It takes time to release and reroute.

This slow-paced work is not primarily about contending with church teachings, although the external work is important. It is about reworking the primary messaging that lives in our bodies. Blameworthiness is not a theological *concept*; it lives as messaging within us that orients us to everything around us.

Second Guide: Simone Weil

Raised with privilege in 1920's Paris, Simone Weil was educated at elite French schools and quickly became recognized for her remarkable intellectual abilities. She viewed societal illness and health from the perspective of the industrial worker and the mercenary soldier. From a young age, she engaged in practices of solidarity with the everyday worker and the mercenary soldier. She was deeply attuned to the mechanisms by which persons can be made into things.[27] Industrialized societies take existence and mechanize it, uprooting persons from human connection. This instrumentalization of the human body—whether for labor or combat—was the theme around which her social analysis and philosophical writings circled.

Her analysis of radical suffering, what she calls affliction, has influenced theologians working in the area of trauma. Affliction is a synonym for the phenomenon of trauma. While affliction has many dimensions, the social dimension, she claims, is the most destructive. Her image of affliction is one of a person crying out but whose cry cannot be heard. This "mute cry" that resounds without the ability to be received; it is the cry at the heart of existence—"Why am I being hurt?"[28] Why are things as they are?" And nowhere is this uprooting and isolation most instrumentalized than in warehouses of industrial production. The guidance she offers comes by reading two of her essays together: "Factory Work" and "Reflections on the Right Use of School Studies With a View to the Love of God."[29] If we think of spheres deeply impacted by the pandemic, these two essays speak directly to them: labor and education.

In late 1934, Weil left her teaching post to work on the factory lines at the Renault auto plant. She penned observations about "direct contact with factory life." She begins the essay with the sounds of the factory, which echo the hums of Disney's Carousel. It is the General Electric vision of the buzz of industry. "Lost in this great hum of labor," she writes, the workingman feels the buzz of energy and creation in his body. "The lamps, the belts, the noise, the hard, cold iron-work, all converge toward the transmutation of man into workingman."[30]

Then she stops. But this is not the case. This harmony of worker and material is not the way things are. Instead, there is no freedom in the workingman's relationship to the materials. Instead, factory workers conform to the rhythms and materials. Instead of mastering them, the conditions constrain and contort. We know that Weil found the metals too heavy to carry and she experienced skin burns from working the

27. Weil, "Factory Work," 60.

28. Weil, "Human Personality," 315.

29. Weil did not pair these essays, but both highlight contexts in which the individual is formed within, and subject to, the conditions of industrialization. In one essay, she focuses on the factory line; in the other, she focuses on the educational line. Weil, "Factory Work."; Weil, "Reflections."

30. Weil, "Factory Work," 55.

industrial furnace. The factory is not a place of freedom. It is a place of servitude. "Time and rhythm constitute the most important factor of the whole problem of work," she writes.[31] Gradually the rhythms of the human body conform to the "cadence" of time (punching the timecard, adhering to the timing of the production line). Instead of leaving our mark on time, time marks us according to the measures of production. "This tick-tock, the barren monotony of which is scarcely bearable to human ears over any length of time, workingmen are obliged to reproduce with their bodies." Time drags; there is an "exhausting passivity."[32]

But it is not the monotony that is most destructive. While numbing, these are predictable rhythms. It is the *interruptions* that produce anxiety. "Nothing is worse than a mixture of monotony and accident."[33] Workers are braced for 'accidents' and 'incidents' that can arise at any time, often initiated by orders from supervisors.[34] "The order" according to Weil, is unnerving, and the worker does not know when an order will come. The worker must be in a state of "constant readiness."[35] Braced for the unexpected, the worker anticipates experiences of humiliation, without having resources to ward again them. This anticipation, according to Weil, is a form of futurity;[36] it anticipates—thinks forward—but for the sake of protecting oneself and avoiding shame.

Throughout the essay, Weil provides a picture of the somatic production of the workingman. It is a commentary on work from the perspective of how time shapes bodies and how central pace and pacing is for vitality. For Weil, freedom requires mobility without anxiety. As a result of these daily repetitions and potential disruptions, Weil says, one's face begins to change. Comportment of anxiety and a weariness sets in. "The faces drawn with anxiety over the day about to begin, dejected looks in the morning subway-trains; the profound weariness, spiritual rather than physical, reflected in the general bearing, the expression, the set of the mouth . . ."[37]

31. Weil, "Factory Work," 69.

32. Weil, "Factory Work," 61.

33. Weil, "Factory Work," 58.

34. She writes: "From the moment one is clocked-in to the time one is clocked out, one must be ready at any instant to take orders." Weil, "Factory Work," 57.

35. Weil, "Factory Work," 59.

36. Weil, "Factory Work," 58.

37. Weil, "Factory Work," 65.

The essay, while written in 1936, was published a decade later. The concluding section begins like this: "The Factory ought to be a place where, for all the inevitability of physical and spiritual travail, working people can taste joy and nourish themselves on it."[38] The editor, responding to the essay, critiques Weil for providing a "positive and programmatic" ending, which he deemed a let-down; this spiritual vision of factory work is insincere.[39] Perhaps so. But this spiritual dimension is important to Weil. The carousels of production destroy the human spirit. This destruction occurs through repetitions of practice that constitute everyday working conditions. Bodily repetition over time conditions persons to perform without thinking. When the body adjusts to the repetition of tasks, an interruption arrests the body. For Weil, this industrial violence constitutes a spiritual condition. When bodies move in particular ways over time and are subject to the jolt of orders and accidents, they result in spiritual weariness. The dehumanization takes place by extracting spirit from the work. The extraction of spirit is physically visible.[40]

For Weil, the antidote to affliction is the practice of attention. If spiritual fatigue seeps deeply into the muscles of workers, then there may be something to considering practices of rehumanization that target body and mind. The rehumanization comes from orienting ourselves to what is around us differently. She uses the illustration of a geometry problem. Instead of taking time to observe the elements and contours, the dimensions of the problem, we teach students to tackle the problem and solve it. And this orientation to what we do not know—mastering—becomes inscribed in us through continual practices of education. But there is another way of orienting ourselves. "If we concentrate our attention on trying to solve a problem of geometry, and if at the end of an hour we are no nearer to

---

38. Weil, "Factory Work," 66.

39. The editor, Dwight MacDonald, notes that Weil felt responsible to give a "positive" conclusion when, in fact, she was disillusioned "about Marxian socialism and the workingclass movement." MacDonald, *Politics*, 377.

40. Jonathan H. Ebel uses the language of "excarnation" to refer to a process by which the fighting nation extracts spirit from the bodies of U.S. soldiers in order to support and sanction the ideals of the nation. He writes: "Excarnation . . . . extracts from the soldierly body . . . that which the nation, the military included, understands to be its spirit and the re-presentation of that spirit to devoted public." This is a productive line of thinking in connection to Weil's description of the worker. So, too, industry relies and even brags about "the worker"; all the while, the spirit is extracted under present working conditions. The spirit is removed, but the worker remains, a vital figure of "American progress. Ebel, *G.I. Messiahs*, 216.

doing so than at the beginning, we have nevertheless been making prog-ress each minute of that hour in another more mysterious direction."[41]

What if, she asks, we sat down with the geometry problem and be-came curious about what you do not know. What if we practice *toward* the problem without anticipating an outcome? We return to it, again and again, to become familiar with not knowing. We lose sight of the end—but in a good way. This approach is un/productive according to the measures of factory time. But it is not aimless. It requires effort in a different direction. "So it comes about that, paradoxical as it may seem, a Latin prose or a geometry problem, even though they are done wrong, may be of great service once day, provided we devote the right kind of effort to them."[42] Practicing *like this* may prepare someone—at some indeterminate moment in the future—to address affliction.

She was writing about industrial France. But she offers insights about the current upheavals in our production lines: factories, schools, hospitals, to name a few. The halt in production brought about by the pandemic has released a different kind of energy—of unrest, agitation, and protest. But those are the designations of factory time. If we follow Weil's analysis, we read things differently. This disruption in the carousels of the production have released the human spirit. The breath of living beings returns; the dry bones revivify.

Weil proposes a wildly *unproductive* posture towards learning. Never assured an outcome. Learning and unlearning, if we return again and again to something, we may allow the encounter to change our pos-ture, like the wedge put in the window to let in air. Weil understands how trauma functions. If trauma is to be witnessed, we cannot assume a mastery posture. A person is not a logic problem to be solved. Instead, we need to approach affliction differently. And just as the combination of monotony and accident create conditions of suffering, the posture of attention to suffering must be differently paced. Hence, a slow theology.

Third Guide: Howard Thurman

If you have ever listened to Howard Thurman *speak,* you are not surprised that I appeal to him for the slow work of theology. His voice is deep, and his rhythm is slow. His cadence itself conjures a spiritual posture.

41. Weil, "Reflections," 45.
42. Weil, "Reflections," 52.

A mystical preacher, he is considered to be a moral anchor for leading activists in the Civil Rights era. He is also part of my local institutional history. He served as the Dean of Marsh Chapel at Boston University from 1953–1965. Throughout the school year, I witness preachers taking the same steps to the pulpit that Thurman did. Thurman wrestled with the invitation to come to Boston University, knowing what he would be navigating his ministry in a predominantly white institution. But he reveled in the spirit of inquiry celebrated at the University and viewed worship spaces as sites of spiritual exploration and testing labs for "common ground" amidst the polarization of American society.[43]

While Thurman is celebrated for many things, he is known for his teachings about the inner life. Each person must confront the questions at the heart of existence: Who am I *really*? What am I *for*? The questions are universal, but each person is responsible for asking them. This quest is challenging, because we live in the busyness—what he calls the "traffic" of life.[44] And in the midst of this traffic, we can get sidetracked and are responsive to everything out of us without ever really coming to terms with who we are.

Thurman presents this inner architecture in marinal terms.[45] We all have a sea within us. And in that sea is an island. And on that island is an altar. Hovering over that altar, guarding it, is an angel with a flaming sword. This meditation is one of Thurman's most referenced meditations. It is from a sermon he delivered in BU's Marsh Chapel in 1952.[46] A lot is missing in excerpted form. After presenting this powerful metaphor of the inward sea, Thurman asks his congregants the question: how does one chart that sea? To find what is most authentic in us and place it on the altar, one must confront oneself. I am not an expert on such matters—not a psychiatrist, he says. One must have a session with oneself, he says. One can find all sorts of external explanations for who we are, and these are not unimportant. But he says that the work of the altar is a confrontation with oneself: "I must deal with myself."[47]

Most of how we explain ourselves comes from outside of ourselves. When I look at my history, I explain myself by talking about all of the

---

43. Thurman, *The Search for Common Ground*, xiv.
44. Thurman, *Meditations*, 28.
45. Thurman, *Living Wisdom*, audio recording.
46. Howard Thurman, *Meditations*, 16.
47. Thurman, *Living Wisdom*, audio recording.

family and forces that have shaped me. You are as you are because your
mother was this way, your father was this way. But Thurman stops. This
is the perspective of oneself as an *object*. But once I stop looking around,
I settle in "for the long pull of me." Thurman stumbles to describe this to
those listening. He keeps reapproaching it from different angles. I imagine him looking out over the pulpit at Marsh Chapel at the perplexed
faces of those sitting in the pews. Hmm, he notes, how do I say this? He
says that our history and the definitions that are placed on us, that tell
you who we are, these are all responsive. We understand that we behave a
certain way, "in response to what happened to [us] the day before and the
day before and the day before."

But if you sit with ourselves, we can train ourselves (with great discipline and courage), to see the "I" that is *not* determined by all of those
things. We can come to see ourselves as *subjects*. And when you do, he
says, "A strange thing begins to happen." A light emerges. What begins
to happen is that "light emerges over the landscape" of your history. And
the view of yourself *as object* fades into the shadows as you navigate the
waters of the inner sea. If you enter the long pull, you begin to clear out
the messages, as if to lift the cloud cover over your landscape.

But what is curious about where Thurman goes next is that he describes this by appealing to various senses. Note that the vision of oneself
that emerges, as *subject,* is not a thought; it is a sensation. Thurman says
you begin to *feel* the warmth of the light. "You begin to feel in some wonderful ways . . . wholeness." He repeats the word wholeness, as if to let it
sink in. The warmth of the light against the skin generates a sensorium
of wholeness.

The figure of this image of the angel with the flaming sword returns
here. When I first worked with this meditation, I parsed the origins of the
angel Uriel guarding the gates of paradise. Uriel, the most mysterious of
the angels, performs different functions throughout the history of interpretation. From a chancellor, to a figure of illumination, to a soldier, Uriel
is positioned at the gates of paradise. Uriel stands guard at the threshold
between the heavenly and the earthly. Thurman scholar Walter Fluker reminds us that the angel is positioned there to guard against any imposters
trying to enter.[48] These imposters will be met with the fire of the angel's
sword. Here, the angel limns the edges of the raging waters of myself as
object and the altar of myself as subject. I suddenly realized that the light,

48. Fluker, "The Archive as Sanctuary," lecture.

the warm glow, is radiating from the flaming sword. It hovers over the altar. The imposters—the objects—cannot be placed there.

The sword provides light, guidance, and protection; but it is still a sword. This is not some peaceful beatific vision. If you listen to the sermon, Thurman's voice gets deeper and louder as if he, in his description, is moving closer to the altar. No one passes by the angel. The altar is fiercely guarded. With trepidation, the nerve center of our consent has been accessed and exercised. For Thurman, the sword staves off the untrue messages that define you from outside of yourself. This is a battle between oneself as subject and object.

You know what is authentic in you, not through cognition but through sensations. When you feel the warmth of wholeness, you know that you are encountering what is authentic in you.

This is the sensorium of groundedness and centeredness amidst the traffic of life. But it is noteworthy that this centering is not an abstract moral compass that is activated within us but, instead, an integration of the senses. When you sit with yourself and have "straight talk," you will feel something shift within you. This is the *long pull*.[49]

Conclusion

All three guides work on the level of reflex and muscle memory, describing how the external messages come to live in us, adhere internally, and create a weariness of body and spirit that cannot be disentangled. It will take effort, as Weil says, in a "more mysterious direction," to release the hold of these messages.[50]

Julian and Thurman are pandemic theologians. Julian is writing amidst the ongoing effects of the bubonic plague and Thurman in the midst of the pandemic of systemic racism. Weil can be understood as such, since she speaks to the conditions of workers when the veil of the carousel production lines is lifted. Considering the effects of industrialization, she positions us to view the effects of globalization. When she is writing about the conditions of the factory, it is not a stretch to consider the conditions operating for Amazon workers at warehouses under conditions subject to the immediate demands of American consumers.

49. Thurman, *Living Wisdom*, audio recording.
50. Weil, "Reflections," 45.

For all three, their writings are hard to categorize, and they sit on the dividing lines between the modern studies of spirituality and theology. Julian and Thurman develop their spiritual insights through the use of parables and metaphors. The dell and the sea become imaginative spaces for reworking previously held teachings. These work indirectly but cause us to slow down. They turn us to the familiar while providing a wedge in the window to let fresh air in. They enable us to release the grip of existing messages, creating space for the inward instruction. When we think about theology's role in addressing contemporary challenges of traumatized bodies, the split between various approaches to theology can separate the external and internal work. The misperception that systematic/philosophical theology works primarily, or even solely, in the cognitive register leaves the reflexes untouched. Each directs us to the limbic register. Weil refers to the anxiety and shame triggered by the orders of supervisors, Julian to the weight of blame that sets in when one is stuck in the dell. Thurman's vision of wholeness is a constellation of embodied sensations.

Right now, we are witnessing strong cultural messages to get the Carousel back on track. *We will get the country running again. We will rise above, stronger and better.* The mixture of nostalgia and promise that drove Disney's core philosophy are still there. These messages live in us at the level of muscle memory. When we hear them, they will remind our bodies of the way things were. And even if the truth is displayed in the daylight, even if there were problems with it, we will be awakened by these familiar tunes. Keep the carousel moving. Tomorrowland is just a dream away.

The stories that America tells about itself are profoundly flawed. And changing our minds is not enough. We need to address our reflexes and muscle memories. Just as many of us Disney-goers inhaled the air of Tomorrow Land, we need to exhale its toxic turns, releasing, through practice the muscle memories of its untruths.

I begin with my own experience of the Carousel, because it illustrates how messages take hold and shape us over time. The envelopment of my childhood senses by this ride illustrates how we come to love what we love. And as we grow up, these affections settle in. We may think that we replace these childish ways. But it is amazing how quickly the sensations can be recalled.

Doing theology in this time requires noticing these sensations. It requires staying close to the skin rather than moving too quickly to our frontal lobe. It requires naming the reflexes at work in our various settings—church spaces, school spaces, neighborhood spaces. And it involves putting in place a spiritual conditioning plan that can target the reflexes and intercept these messages.

This is spiritual work. It is slow work. There is no short cut. This is, in Thurman's words, the "long pull . . . of me." The long pull . . .of us.

Bibliography

Association of Theological Schools Commission on Accrediting. "Degree Program Standards." Posted January 21, 2015. https://www.ats.edu/uploads/accrediting/documents/degree-program-standards.pdf.

Crenshaw, Kimberlé Williams, "Fear of a Black Uprising: Confronting the White Pathologies that Shape Racist Policing," *New Republic*, August 13, 2020. https://newrepublic.com/article/158725/fear-black-uprising-confronting-racist-policing.

Coates, Ta-Nehisi. *Between the World and Me*. New York: Spiegel & Grau, 2015.

Cone, James. *The Cross and the Lynching Tree*. Maryknoll, New York: Orbis, 2013.

Ebel, Jonathan H. *G.I. Messiahs: Soldiering, War, and American Civil Religion*. New Haven, CT: Yale University Press, 2015.

Fluker, Walter Earl, "The Archive as Sanctuary," Report from the Archives Panel. Boston University's Gottlieb Center, Lecture at Boston University, Boston, MA, February 6, 2018.

Herman, Judith Lewis. *Trauma and Recovery*. Rev. ed. New York: BasicBooks, 1997.

Jantzen, Grace. *Julian of Norwich: Mystic and Theologian*, New ed. Mahwah, NJ, Paulist, 2000.

Jennings, Willie James. *The Christian Imagination*. New Haven, CT: Yale University Press, 2010.

Jennings, Willie James. *After Whiteness: An Education in Belonging*. Grand Rapids, MI: Eerdmans, 2020.

Julian of Norwich. *Showings*. Translated and edited by Edmund Colledge and James Walsh. Classics of Western Spirituality. New York: Paulist, 1978.

Kempe, Margery. *The Book of Margery Kempe*, edited by B.A. Windeatt. New York: Penguin, 2004.

Kendi, Ibram. "Is This the Beginning of the End of American Racism?," *The Atlantic*, September 2020. https://www.theatlantic.com/magazine/archive/2020/09/the-end-of-denial/614194/.

MacDonald, Dwight. *Politics*. Radical periodicals in the United States series. New York: Greenwood Reprint CO, December 1946.

Menakem, Resmaa. *My Grandmother's Hands: Racialized Trauma and the Pathway to Mending Our Hearts and Bodies*. Las Vegas, NV: Central Recovery, 2017.

Moltmann, Jürgen. *The Trinity and the Kingdom: The Doctrine of God*. Minneapolis, MN: Fortress, 1993.

Sherman, Robert B. *Sherman Brothers Songbook*. Walt Disney Records, 2009, compact disc.

Rathbone, Cristina. Talk, Distinguished Alumni panel, Boston University School of Theology, Boston, MA, September 16, 2020; http://www.bu.edu/sth/news-media/live-streaming/.

Richard M. Sherman and Robert B. Sherman, "The Best Time of Your Life," in *The Disney Song Encyclopedia*, edited by Thomas S. Hischak and Mark. A Robinson, 17–18. Lanham, MD: Scarecrow, 2009.

Thurman, Howard. *Meditations of the Heart*. Boston: Beacon, 1953.

Thurman, Howard. *The Living Wisdom of Howard Thurman: A Visionary for Our Time*. Louisville, CO: Sounds True, 2010. Audible audio ed.

Thurman, Howard. *The Search for Common Ground: An Inquiry into the Basis of Man's Experience of Community*, New York: Harper and Row, 1986.

Weil, Simone. "Factory Work." In *Simone Weil Reader*, edited by George A. Panichas. Wakefield, RI: Moyer Bell, 1977.

Weil, Simone. "Human Personality." In *Simone Weil Reader*, edited by George A. Panichas. Wakefield, RI: Moyer Bell, 1977.

Weil, Simone. "Reflections on the Right Use of School Studies With a View to the Love of God." In *Simone Weil Reader*, edited by George A. Panichas, Wakefield, RI: Moyer Bell, 1977.

6

Mourning, Raging, Loving, Learning
Embodied Theologies during the COVID-19 Pandemic

GABRIELLA LETTINI

IN THE EARLY PART of 2020, the COVID-19 virus shook many societies to their core. As we faced the brutal effects of an unknown virus that could not be stopped by any human-made border, and scientists tried to understand its patterns, it felt like we were looking into the unknown. Nevertheless, we were also looking at a mirror reflecting back the images of our societies and conjuring shadows of our past. Rather than bringing us merely new issues, the COVID-19 pandemic forced us to face more urgently and dramatically the realities and emergencies that were already embedded in our lives and societies, and that were already part of daily life for too many.

The way I faced this pandemic and reflected on it is shaped, among other realities of my social location,[1] by the fact that I am Italian and

---

1. While I acknowledge that identity is fluid, everchanging and more complex than any label, my life has been strongly shaped by being a white cisgender straight woman of Italian nationality, from a poor working-class background, first generation in higher education, from a religious minority (Waldensian), and living with invisible disabilities.

lived the second half of my life between New York City and Northern California: my home is in all the places where my loved ones are and where I have communities, roots, and deep connections. Therefore, my reflections are shaped by these different locations and what I saw happening there during this pandemic. They are also based on the mourning, raging, learning, and loving I speak about in the title of my lecture. I had visceral embodied reactions to what I experienced and witnessed. They are important sources in my theologizing. While I kept reading and researching about the effects of the pandemic, I was certainly no passive or objective observer of the devastation happening around me.

In the winter of 2020, before the virus became a main news item in the US, I witnessed the growing numbers of death in China, Iran, and Italy. I felt simultaneously shaken by massive grief and anxiety and also somehow prepared in already knowing some fundamental truths of what we will witness: this pandemic would not affect everyone equally. We will live it according to the patterns of injustice already present in our lives, and the most marginalized and oppressed will suffer the most. These truths needed to be voiced and addressed with renewed urgency to avoid ever-increasing massive suffering. I knew that we needed to face the urgent now, yet in a way that could also create a path to a better future.

My thoughts in this chapter will be organized in three sections. First, I will reflect on some pronouns, words, and phrases we have heard used very often as people dealt with the early months of the pandemic, questioning their theological and ethical significance. Later, I will address the topic of moral injury, a term we have started to hear about in relation to the spiritual effects of the pandemic, especially in connection to health care workers. Finally, I will ask how we may live in the present not only to survive but so that our future may be different, and especially for those already more dramatically impacted by the pandemic. What kind of theological and ethical paradigm shifts and political and cultural changes do we need?

Pandemic Pronouns, Words, and Slogans

While post-pandemic writings will offer us ways to reflect more comprehensively and with more critical distance about the experiences of these months, it is important to keep chronicling and reflecting upon the lived realities of these days as we live them, so that we will not forget too easily how our communities reacted to and dealt with this challenge, and so that the records of our mistakes and learning may inform the communities of the future.

Tragically, but unsurprisingly, from the early days of the pandemic we witnessed the use oppositional use of the pronouns "I-them" and the adjectives "disposable-essential."

The pronoun "them" stands for "the others." As I was following the early spreading of the COVID-19 virus in Italy, before it became a popular news item in the US, I witnessed how quickly people started talking about it as something that "they" caused, they brought, meaning people from Asia, independently from where they came from, being tourists or immigrants, or somehow even Italian citizens of Asian descent that had maybe never traveled to Asia. Fear of something unknown quickly generated scapegoating, gave free rein to the expression of racist tropes, and generated racist aggressions. Weeks later, I witnessed the same in the United States, with the difference that instead of having a president that swiftly and forcefully condemned these racist responses, the US had a president that spoke of the "Chinese virus," and intentionally continued to do so for months. These two different institutional answers shaped the popular responses in the two countries. Italy was not cured of its racism, yet people were quickly admonished by the highest institutional powers against the scapegoating of the other. In the US, such scapegoating worked to temporarily shift the focus from the crisis and from taking accountability for it, while its effect on Asian communities will be felt for a very long time.

The other pronoun we have heard often is "I," as an identity that can exist in isolation from you, us, and them: "I have the right not to wear a mask, not to keep at a safe distance, or be sheltered in place, to believe in ideas on COVID-19 that have no scientific bases." The isolated I of some white US Christian culture once again hindered community thinking and community care in vast parts of this country. The most naked egoism. The culture of white supremacy. Echoing the Jewish philosopher Emmanuel Levinas, who wrote that Western philosophy was "egology,"[2] I think we saw some pathetic displays of White Christianity as "egology," something that unfortunately is embedded in the fibers of this country.

2. "The ideal of Socratic truth thus rests on the essential self-sufficiency of the same, its identification in ipseity, its egoism. Philosophy is an egology." In Levinas, *Totality and Infinity*, 44.

As we realized that we were dealing not with a virus that would affect just some "over there," but with a pandemic that would touch us all, across any human-made border, some of us with disabilities, chronic health conditions, and living in mid-life witnessed with horror how quickly mainstream media and even our neighbors and friends started finding solace in the fact that the virus seemed to affect especially senior people or people with pre-existing conditions. Therefore, others did not have to worry or use caution, as the problem was serious only for people that were already, somehow, defective, and therefore disposable. As more people were hospitalized for treatment, we started hearing of triage and how hospital and medical personnel should prioritize the treatment of some at the expense of the aforementioned disposables, as it were an obvious and easy choice. I knew I was somehow a disposable one, having lived with Lupus for decades, and being middle aged. We even witnessed people taking hydroxychloroquine to manage their autoimmune diseases were taken off from their medication, as it was touted as a cure for CO-VID-19. I received a note from my health insurance thanking me for my "sacrifice" in doing without my medication for the foreseeable future, a sacrifice I did not know I was about to make and I had not chosen to make. Mine is only a tiny example of a larger pattern at work: the "disposables" of society became sacrificial victims with the pretension that they had chosen the path of self-sacrifice for the healing of the community. This pattern espoused and reinforced a very problematic theology of sacrifice, which has been criticized by the work on atonement, scapegoating and surrogacy by scholars like René Girard[3] and womanist theologian Delores G. Williams.[4]

As people became more transparent about who saw as disposables, we also witnessed some newly found realization of who was truly helping the larger community to function: the essential workers, starting from medical personnel, but also store clerks, delivery people, postal and transportation workers. There was some minor acknowledgment of farmworkers, many of which are undocumented citizens. Yet, while we saw children's drawings and big signs thanking the essential workers, we did not witness yet the same kind of impetus to make sure the essential workers receive justice, are paid a sustainable living wage, and can afford health care. In effect, praising the "essentials" is also an easy way out from

3. See: Girard, *The Scapegoat* and *Things Hidden Since the Foundation of the World*.

4. Williams, *Sisters in the Wilderness: The Challenge of Womanist God-Talk*.

dealing with the fact that so many really see them as disposable, the one that have to put their lives in jeopardy because they cannot afford to do otherwise. Essential workers are disproportionately people of color, and part of the working poor. They are called heroes now, but soon they will be forgotten again by most.

Some phrases that we also heard often are "The virus is the cure," "We are all in this together," "All will be different now," and "It will all end well." The last slogan was widely used in Italy, accompanied by rainbow drawings that people posted on their windows. My question as a theological ethicist is: which voices are we centering in these statements? Who are the people and communities at the center of our concerns? Is it something we are even consciously asking?

"The virus is the cure" stemmed from an effort to find spiritual meaning and comfort and honor earth-based learning, and out of genuine concern for ecological disruption. Yet often, it was a statement made by people who were mainly looking from afar at the virus's ravages. Certainly, there is a lot to learn from the experience of this pandemic, as from any event in life, and yet to see it as something positive that will singlehandedly solve all issues of humanity was in my view naïve and misplaced, and hurtful to many. The virus did affect disproportionately those who were already the victims of systems of economic and racial injustice. In the US Black children were disproportionately affected by the virus compared to white children: I don't think this suffering is any cure. It is the fruit of centuries of systemic injustice. This is why to say "we are all in this together," while heartwarming and potentially true, may also be hypocritical and even dangerous as it hides the extremely different ways in which people are affected by COVID-19. To speak about community and interrelation without addressing injustice and differences is disingenuous at best and possibly lethal.

"All will be different now," and "All will end well" do not ring true. Nothing will be better and end well unless we address the theological, ethical, political, and cultural roots of the kind of thinking and acting that what made this pandemic such a crisis as we were too unprepared for it, even if scientists had warned us that it would happen, and a crisis that once again we did not face equally with the same resources and outcomes. People coming from marginalized and oppressed communities had experienced this before.

Moral Injury

In the last months, we witnessed and maybe experienced firsthand heartbreaking situations: 220,000 deaths in the US that could have been avoided, people dying without receiving adequate treatment, in solitude, without being able to say goodbye to their families. We saw families that could not come to grieve together. Medical personnel had to work in grueling shifts without adequate protection and resources to support their patients. People considered essential workers had to put their lives in jeopardy to pay their bills, and many have lost their sources of income and fear for the future of their families, often having to admit that they were a paycheck away from food security and houselessness. This situation should not be surprising and should not be blamed on the virus itself: it is results of centuries of systemic racism and injustice.

As we deal with so much unprocessed grief, constant every-day financial challenges, and a bleak future, the mental health of so many of us, so many around the world, has been affected, bringing us on the verge of another crisis,[5] as more people fall into addictions and die of suicide. As we addressed this dramatic outcome of the pandemic, it is also important to ask about the spiritual impact of what we are experiencing. How is it affecting not only people's mental health but also their spiritual life?

Recently even mainstream media have reported about the moral injury of health care workers facing this pandemic. Some scientific studies about it have already been published, like the recent one led by Rachel Schwartz. It argues that the COVID-19 pandemic presents unique challenges that surpass those of previous pandemics, that also had a significant mental health toll on medical workers.[6]

Moral injury is a concept more often discussed in relation to military personnel. There are different ways to understand it, yet in general it refers to the spiritual outcome of having to deal with situations of betrayal by people in position on authority, as for Jonathan Shay's approach, or having perpetuated, failed to prevent or being a witness to acts of violence and great harm, like in the work of Brett Litz. My definition encompasses both understandings, with a focus on the systemic causes of

5. This crisis had been foreseen and is now being assessed: Rajkumar, "COVID-19 and mental health: A review of the existing literature"; Petterson, Steve et al. "Projected Deaths of Despair During the Coronavirus Recession."

6. Schwartz, Sinskey, Anand, and Margolis, "Addressing Postpandemic Clinician Mental Health: A Narrative Review and Conceptual Framework."

moral injury and the need to address justice issues as part of the process of healing or soul repair.

The effects of moral injury are deep spiritual despair, guilt, unworthiness, a sense that one can no longer see oneself and the world as good, lack of trust, a deep sense of void and meaninglessness. In some cases, this spiritual despair leads to suicide, as has it has been studied in relation to veterans. Moral injury has often been described as the hidden wound of war. Today, it is one of the hidden, less obvious wounds caused by COVID-19 on individuals and on whole societies at large.

Talking about moral injury in relation to medical personnel is not new, as in the last decades several studies have been dedicated to this experience. Doctors and health care workers always faced every day difficult decisions, witnessed tragic situations, functioned in societies where people often did not have the access to the health care they needed and deserved, like in the United States, or where a good universal health care system has been gradually dismantled by neoliberal forces, like in Italy. Nevertheless, in this pandemic, medical workers are experiencing moral injury in a very acute way, and finally, even mainstream media noticed the effect this pandemic is having on their mental health and spiritual wellness. Scholars and chaplains have been trying to understand what learning and protocols that proved useful in addressing the moral injury of military personnel can also be effective with medical ones.

Erik De Soir, a Belgian psychologist, crisis expert and formerly a member of the Belgian armed forces, has recently shared a protocol that he has started implementing in some European hospitals. It is very comprehensive as it looks at a hospital as an organic system, aiming to create a supportive environment where all the mental and physical health of the personnel are genuinely valued. The first step in this protocol, for De Soir, is the ability to identify the issue affecting the medical staff, as still many are unfamiliar with moral injury. The approach includes leadership policies that include timely referral to peer support and professional counselling for personnel; the creation of peer support groups; self-care education; appropriate rotation of staff in health care; and regular short debriefing moments. After each wave of the virus there should be decompression retreats, similar to the post-mission decompression and adaptations retreats for soldiers. These are programs that monitor and support the well-being of health care workers, facilitating their reintegration in everyday life and fostering their resilience.

This protocol comes from a European country where significant resources have been traditionally devoted to the public health care and senior care systems. It shows what is possible when the well-being of health
care workers is taken into serious consideration and is understood as part
of collective well-being. It is not only fair but also vital to the optimal
functioning of the system and to the overall health of the community. In
the Unites States, we have seen parallel important work being done by
some scholars and chaplains that feel called to serve both patients and
health care professionals.[7]

As De Soir points out, the first step to take is the identification of
the issue. We need to talk about moral injury in relation to the pandemic
and understand it. It is important to create adequate structures of work,
support, and accompaniment to engage not only the stress and mental
health of health care workers but also their spiritual well-beings, as we
may be about to experience a new wave of the virus. This kind of learning
will not only ensure the resilience of our medical personnel now but will
be beneficial for the future of health care in general. We are just learning
that we need to take care of the people who are taking care of others, in
every helping profession. When they struggle, they are not experiencing
an individual failure but having a normal reaction to flawed structural
situations where the burden they are asked to carry is unbearable.

As we speak about the moral injury of health care workers, we also
need to bring our attention to the many others who may be experiencing
it, like all the essentials workers that are treated as disposable and sacrificial beings, the people who lost their livelihoods and are not receiving
appropriate structural support, and the people who are facing the pandemic unhoused or within the prison system. All the people who have
been betrayed and forgotten by society. There will be no special healing
programs for most of them, and the kind of betrayal and harm experienced during the pandemic is not something that could be addressed and
healed only with such programs.

---

7. The most recent resources of the Chaplaincy Innovation Lab based in Boston,
or Volunteers of America are very good examples of the collective learning and wisdom that has been produced, collected, and shared during the COVID-19 pandemic.

Systemic Injustice, Systemic Healing, and Liberation

When speaking about moral injury, it is crucial not to address it as an issue of particular individuals, but as a collective one. The structural realities that cause moral injury need to be named and addressed, so that responsibilities for the harm can be placed in the most appropriate places, people and institutions can be called into accountability, and the processes of reparation and healing can begin. This is true in the case of war, as the whole armed forces and the whole society who go to war should be addressing moral injury, and this is true during this pandemic. No amount of mindfulness training or resilience protocols will be enough to address the depth of harm caused by the centuries of racial and economic injustice that build our current capitalist system. Generations of liberation, feminist, womanist, mujerista, and queer theologians have asked us to address the suffering caused by systemic oppression as a central theological question.

The outcomes of this pandemic are determined largely by the political, theological, ethical decisions that were made by those in power. They betrayed even our basic expectations of safety and community care. Scientists have been warning heads of states and decisionmakers that a pandemic, most likely affecting the respiratory systems, was likely on the horizon. In January 2017, Anthony Fauci, director of the National Institute of Allergy and Infectious Diseases (NIAID), during a forum on Pandemic preparedness at Georgetown University, affirmed that the Trump administration was likely going to experience an infectious disease outbreak.[8] Nevertheless, adequate funding was not directed to research in this area. Hospitals, and senior centers, even in large cities, were not properly equipped for the basic protection of their staff and patients. We were repeatedly lied to about the severity of the situation and the level of dismal preparation for it. In the early day of the pandemic, even medical professionals were often disciplined for wearing a mask during their shifts to cover for the fact that it was a basic necessity that was unfortunately missing.

In Italy, the virus spread mostly in the North, with the highest concentration in the area around Milan, Lombardy, which is Italy's business center, is very international and is one of the wealthiest areas in the country. I was shocked, numb, then furious. I realized that, again, all of this

8. Gallagher, "Fauci: 'No doubt' Trump will face surprise infectious disease outbreak."

suffering could have been preventable by putting people before profits. First, while having the benefit of the warning coming from China, Italy did not take the situation seriously enough to stop business right away in order to prevent the spreading of the virus. Even after a severe lockdown was put in place, many factories were still operative, something that widely underreported by the media. Businesses in Milan and other big cities started media campaigns about the importance of being resilient, not giving in to fear, and going back to work, shop and consume. "Milano non si ferma" ("Milan does not stop") was the name of a campaign. Eventually, it had to stop, as thousands of more people suffered because of this centering of profit instead of public health.

Something that caused profound distress was also the coming to terms with how much weaker, inadequate, and ineffective the Italian public health care system had become. Decades of neoliberal governments had chipped away at our universal health care system, as Berlusconi and others claimed that the US model was more efficient and defunded the public system in favor of the private one. This is why even large public hospitals did not have enough ventilators for people in respiratory crisis and testing was so hard to implement.

Another effect of the current pandemic is a deep economic crisis that puts the survival of millions at risk. In the US, one in four people faced food insecurity, while the mostly white billionaires gained over $400 billions by May 2020.[9] Yet even this was not mainly caused by the virus itself. Theologian Jeorg Rieger has been an important voice in raising issues of economic justice in the US and the world as central theological issues well before this pandemic. Rieger pointed out what he calls "the ugly truth of the pandemic" as he quotes something that Jewish philosopher Walter Benjamin articulated in the 1940s as he faced Nazism: "The tradition of the oppressed teaches us that the 'state of emergency' in which we live is the not exception but the rule."[10] Rieger stresses that most people in the US, the 99%, had never really recovered from the 2008–2009 economic downturn. I think this is true for Italy as well. And the systemic problems that we are now facing are directly connected to the ones that generations before us experienced, well before the XX1st century: a capitalist system that is based on exploitation, is embedded in neo-colonialist and racist practices, reckless exploitation of natural

9. Frank, "American billionaires, mostly white, gained more than $400 billion during the crisis."

10. Rieger, "The Ugly Truth of a Pandemic and the Logic of Downturn."

resources and disruption of the Earth natural capacity to function, heal, and adapt to change.

As I write, California is once again being ravaged by fires. As I witness this apocalyptic scenario, I think again of moral injury. We can learn to be more resilient and adaptive, yet no amount of training, debriefing, spiritual care, and practices will heal society and souls from the moral injury caused by the systemic injustice rendered more visible and acute by the pandemic: addressing this moment spiritually must include faith in actions, both as measures of harm control, such as voting in the upcoming election, but more importantly as political and restorative practices that will transform the way we live, who and what we value, and whose needs we put at the center of our theology, ethics, budgets, and policy decisions.

Nothing will be different after the pandemic if we do not address the structural issues that plague us. It can possibly get worse, as the pandemic is far from over. In order to address the harm done, we need to name it in its greater complexity, and challenge systems, institutions, and people into accountability. There should be no moral bail out.

To address the structural realities that caused the unnecessary tragedies related to the COVID-19 pandemic, it is necessary and urgent for communities and faith traditions to radically question the ethical viability of capitalism and their relationship to it. This pandemic has exposed once again that capitalism is a system of relationships based on exploitation, where few can become wealthy at the exploited masses' expense. It is an economic system that justifies unequal power relationships and the trampling of fundamental human rights for the very few's profit, and the illusion of relative safety and wellbeing for a larger number of privileged people, mainly white. As it became painfully clear, in the last decades, the number of people that genuinely benefitted from capitalism has been shrinking dramatically, as the former middle class manages to survive while being immersed in debt and a few medical crises away from bankruptcy and possible houselessness.

Capitalism has always been perpetrated by the constructions of false myths and the perpetuation of lies. In the US, we can still not think that access to health care, sustainably living wages, housing, education, and work safety are fundamental human rights. Anyone fighting for it is still labeled negatively as a danger to society and a supporter of totalitarian forms of communism. Wealth is supposed to be the fruit of hard work and good morals, while it is most often inherited and built on exploitation. Nevertheless, the myth of the solitary self-made individuals that lifted

themselves by their individual boot-straps persists. Taking seriously the
suffering of people under COVID-19 means to unequivocally denounce
these lies, renouncing theologies that sustain them and embracing ones
that create alternative ways of living.

Conclusion: Healing Is/in Resistance

Even in a world so marred by suffering and long-standing systems of
economic and racial oppression and ableism, that made this pandemic so
dire, we can still witness and experience love as deep care, as compassion,
as creative grassroots attempts to live according to a different logic from
capitalism. The spiritual and political will to transform societies still exist.
They are nurtured by relationships of accountability, interdependence and
care, by a sense of the sacredness of community, coming from different
spiritual and philosophical perspectives, instead than an idolatry of one's
individual rights. Within these communities of struggle and resistance,
there is also a centering of the voices and needs of the most affected by
injustice in this society, and a willingness to listen directly to their voices,
their strategies, and follow their leadership. This can be seen in the movements supporting Black Lives Matter or the Poor People's Campaign.

These movements of resistance to the oppressive structures of
capitalism are not striving for unattainable purity outside the system but
embody the belief that other ways of living are possible and necessary
and may transform reality. They witness that communal resistance and
collective struggle for justice are essential to the healing process from
the moral injuries of oppression. In this healing resistance, I see God's
transformative power at work.

Bibliography

De Soir, Erik. "Lived Experiences of Nurses in Emergency and Intensive Care Medicine:
    Post COVID- Decompression to Cope with Burden Trauma and Moral Injury?"
    Military Psychology Response to Post Pandemic Reconstruction, Samir Rawat, Ole
    Boe, and Andrzej Piotrowski eds. Vol. I, New Delhi: Rawat, forthcoming October
    2020.
———. "Psychological Adjustment After Military Operations: The Utility of
    Postdeployment Decompression for Supporting Health Readjustment." *Handbook
    of Military Psychology: Clinical and Organizational Practice.* Stephen V. Bowles
    and Paul T. Bartone eds. New York: Springer, 2017, 89–103.

————. "The Belgian End of Mission Transition Period: Lessons Learned from Third Location Decompression after Operational Deployment. *Proceedings of NATO-RTO-MP- HFM-205, 11*:1–18, 2010.

Dzau, Victor J., Darrell Kirch, and Thomas Nasca. "Preventing a parallel pandemic—a national strategy to protect clinicians' well-being." *New England Journal of Medicine* (2020).

Frank, Robert. "American billionaires, mostly white, gained more than $400 billion during the crisis." CNBC May 21, 2020.

Girard, René. *The Scapegoat*. Baltimore: John Hopkins University Press, 1986.

————.*Things Hidden Since the Foundation of the World*. Stanford, CA: Stanford University Press, 1987.

Haseltine, William A. "The Moral Trauma of COVID-19: How failures of our national leaders have torn the moral fabric of our lives." *Psychology Today*, posted August 21, 2020.

Jun, Jin, Sharon Tucker, and Bernadette Mazurek Melnyk. "Clinician Mental Health and Well-Being During Global Healthcare Crises: Evidence Learned From Prior Epidemics for COVID-19 Pandemic." *Worldviews on Evidence-Based Nursing* (2020).

Lettini, Gabriella. "Moral Injury and Its Causes, Symptoms and Responses." *In Moral Injury: A Guidebook for Understanding and Engagement*. Brad E. Kelle ed. New York: Lexington, 2020.

Levinas, Emmanuel. *Totality and Infinity: An Essay on Exteriority*, translated by Alphonso Lingis. Pittsburgh: Duquesne University Press, 1969.

Litz, Brett T., Nathan Stein, Eileen Delaney, Leslie Lebowitz, William P. Nash, Caroline Silva, and Shira Maguen. "Moral injury and moral repair in war veterans: A preliminary model and intervention strategy." *Clinical Psychology Review* 29, no. 8 (2009): 695–706.

Mantri, S., Lawson, J.M., Wang, Z. *et al*. Identifying Moral Injury in Healthcare Professionals: The Moral Injury Symptom Scale-HP. *J Relig Health* 59, 2323–2340 (2020). https://doi.org/10.1007/s10943-20-01065-w

Nelson, Anitra. "COVID-19: Capitalist and Postcapitalist Perspectives." *Human Geography* Volume: 13 issue: 3, page(s): 305–9, November 1, 2020, https://doi.org/10.1177/1942778620937122

Paravati, Claudio, ed. COVID19: Costruire il Futuro. Economia, Ambiente e Giustizia Sociale. Roma: Com Nuovi Tempi, 2020.

Petterson, Steve et al. "Projected Deaths of Despair During the Coronavirus Recession," Well Being Trust. May 8, 2020. WellBeingTrust.org.

Rajkumar, Ravi Philip. "COVID-19 and mental health: A review of the existing literature." *Asian journal of psychiatry* vol. 52 (2020): 102066. doi:10.1016/j.ajp.2020.102066.

Rieger, Jeorg. "The Ugly Truth of a Pandemic and the Logic of Downturn" *Faith and Reason*, April 9, 2020.

Ripp, Jonathan, Lauren Peccoralo, and Dennis Charney. "Attending to the emotional well-being of the health care workforce in a New York City health system during the COVID-19 pandemic." *Academic Medicine* (2020).

Shay, Jonathan. *Achilles in Vietnam: Combat Trauma and the Undoing of Character*. New York: Scribner, 1984.

————. "Casualties." Daedalus 140, no. 3 (Summer 2011): 179–88.

————. *Odysseus in America. Combat Trauma and the Trials of Homecoming.* New York, Scribner, 2002.

Schwartz, Rachel, Jina L. Sinskey, Uma Anand, and Rebecca D. Margolis. "Addressing Postpandemic Clinician Mental Health: A Narrative Review and Conceptual Framework." *Annals of Internal Medicine* M20–4199. 21 August 2020, doi:10.7326/M20–4199.

Simon, Joshua. "Society for Sick Societies: The Tiny Hands of the Market." *Social Text*, June 16, 2020.

Talbot, Simon E. *and* Wendy Dean. "Physicians aren't 'burning out.' They're suffering from moral injury." STAT. July 26, 2018.

Taylor, Warren D, and Jennifer Urbano Blackford. "Mental Health Treatment for Front-Line Clinicians During and After the Coronavirus Disease 2019 (COVID-19) Pandemic: A Plea to the Medical Community." *Annals of internal medicine* vol. 173,7 (2020): 574–75. doi:10.7326/M20–2440.

Watkins, Ali, Michael Rothfeld, W. K. Rashbaum, and B. M. Rosenthal. "Top ER doctor who treated virus patients dies by suicide." *New York Times* 27 (2020).

Williams, Delores S. *Sisters in the Wilderness. The Challenge of Womanist God-Talk.* Maryknoll: NY: Orbis, 1992.

7

Readings for Resilience

Biblical Reflections on the COVID-19
Pandemic and Beyond

RACHEL S. MIKVA

As THE WORLD WAS consumed by the COVID-19 pandemic, its other problems did not disappear. So humanity has been pressed into service in a global emergency room and forced to do ethical triage. Racism still rages through our body politic; health disparities and police violence have been laid bare, but it infects every aspect of our society. Domestic violence is on the rise and the vulnerable are more stuck than ever to deal with their abusers alone. The climate crisis grows more acute. Ethnic and religious tensions keep exploding into violence. Refugees—driven from their homes by war, famine, climate change, and other unbearable conditions—are too often turned away, dying en route, imprisoned, separated from their children. Autocrats and ultranationalists multiply. Wealth disparities widen. America's social fabric continues to shred as truth takes a back seat to politics; it is not even certain that our experiment in democracy will hold.

In the face of such sustained and multifarious trauma, we need to cultivate resilience. Philip Gulley, a Quaker minister, tells a story about a neighbor with a lot of land who wanted to create a forest. Each year, he planted a bunch of trees but he never watered them. Instead, he would go out and give them a modest whack every now and then with his morning newspaper. He said he did it to get their attention. And why did he refuse to water them? He wanted them to grow deep roots. Gulley thought about this when he tucked his kids into bed at night and prayed that no harm would ever come to them. Everyone encounters hardship, he realized, and eventually he changed his prayer. He prayed for his children's roots to grow deep so when the rains fall and the winds blow, they would not be swept asunder. They would bend, and change, and continue to grow. He prayed for resilience.[1] Resilience is not simply the ability to endure suffering, or to bounce back afterwards. It is about the strength and speed with which we *adapt* to adversity. It is about how we might or even must change.

My roots dig deep into the soil of Scripture, so it is there I turn to reap insights for facing the social, political, physical, psychic, and spiritual challenges before us. Entangled in a web of interwoven tragedies, the COVID-19 crisis serves as the primary thread of contemporary theological and exegetical reflection. At the same time, it is impossible to separate the pandemic completely from other concerns that swirl around us, so the interpretations have broader implications as well. Viewed through this lens, the books of Lamentations, Ruth, and Job illuminate vital elements of human response to adversity and our capacity to adapt. These readings are not a recipe for personal or social resilience—but sampling the menu of questions they raise can provide needed sustenance in dark times.

Lamentations—Resilience Requires Space for Mourning

I begin with reflections on the Book of Lamentations, a collection of poems composed after the destruction of Jerusalem at the hands of the Babylonian Empire in 586 BCE. At first it would seem to be of little theological value; many people reject the idea of suffering as divine retribution that is evident throughout the book, and the concept has proven dangerous in our day. Intended as an exercise in self-critical faith to help make sense of catastrophe and reclaim a sense of agency, the idea of retributive justice too often gets wielded as a weapon against others, with self-righteous bigots who blame people they do not like for our collective plight. These contemporary interpretations also ignore substantial

---

1. Gulley, "Growing Roots," 17–19.

teachings about restorative and distributive justice that are just as integral to biblical thought.[2] In fact, the Book of Lamentations is not particularly interested in why calamity has struck. It is asking "how"—*How could this be happening?* This focus is captured by the Hebrew title of the book, chosen simply by its first word: *Eicha.* "How" resists explaining away suffering; its primary purpose is to give expression to the fact that it happened.

"Lament is language traumatized," Rachel Adler explains.[3] The verses in Lamentations give voice to the death of thousands, the loss of sovereignty, the burning of the Temple, the exile of the people, the theological crisis, and the miseries of trying to survive. Shifting between singular and plural, they reveal how communal mourning contains a myriad of individual stories of suffering. They also unpack the polymorphous nature of loss because there is so much at risk—real, imagined, and merely hoped-for—qualities of life that provide meaning, wholeness, security, joy, and fulfillment. Rooted in antiquity, these expressions are nonetheless profoundly resonant, bound to the current moment through tragedy.

Let us begin at the beginning: "How lonely sits the city that was once great with people!" (Lam 1:1). I did not know what a lonely city looked like until I saw the empty streets of Chicago, heard the eerie silence of my normally bustling neighborhood, felt the isolation of a million neighbors afraid to come outside as the pandemic took hold. I could sense the web of relationships being torn apart by the virus, unmooring emotional anchors that keep us from floating away. And suddenly I wondered—as if for the first time—why we accept that some people feel lonely all the time. The Book of Lamentations recognizes that experiences of loneliness, poverty, and hunger are not acceptable social ills but actually violations of our humanity. The poets feel they are dwelling in darkness like people already dead (3:6); they are appalled seeing infants die on every street corner (2:19) and even individuals of privilege hugging garbage piles (4:5). "All her inhabitants sigh as they search for bread; they have bartered their treasures for food to keep themselves alive. See YHWH, and behold how abject I have become" (1:11). It is not simply an issue of desperation, but of how such circumstances chip away at personhood.

The book also grapples with the sense of betrayal, of being besieged and trapped in narrow places (1:2–3), of leaders who utterly fail; each struggle has its present parallels. "Panic and pitfall are our lot, death and

2. See Mikva, "Change the Conversation About Justice."
3. Adler, "For These I Weep: A Theology of Lament," 18.

destruction" (3:47) evokes images of overwhelmed hospitals, with bodies piling up in rented storage containers. "We get bread at the peril of our lives" (5:9) now speaks to the dilemma of essential workers and others who have to expose themselves to contagion in order to keep their jobs. We betray them by not providing adequate protective equipment. In our context, of course, it is compounded by race and class inequities that force people of color, immigrants, and poor people to bear disproportionate risk of both illness and economic dislocation. "Your seers prophesied to you delusion and folly" (2:14) mirrors the Trump administration's facile denial of the severity of the crisis, wasting crucial weeks of preparation and continuing to undermine our resolve with misinformation.

Lamentations speaks of shame as adversaries rejoice and allies are bewildered (e.g., 1:21, 2:15, 3:14)—prompted now by our own nation's missteps—and the deeper shame of worrying about how we are complicit in them. "See YHWH the distress I am in! My gut is wrenched, my heart capsized within me because I rebelled. Outside the sword deals death, inside the plague" (1:20). We are all feeling vulnerable but—whether it be police violence (the sword) or health disparities (the plague)—people of color and people who are poor are more so. We are all implicated in these injustices. They eat at our heart as rebellion against God. Our gut is wrenched.

The virus has utterly transformed how I read one verse: "For these things do I weep, my eyes flow with tears: far from me is any comforter who might revive my spirit" (1:16). Part of the pain, the poet realizes, is that there is no one to comfort the afflicted city. Now I cannot help but think of coronavirus patients in hospitals and nursing homes, unable to have family and friends present as they struggle to breathe or to hold on to reality amidst the disorienting cocktail of fever and medication. As they lay dying, those who could best comfort them are absent.

The deeper terror of Lamentations is expressed by describing the reverberations of a world turned upside down. Instead of infants sucking at their mothers' breasts, the women eat the fruit of their womb (2:20). The physical, emotional, and spiritual debasement that the people suffer make them unrecognizable to themselves and others as they turn unbearably cruel (4:1–10). It calls us to look hard at our own upside-down country, only some of which results from COVID-19. Social illness has wracked our national body for quite some time, even as the symptoms have varied. Why does someone spit on a minimum-wage worker who asks them to wear a mask before entering the store? How did it come to be that face coverings have become so politicized that some people cannot perform even this modest act to protect others? Why would a health care system be driven by profit rather than human flourishing? How could so many people turn their backs on science just because it reveals inconvenient truths about viral transmission or human evolution or climate change? What makes a white woman want to call the police because a black man has the audacity to ask her to leash her dog, as park rules require? What prompts dozens of citizens to drive their cars into peaceful protests against systemic racism? How can it be that so many people of color are murdered at the hands of a police force called to serve and protect? We are currently being disciplined to view other human beings as sources of contagion, so the dangers of misanthropy are growing. But did our society's own intellectual and spiritual debasement make us unrecognizable to each other long ago?

Lament is a crucial religious language, in part because of its capacity to force such questions. As Theodor Adorno writes, "The need to lend a voice to suffering is a condition of all truth."[4] It is also an essential posture before God. What difference does it make, asks Walter Breuggemann, that religion permits or even requires lament as a form of prayer? Without it, people of faith risk becoming "yes-men" who simply accept whatever they believe God dishes out. Lament is an observation that something is not right—as bursting with transformative potential as Black Lives Matter protesters who assert with their bodies that the system is broken. Lament challenges the divine power dynamic to insist that God see, hear, remember, and participate in change. Lament makes a moral claim. Like Abraham, it demands that the God of justice advance the cause of justice.[5]

Lament is also a spiritual necessity. The importance of expressing loss, of making room for mourning, cannot be overstated. Its value must be acknowledged amidst the plight of our current pandemics. Activist Benji Hart comments, "Pretending I am not sad, hiding my sadness, will not make me stronger. Suppressing my true self, denying the fear and rage that surround loss, is what in the long run will weaken me. When we talk of self-care, self-preservation, we need to talk not just about overcoming our feelings of grief, but allowing them, making room for them." They

---

4. Adorno, *Negative Dialectics*, 17–18.

5. Brueggemann, "The Costly Loss of Lament," 59–60.

want to create space for this work within justice movements, not to "bottle up our sadness in the name of organizing, leadership or activism."[6]

I wonder whether we have sufficient space for this work in our religious institutions. Some grow queasy, seeing lament as failure of trust in God; too many fail to embrace doubt and rage as handmaidens of faith. The challenge is compounded by American positivism with its prejudice toward success and the expectation that we should just muscle through. Suffering can cause what Adler calls "spiritual vertigo." Like physical vertigo, when our brain cannot process what our eyes see and we are left spinning, forthright faith can have trouble processing what we experience. We need lament to regain our balance.

Recognizing the essential nature of lament in our broken world, rabbinic tradition ritualized it—most particularly on Tisha b'Av, a day of fasting that commemorates the Temple's destruction and many other catastrophes in Jewish history. Worshippers sit on low stools or on the floor and chant the sorrowful verses of Lamentations. They add the cries of later generations, layers of human suffering, hope, and resilience. Recognizing that the work of healing does not happen overnight, the sages framed a ten-week cycle: three weeks descending into the darkness, culminating in Tisha b'Av, followed by seven weeks of consolation leading to the new year (Rosh haShanah) fresh with new possibilities.[7] They also assembled a midrash on Lamentations, *Eichah Rabbah*, a fourth- or fifth-century text that was not satisfied with the biblical book's conviction that God would hear and understand the traumatic experience of the people. It presents God *responding*. That may appear as an impiety, to put words in God's mouth, but it sustains faith through ongoing dialogue with the divine. David Wolpe calls midrash "the free verse of theology," inviting creative exploration of our deepest fears, our most important questions, and our highest hopes.[8]

Hope is intrinsic in the theological work of lament. Consider the question that appears in so many of the lament psalms (e.g., Pss 6, 13, 74, 80, 82, 90, 94), one that haunts us now as well: *How long* will this continue? Implicit in the question is an expectation of an end to the suffering. The poet of Lamentations 3 writes, "This do I call to mind and therefore have hope: The kindness of YHWH has not ended, God's mercies are not

6. Hart, "Feeling Is Not Weakness."

7. See Stern, *From Rebuke to Consolation*; Anderson, *A Time to Mourn, a Time to Dance.*

8. Wolpe, *Healer of Shattered Hearts*, 55.

spent. They are renewed each morning—Your faithfulness is abundant"
(3:22–23). Lament is about rupture and repair. It is a tool of resilience.

Ruth—Lovingkindness and Social Justice
Make Transformation Possible

The Book of Ruth, an exercise in imaginative storytelling that comes to
teach deeper truths than would be possible if it was history, offers another
opportunity to contemplate human trauma and resilience. It begins with
Naomi, her husband Elimelech, and their two sons departing the Land
of Israel on account of famine. It cannot be an easy thing to be forced to
leave their home, but they adapt by moving to Moab and settling there. All
seems well enough until Elimelech dies. Even at that point, the family car-
ries on. Naomi's sons marry and life seems to be bouncing back—except
that the young men are named Sickness and Consumption (Mahlon and
Chilion), so you can guess that this "new normal" might be short-lived.
Sure enough, Naomi's sons die too. All this happens in the first five verses.

We each have a psychological immune system. Essential for survival, it looks for meaning in our experience, prepares us to endure, and
focuses our attention inward. But trauma can send this immune system
into overdrive and we fall prey to what psychologist Martin Seligman
calls the three P's: personalization, permanence, and pervasiveness.[9]
Understandably, Naomi exhibits these behaviors in response to the com-
pound trauma of economic scarcity, losing her home, her husband, and
her children.

She *personalizes* her plight. The overwhelming loss is somehow her
fault, she concludes, presuming that God's hand is striking out against
her and that her suffering is unparalleled—even though her daughters-
in-law, Ruth and Orpah, are widowed and childless as well (1:13). She
assumes the condition is *permanent*: she will feel this way forever. When
Naomi decides to go back to Bethlehem and her daughters-in-law offer
to return with her, she puts them off, arguing that there is no hope for her
future (1:11–13). She also experiences the suffering as *pervasive*: everything in her life is terrible. Naomi is almost oblivious to Ruth's stunning
declaration of fidelity, "Wherever you go, I will go; wherever you lodge,
I will lodge. Your people shall be my people, and your God my God.
Where you die, I will die, and there I will be buried" (1:16–17). When

9. Seligman, *Learned Optimism*, 43–48.

the women of Bethlehem greet Naomi upon her return, she says, "Do not call me Naomi [pleasantness]. Call me Mara [bitterness], for Shaddai has made my lot very bitter. I went away full and YHWH has brought me back empty" (1:20–21). She is romanticizing how good it was, since her family left amidst a famine, but she did have her husband and sons. Still, it is heartbreaking to hear her describe her current state as empty. Empty!? Naomi has no capacity at that point to see the restorative power of Ruth by her side.

COVID-19 has triggered variations on these traps of trauma. *Personalization:* For many people, the sustained discomfort, inconvenience, and worse of sheltering in place can breed a narcissism akin to Naomi's. Loss of physical presence has caused us to lose sight of one another in profound ways, so we personalize the crisis by making it all about us (with Trump as narcissist-in-chief).

Permanence: Anxious to return to business as normal, some elected representatives have continually minimized the patience and sacrifice that are required. Scientists warn of a second wave. Some aspects of life may never return to normal. Increasingly, the uncertainty of the moment starts to look like the permanence of misery.

Pervasiveness: The crisis has made it difficult to access many of our spiritual resources, such as the physical presence of and relationship with friends or family, the cultural richness of theater and art, the gathering of community in prayer, even parts of the great outdoors. Impacting so many aspects of our daily lives, it can blind us to the blessings that endure. Is *everything* terrible? Rabbinic tradition guards against this perspective by fostering the recitation of daily blessings—one hundred blessings a day, to take nothing for granted. Blessing that I woke up this morning. Blessing that I can see. Blessing that creation is renewed. Co-founder of Blavity, Aaron Samuels, speaks of resisting pervasiveness this way: "We find time to dance, and drink, and love, even when we are surrounded by a vortex of impossible."[10]

Our current tsunami of suffering makes it hard to resist the three p's—especially the sense of permanence that makes working for change so exhausting. Racism has been built into the very foundations of our nation; how will we ever remove its stain? Climate change threatens to multiply disaster after disaster as we continue to make our planet uninhabitable. Police violence is an integral part of our carcerative imagination; how

10. Samuels, "The Poetry of Black Jewish Identity."

is reform possible? The polarization of post-truth politics, where people feel entitled to their own facts as well as their own opinions and have no interest in hearing another perspective, derails any potential for progress. How do we even endure, much less triumph over adversity?

Seligman believes that we can learn resilience by training our minds not to succumb to this way of thinking. We can externalize the problem: it is not all my fault or all about me. We can recognize our own agency and the possibility of change; it will not last forever. And we can explain hardship with specificity rather than globalizing our despair. In the Book of Ruth, we see Naomi grow in these capacities, transcending the debilitating effects of trauma. But she does not do it alone. The transformation of suffering is helped in large part by other human beings acting with decency and compassion. Hebrew Bible calls it *chesed*, a lovingkindness that does not expect reciprocity, that may not even be deserved—except that you are a creature in need.[11]

We do not know what motivates Ruth's decision to stay by her mother-in-law's side because Hebrew Bible does not talk much about characters' feelings. But we see her take initiative to glean among the fields in Bethlehem to provide sustenance for herself and Naomi. We see how her courage and endurance inspire grace from Boaz as well. First it is simply that, as owner of the field, he supports Ruth's gleaning with water and protection because he has heard about all that she did for Naomi. Then he gives her access to intact stalks of grain, substantially augmenting her harvest. Such bounty in turn inspires Naomi to see blessing where before there was only bitterness, especially once she learns that the landowner is her kinsman Boaz. Eventually she can see past her own situation—a vital stage in healing—and work toward Ruth's welfare as well. *Chesed* is not only God's to bestow. Naomi encourages Ruth to persuade Boaz to act as redeemer by restoring the family land and marrying Ruth. She glimpses a possible future and seizes the agency available to her through knowledge of local custom. Since this path potentially restores the fortunes of both women, Boaz is even more moved by Ruth's *chesed* in this instance than before—and he stands up as redeemer. *Chesed* is self-replicating, contagious, transformative.[12]

Adversity is never evenly distributed, however; personal courage and interpersonal kindness are not enough. Ruth and Naomi's resilience

---

11. In the book of Ruth, *chesed* appears three times. In 1:8 and 2:20, it is invoked as a kindness from God. In 3:10, Boaz explicitly affirms that Ruth acts with *chesed* as well.

12. See Pardes, *Countertraditions in the Bible*, 109–10.

and recovery are possible only because they are supported by the law of the land. The laws of gleaning ensure that they have plenty to eat even though they arrive with nothing and one of them is an immigrant. The laws of redemption for persons and property enable them to rebuild their lives.[13] These are laws of *tzedakah*, distributive justice. *Tzedakah* is not charity but rather a fundamental building block of a just society. The Book of Ruth testifies to the essential linkage between laws that support the marginalized and the welfare of the state: it is the redemption of Ruth and Naomi, after all, that leads to the birth of King David. And it is David's royal house that is destined to build up the nation.[14]

Systemic problems require systemic change. This is why we fight for restorative and distributive justice in our legal systems. We should not pretend that people can overcome structural inequality with grit, or that charity will suffice; such an assumption is wrong-headed and heartless.[15] We should acknowledge that the body politic grows stronger by supporting all of its members. It is astounding that these truths, known in antiquity, are up for debate. Resilience is forged together.

Job—Comfort from Dust and Ashes

In the New Testament, James mentions the patience of Job (James 5:11) and it makes me wonder if he read the same book we have. Yes, Job endures substantial and undeserved hardship, but he sure makes a lot of noise about it—especially compared to Ruth and Naomi who simply deal with their adversity. The Book of Job is over forty chapters, with the character demanding at great length that his complaint be heard. So, like lament, the wisdom tradition transmitted in the Book of Job calls God to account for the moral order of the cosmos. At the same time, it challenges readers to reexamine their own worldview—not to let rigid theological

13. Many Bible scholars talk about the law as a variation on levirate marriage, but it does not align well with the language. I see the actions here as an outgrowth of Lev 25:24–34 and Ex 21:7: If Israelites are forced to sell land due to poverty, a kinsman is obliged to buy it back for them, if possible, and allow them to enjoy the usufruct of the property. In Ex 21, when a man has to sell his daughter as a handmaid due to poverty, the buyer has an obligation to marry her. (Ruth refers to herself as a handmaid in 3:9.) These are laws of redemption for persons and property.

14. The royal house of David is seen as the legitimate ruler over the people of Israel throughout history. See, e.g. Nathan's prophecy in 2 Sam 7:16, "Your house and your kinship shall ever be secure before you; your throne shall be established forever."

15. See, e.g., Yeh, "Forget Grit. Focus on Inequality."

perspectives limit their understanding of the universe. This summons, and the literary construction of it, can also be instructive amidst our current pandemic.

Similar to the Book of Ruth, calamity is conveyed in short order: Job's children are all killed, his property is destroyed, and his body is afflicted with sores from head to foot (Job 1:13–19, 2:7). As Job's troubles multiply, his three friends come to sit with him in the dust for a long time before they even speak, a commitment to accompaniment that is often overlooked. Then they begin rather gently to explore the meaning of his experience. "If one ventures a word with you, will it be too much?," (Job 4:2) asks Eliphaz, the first of the friends to speak. "You have encouraged many, you have strengthened failing hands. Your words have lifted up those who stumble; you have braced knees that gave way. But now that it overtakes you, it is too much. It reaches you and you are horrified. Is not your piety your confidence, your integrity your hope?" (4:3–6).

As Job continues to stand his ground, however, they blame the victim in increasingly vociferous tones, inventing all sorts of terrible things he must have done to fit the measure of his pain. "Is it because of your piety that God arraigns you, and enters into judgment with you? You know that your wickedness is great, and that your iniquities have no limit. You exact pledges from your fellows for no reason and strip the naked of their clothes. You do not give the thirsty water to drink; you deny bread to the hungry" (22:4–7). The accusations are all false, but Job's friends apparently care more about vindicating their theological assumptions and justifying God than showing compassion for the afflicted. In the final chapter of the book, God is portrayed condemning them for it: "I am incensed at you and your two friends, for you have not spoken the truth about Me as did My servant Job" (42:7).

People tend to respond to crisis by relying on pre-existing beliefs: Eliphaz, Bildad and Zophar are certain that suffering is punishment for sin. Yet it is announced in the first verse that Job is "blameless and upright," so readers know it cannot be that simple. Carole Newsom astutely identifies the character of Elihu, a fourth "friend" who suddenly appears three quarters of the way through the text and disrupts the flow of the book, as the later insertion of one such dissatisfied reader. Elihu offers a different explanation. He refuses to blame the victim, instead asserting that Job's suffering is a divine means of his education and purification. The prose frame around the poetic dialogues suggests a third possibility: it is a test of faith, and God's justice will prove true if Job's faith is.

This polyphonic construction, according to Newsom, is crucial to the theological work of the book: "The truth about piety, human suffering, the nature of God, and the moral order of the cosmos can be adequately addressed only by a plurality of unmerged consciousnesses engaging one another in open-ended dialogue."[16]

For Job, however, suffering is not a theological question to be resolved. It is a human experience to be recognized, and the articulations of faith offered by his friends do him no service. As Martin Buber describes it, "There now came and sought him on his ash heap *religion*, which uses every art of speech to take away from him the God of his soul."[17] Job wants the living God to answer for his very real torment which, no matter the minor sins he may have committed, has no discernable moral justification. He demands to know God's relationship to our existence and our suffering. Job eventually gets his day in court—YHWH is present to his suffering—but the response is not quite what he might have hoped (chapters 38–41). God argues that humanity's knowledge and sensibility do not order the universe: "Where were you when I laid the earth's foundations? . . . Who closed the sea behind doors when it gushed forth out of the womb? . . . Have you ever commanded the day to break, assigned the dawn its place? . . . Have you penetrated to the sources of the sea, or walked in the recesses of the deep? Have the gates of death been disclosed to you?" (38:4, 8, 12, 16–17).

It is too strident to equate with divine mystery or a soothing reassurance that we may not understand God's ways but can trust it is all for the best. The character of God almost dares Job to try taking charge, to enforce one small part of his humanly-constructed ethical expectations. "Deck yourself now with grandeur and eminence, clothe yourself in glory and majesty. Scatter wide your raging anger, see every proud man and bring him low. See every proud man and humble him, and bring them down where they stand . . . Then even I would praise you for the triumph your right hand won you" (40:10–12). Knowing this is beyond his ken, God goes on to describe untamable animals of the wild, behemoth and

---

16. Clues that signal the later insertion of Elihu include: In the epilogue, the text still speaks of Job's three friends, not four (42:7). Job does not answer Elihu as he does the others (ch. 32–37). When Elihu is done speaking, the text reads, "Then YHWH replied to Job out of the tempest" (38:1) even though Job has not been speaking since Chapter 31, when Elihu first began. See Newsom, *The Book of Job*, 24, 200–233.

17. Buber, *The Prophetic Faith*, 237.

leviathan, as irrefutable evidence that we are not the pinnacle of creation. We are merely creatures like the rest.

God's response to Job challenges our own anthropocentric tendencies. There are forces and living beings in the universe that humanity does not control; the world does not revolve around us. While the Book of Job relies on polyphonic complexity to grapple with the human condition, to some degree it privileges this perspective that it puts into the mouth of the Most High.

Job's experience of the divine presses him to reshape his worldview. Recognizing himself as dust and ashes, he withdraws his protest. Or in Stephen Mitchell's provocative and insightful translation, using the more frequent connotation for the root *n-☒-m*, Job finds solace in the realization that humans are but a speck in the vastness of the universe: "Therefore I will be quiet, comforted that I am dust" (42:6).[18] We live in a world where countless species compete for space and survival, including a microscopic virus that can fell the mightiest among us. In honoring the complexity of creation, can we—like Job—find some comfort in our vulnerability, from the fact that we are but dust and ashes? What might we learn from this virus, besides how to kill it?

Perched on the precipice of climate catastrophe, it is hard to think about humanity's place in the universe without wondering how long we will be here. Like the novel coronavirus, we moved along for some time without noticeably harming our planet host. But then we made it sick and, if we do not evolve to become less toxic to it, we invite our own destruction. Many people have reflected on the way that human quietude while sheltering in place has allowed aspects of the natural world to reassert themselves. Are we prepared, however, purposefully and permanently to take up less room? This, too, is a dimension of resilience.

Jem Bendell talks about resilience as a meaning-making exercise, determining what is most valued, most essential to our individual and collective identity. In the process of adaptation, we try to preserve these. At the same time, we need to relinquish ideas, habits, and things that are not sustainable or equitable. And we can seek to restore simple pleasures that were somehow lost. This is the deep adaptation of resilience.[19] We have had to do this to some extent in response to the pandemic; the climate crisis will press us further.

18. Mitchell, trans., *The Book of Job*, xxxii, 88.
19. Bendell, "Deep Adaptation," 19.

Readings of Resilience and the Role of Religion

These biblical readings of resilience can facilitate our deep adaptation. Hope looms large among core values they seek to preserve. Social scientists have demonstrated that, if you tell people something must be done or we are all going to die, most people opt for Door #2, however strange that seems. I guess we'll just die then.[20] Overwhelming fear leads people to give up or disengage. The prophet Isaiah knew this; the biblical book that bears his name relates how God called the Israelites to change their ways in order to avert catastrophe, but instead they succumbed to the temptations of fatalism: "Eat and drink, for tomorrow we die" (Isa 22:13). Lament is a different kind of response. It not only makes space to express our grief, individual and collective; it also enables us to recognize how hope accompanies the pain. Lament turns us toward God and toward the world when fear and sorrow tempt us to run away. The world has been turned upside down before, but it is not a permanent condition.

Hope is not idle optimism that all will turn out for the best, but active faith that the world can be different than it is and that we play a part in shaping it. During the Days of Awe, Jews recite *Un'taneh Tokef*, a litany that speaks of God determining who shall live and who shall die in the coming year. To me, it cannot be a literal description of divine decrees, but rather a vivid reminder of our mortality so that we may treasure the life we are lent and work to become the human beings God hopes for. It is less a time of God's judgment than our own, as the prayer's refrain intimates: "Prayer, repentance, and *tzedakah*"—the last of these ultimately fostering construction of a just society—"transforms the severity of the decree." We have agency.

Yet when the shadow of death overtakes so many, as it does now, it is particularly challenging to recite the words even as metaphor: "Who by fire and who by water, who by war and who by beast, who by famine and who by drought, who by earthquake and who by plague . . ." The forces arrayed against our continuing existence are overwhelming; as Job learned, we are just a speck in the eye of the universe. In the biblical reading of resilience, we take some comfort from being but dust and ashes—and relinquish claims of mastery over the world. Agency must not mutate into arrogance. While we will fight the coronavirus with all the intellectual and other resources at our disposal, we need humility to let the pandemic reset our habits, to relinquish what we must to keep each other

20. O'Neill and Nicholson-Cole, "Fear Won't Do It," 355–79.

safe. Other crises before us press us to acknowledge that there are limits to what can be extracted from the earth and from other human beings. We try to imagine instead what Kathryn Tanner calls "an economy of grace."[21]

In this economy, we reawaken communitarian impulses laid dormant in our highly individualized society. We recognize how our choices, our actions shape each other's quality of life. We are pressed to grapple with the rippling effects of loss and to see the manifestations of injustice that flow from them, especially the ways in which poor and marginalized people bear a disproportionate burden. As Robert Bullard, often considered the father of environmental justice, and Beverly Wright wrote long before the current pandemic, "When societal resources are distributed unequally by class and race, it should be no surprise that population health is distributed along those lines as well."[22] Readings of resilience restore our commitment to an economy of grace in which everyone has the resources they need to thrive—a vision woven into the warp and woof of biblical tradition. We are reminded that we are better together—not only because physical separation is making us lonely, but also because we have the power to transform each other's trauma with *chesed* and *tzedakah*. This is how we adapt to adversity.

Most spiritual lifestances have multiple methods by which they make meaning, cultivate gratitude, foster community, value sacrifice, and engender self-critical faith. Reading scripture is but one of them. It is itself an exercise in meaning-making, offering a lens for viewing the world—perhaps seeing more clearly how to treasure what we have, relinquish things we thought we could not do without, and restore simple pleasures we unnecessarily gave away.

Of course, scripture and tradition do not automatically or consistently hone these tools of resilience, especially those that operate on the societal level. Examining the role of religion in many of our current crises, the record is not all that flattering. During the spring COVID-19 lockdown in the U.S., many houses of worship fought to be seen as essential businesses so they could meet for prayer despite the risks of gathering in groups and the lack of preparedness to manage them. Some congregations disseminated misinformation that suited their institutional or political purposes. Facing the pandemic of racism, religious institutions

---

21. Tanner, *Economy of Grace.*

22. Bullard and Wright, *The Wrong Complexion for Protection*, 181.

have often been instrumental in preserving white supremacy—from justifying slavery and Jim Crow, to undermining reproductive justice, to suing for the right to be exempted from anti-discrimination laws of all sorts. In terms of climate action, influential Christian communities have exerted their power to shut down public discourse about meaningful change in America. They have resurrected a medieval battle between faith and science.

At the same time, there are religious institutions that have demonstrated phenomenal courage and strength in troubling times. During the COVID-19 crisis, they have focused on providing support to their communities with pastoral care, food distribution, spiritual uplift, and other essentials—even from afar. For decades, they have fought to expand civil rights, and currently invest in substantive anti-racism training and self-transformation. They hold themselves to high standards of fairness rather than claim religious freedom for their biases. They have organized themselves and others to promote climate action.

What role do exegesis and theology play in these disparities? Historically, researchers assumed that religious identity shaped one's politics—but that consensus is dissolving.[23] Politics have become the most challenging difference to bridge as Americans increasingly demonize those who disagree. People of a different religion might make it into heaven, to put a colloquial Christian spin on it, but people of the other party never will. This polarization makes it feel that politics have become what Paul Tillich calls our "ultimate concern," the wellspring from which all convictions flow. In truth, religion and politics are reciprocal in their impact, inextricably intertwined. Exegesis and theology are not by themselves determinative, but they are interwoven in the way we wield our faith.

The coronavirus is a bit too recent to trace this interdependence with much detail, but it shows up in the climate debate. Last summer, I was chatting with an acquaintance who wanted me to understand that his resistance to doing anything about the climate crisis was not that he doubted the science. He just believes that God has a plan. Either the Second Coming of Christ is upon us, he asserted, or else God will not allow us to destroy ourselves. Since he is a faithful Catholic, I tried citing Pope Francis's encyclical, *Laudato Si*, and its clear charge to take care of our common home in peril, to acknowledge the human roots of the crisis,

23. See, e.g., Margolis, *From Politics to the Pews.*

and to recognize abuse of creation as ecological sin. It turns out he is not such a "Pope-y" Catholic.

White evangelical Christians and white Catholics in the U.S. are most resistant to accepting climate science. One reason is that 58% of white evangelicals believe that Jesus will return by 2050.[24] The worse the world gets, the more it seems to align in their imagination with the Book of Revelation, which David Wallace-Wells called "the inescapable sourcebook for Western anxiety about the end of the world."[25] So, in an unholy alliance with the fossil fuel industries, the Religious Right has taken the Republican Party hostage—the party that created Yellowstone National Park under President Grant, the first national forest preserves under Benjamin Harrison, the Environmental Protection Agency under Richard Nixon (who also signed major legislation like the Endangered Species Act). Even as recently as George H.W. Bush, Republicans pushed to stem acid rain.[26] Eschatology plays a role in dulling the political will to take responsibility for change and Christianity is not alone in its expectations. Substantial majorities of Muslims in Turkey, Iraq and Afghanistan (68–85%), for example, believe the *mahdi*/messiah will come in their lifetime.[27] Multiple lifestances have conjured visions of the end, with their own versions of upheaval and cataclysm that can rationalize inaction.

Yet these same traditions can forge a different path. There are evangelical Christians committed to "creation care," like those involved in the Evangelical Environmental Network. African-Americans of various religious stripes helped build the US movement for environmental justice. They have seen how poor people suffer the effects of ecological destruction first and worst, and they are not sanguine about apocalypse.[28] Alongside a range of religiously-inspired organizations—including GreenFaith, the Indigenous Environmental Network, Hazon, Green Muslims, Buddhist Climate Action Network, Faith in Place, the Bhumi Project, the Coalition on the Environment and Jewish Life, and the Parliament of the World's Religions Climate Action Task Force—they demonstrate how people of

24. See Pew Research, "Jesus Christ's Return to Earth."
25. Wallace-Wells, *The Uninhabitable Earth*, 230.
26. Solomon, "The GOP Has Turned its Back on Conservation."
27. Torres, "How Religious and Non-religious People View the Apocalypse."
28. See, e.g., Harris, *Ecowomanism*.

all backgrounds find that their faith inspires and even requires them to address the climate crisis.[29]

It is not difficult to find environmental wisdom in our traditions if we choose to look for it, with messages that mirror the lessons of resilience we found in the biblical texts. I offer two small examples from Jewish thought from among hundreds of teachings across diverse lifestances. A tenth-century midrash, *Tanna d'bei Eliahu,* affirms our interconnectedness: "The whole world of humans, animals, fish, and birds all depend on one another. All drink the earth's water, breathe the earth's air, and find food in what was created on the earth. All share the same destiny—what happens to one, happens to all." In a fourteenth-century commentary on Deuteronomy 22:6–7, Joseph ibn Kaspi echoes the teaching in Job that we acknowledge our creatureliness, "The Torah inculcates in us a sense of our modesty and lowliness, so that we should be ever cognizant of the fact that we are of the same stuff as the ass and mule, the cabbage and the pomegranate, and even the lifeless stone." Faith both catalyzes the commitment to creation and is in turn shaped by it.

Reading for collective resilience depends on how we search out and understand our spiritual inheritance. Every religious tradition *can be* interpreted in ways that foster complacency. Detachment in Buddhism, for example, is sometimes imagined as a lack of concern for the created world—but I learned it as a commitment to do what is right without investment in the outcome. Observance of halakha in Jewish tradition can mistakenly be reduced to ritual meticulousness, even though ritual is supposed to be wholly bound up with the ethical. Moksha in Jain or Hindu traditions can be seen as concern only for the fate of one's own soul, but there are numerous teachings that connect the fate of your soul with work to ease the suffering of others and to seek collective liberation.

Harold Dean ("Doc") Trulear has suggested, only half in jest, that if Rosa Parks was arrested today, "the church" would respond by offering to pray for her, or organizing a van ministry so she would not need to take the bus, or launching a study group, or suggesting that she pray to Jesus for a car. Prayer, service, study, fostering faith in God's blessings—these are fine things for churches to do. But the prophetic voice, he argues, is the one that

---

29. Parts of the climate change discussion in this chapter have been adapted from Mikva, "Does Interreligious Understanding Matter if the World Is Coming to an End?," 12–17.

changes the society in which we live and breathe for the better.[30] It is where faith meets politics—and resilience moves through the intersection.

Bibliography

Adler, Rachel. "For These I Weep: A Theology of Lament," *The Chronicle* 68 (2006): 16–21

Adorno, Theodor. *Negative Dialectics.* Translated by E.B. Ashton. New York: Continuum, 2007

Anderson, Gary A. *A Time to Mourn, a Time to Dance: The Expression of Grief and Joy in Israelite Religion.* University Park PA: Penn State University Press, 1991

Bendell, Jem. "Deep Adaptation: A Map for Navigating Climate Tragedy" (July 27, 2018). https://jembendell.com/2019/05/15/deep-adaptation-versions/.

Brueggemann, Walter. "The Costly Loss of Lament," *Journal for the Study of the Old Testament* 36 (1986): 57–71.

Buber, Martin. *The Prophetic Faith.* Princeton: Princeton University Press, 2016.

Bullard, Robert and Beverly Wright. *The Wrong Complexion for Protection: How the Government Response to Disaster Endangers African American Communities.* New York: NYU Press, 2012.

Gulley, Philip. "Growing Roots." In *Front Porch Tales: Warm-Hearted Stories of Family, Faith, Laughter, and Love.* New York: HarperCollins, 2001, 17–19.

Hart, Benji. "Feeling Is Not Weakness: Sadness, Mourning and Movement." https://radfag.com/2015/05/14/feeling-is-not-weakness-sadness-mourning-and-movement/.

Harris, Melanie L. *Ecowomanism: African American Women and Earth Honoring Faiths.* Ossining NY: Orbis, 2017.

Margolis, Michele F. *From Politics to the Pews: How Partisanship and the Political Environment Shape Religious Identity.* Chicago: University of Chicago Press, 2018.

Mikva, Rachel S., "Change the Conversation About Justice," *Tikkun* (August 14, 2015). https://www.tikkun.org/change-the-conversation-about-justice-by-rachel-mikva/.

———. "Does Interreligious Understanding Matter if the World is Coming to an End?" In *Deep Understanding for Divisive Times.* Edited by Lucinda Allen Mosher, et al., 12–17. Newton Centre, MA: Interreligious Studies, 2020.

Mitchell, Stephen, trans. *The Book of Job.* New York: HarperCollins, 1987.

Newsom, Carole. *The Book of Job: A Contest of Moral Imaginations.* Oxford: Oxford University Press, 2009.

O'Neill, Saffron and Sophie Nicholson-Cole. "Fear Won't Do It: Promoting Positive Engagement with Climate Change Through Visual and Iconic Representations," *Science Communication* 30:3 (March 2009): 355–79. https://doi.org/10.1177/1075547008329201/.

Pardes, Ilana. *Countertraditions in the Bible: A Feminist Approach.* Cambridge MA: Harvard University Press, 1993.

Pew Research. "Jesus Christ's Return to Earth," (July 14, 2010). https://www.pewresearch.org/fact-tank/2010/07/14/jesus-christs-return-to-earth/.

30. Trulear, "Theological Education and Social Justice as Vocation."

Samuels, Aaron. "The Poetry of Black Jewish Identity" (December 17, 2013). https://www.myjewishlearning.com/jewish-and/the-poetry-of-jewish-black-identity/.

Seligman, Martin. *Learned Optimism: How to Change Your Mind and Your Life*. New York: Pocket, 1991.

Solomon, Christopher. "The GOP Has Turned its Back on Conservation," (September 11, 2018). https://www.outsideonline.com/2342301/how-gop-turned-its-back-conservation/.

Stern, Elsie R. *From Rebuke to Consolation: Exegesis and Theology in the Liturgical Anthology of the Ninth of Av Season*. Providence, Brown Judaic Studies, 2004.

Tanner, Kathryn. *Economy of Grace*. Minneapolis: Fortress, 2005.

Torres, Phil. "How Religious and Non-religious People View the Apocalypse," (August 18, 2017). https://thebulletin.org/2017/08/how-religious-and-non-religious-people-view-the-apocalypse/.

Trulear, Harold Dean. "Theological Education and Social Justice as Vocation." Presentation at *Current and Future Trends in Theological Education*, June 2018.

Wallace-Wells, David. *The Uninhabitable Earth: Life After Warming*. New York: Tim Duggan, 2019.

Wolpe, David. *Healer of Shattered Hearts: A Jewish View of God*. New York: Penguin, 1991.

Yeh, Christine, "Forget Grit. Focus on Inequality," *Education Week* (April 14, 2017). https://www.edweek.org/ew/articles/2017/04/14/forget-grit-focus-on-inequality.html/.

Note: Biblical translations are adapted from NJPS.

8

You Can't Do This Alone

Leadership in Times of Crisis

CHRISTINA AMALIA REPOLEY AND PATRICK B. REYES

Introduction

THE LEADERSHIP CHALLENGE HAS always been one of survival, especially in times of crisis. We crafted our principles of shared leadership in the Fall of 2020. This was a time of great upheaval in the United States and the world. A global pandemic raged for most of the year with no end in sight, police killings of Black and Brown people had sparked an outcry that resulted in a racial reckoning moment at the national level unlike anything we had experienced in recent decades, violence and abuse of children and families at the border was in our news feeds daily, the climate crisis had never felt more real as wildfires ravaged some parts of the country, hurricanes, and floods others. An unbelievably contested presidential election was fast approaching, calling into question certain political principles we had previously taken for granted. Early in 2021, an attack on Congress by white nationalist and domestic terrorists spurred on by the President, brought into stark relief the difference between Black and white life. It often felt like we were living in a dystopian future, hardly able to take in yet more news of violence, hatred, injustice, and despair.

In this context, we came together to reflect on our task as leaders, on our shared calling to accompany the next generation of Christian leaders as they discern their meaning and purpose. The task of leadership has always been about stepping into the moment, about knowing what time it is.

Indeed, shared leadership, for us, is a way of surviving. It is a way of knowing we are not alone and that our individual gifts and talents are made fuller and stronger through partnership. Shared leadership is counter-cultural in crisis. Too often, the patriarchal white-savior complex kicks in and we believe we are the solution to the many problems we face. For so many others who feel overwhelmed by the moment, we often end up waiting for Superman or Wonder Woman, someone with out-of-this world abilities who can save us. These toxic models of singular leadership fail in moments of great crisis because the problems facing our world today are bigger than any one person, superpowers or not.

We found ourselves asking: How do you lead and accompany the next generation of Christian leaders to find meaning and purpose when communities are struggling to survive? Drawing on 70 years of supporting the next generation of Christian leaders, Forum for Theological Exploration (FTE) has discovered some core principles of a shared leadership model. The principles create the conditions for clarity of purpose when leading and accompanying the next generation in moments of crisis. More importantly, they are the foundation for understanding that no one person leads an organization in this work. As leaders in the organization and in the field, the principles are the foundation for shared leadership that supports, honors, and values people.

In our experience of shared leadership, especially in times of crisis, it requires at least four key components: Stories, Stakes, Support, and Showing up. These principles of shared leadership are not important only in times of crisis. In fact, the more we can build the muscle and the habit of these shared leadership practices over time, we will be better equipped for times of crisis because we already know how to lead together. In order for us to do our work well together at any time we need to understand, care for, and embody these four elements of shared leadership.

As we reflected on shared leadership together, we remembered the context and history of the work we do. We are both senior directors at the Forum for Theological Exploration (FTE), an organization with a long and rich history of supporting the next generation, through crisis, utilizing a model of shared leadership.

Shared Leadership in the Context of Our Work

The work at the Forum for Theological Exploration has never been the work of one person. It has always been by, for, and with the community of faith. Since 1954, FTE has supported the next generation of pastors and scholars. During the 1960s, in a time with social unrest, then director Rev. Dr. Charles Shelby Rooks and board chair Dr. Benjamin Elijah Mays, the 29-year president of Morehouse College, shifted our work to meet the times. The backdrop of the events of 1968 necessitated a shift in our work. These events included the death of Rev. Dr. Martin Luther King Jr., John Carlos and Tommie Smith lifting their black-gloved fists at the Olympics in Mexico reminding us all of Black power and Black life, the same Olympics that young college students protested and were slaughtered for raising their voices against the human rights abuses of their time. It was the same year that César Chávez leading the UFW participated in his first spiritual fast, breaking it with Holy Communion with presidential hopeful Robert Kennedy by his side. Later that year, the world witnessed Kennedy's assassination, where a young Latino migrant, Juan Romero placed a Rosary in his hand as Kennedy said his final words, "it's going to be alright."

During that same year, we remember there were only 18 doctoral students of color in religion. If FTE was going to address the social ill of racism and teach the next generation Christian leaders to address the crisis of the racism, imperialism, and poverty, if FTE was going to help prepare the next generation of Christian leaders in the wake of our heroes being slain in the street, FTE had to do something. Crisis created conditions where business-as-usual would not suffice. Rooks and Mays began a powerful program to honor our fallen heroes and legends, and capture, re-member, and to reimagine the spirit of the movement. We are reminded of those who we benefit from now more than 50 years later that we have a James Cone, *Black Theology and Black Power*,[1] and Vine Deloria's, *God is Red: A Native View of Religion*.[2] The foundations were laid just following 1968 for Latin American liberationists, Minjung theologies of the 1970s, womanists and Mujerista theologies of the late 1970s and 1980s. And FTE, launched its historic work supporting scholars of color in religion and young adults discerning a call to ministry in 1968 with support for African American and Black students. In 1976 following the

1. Cone and West, *Black Theology and Black Power*.
2. Deloria Jr., Silko, and Tinker, *God Is Red: A Native View of Religion*.

leadership of Dr. Justo Gonzalez and Rev. Dr. Ruben Armendariz, supporting Latinos pursuing calls to ministry and theological education. We continued to expand our programs in the 1980s to support first nations and Indigenous communities. Our ministry programs have been keen to support women in leadership. Our ministerial programs always serve more than 60 percent women who are seeking to serve the church, and often, in traditions that still do not recognize their leadership.

The field now has a substantial theological academic corpus of material to stand on, though we always had the stories of ancestors streaming below the surface. This is the legacy we are stewarding, together. And we find ourselves in this moment in our leadership discerning with each other how we will lead in this moment that has specters of 1968. Like the crisis then, 2020 necessitated a fundamental shift in explicit articulation about how we were to lead together.

Definitions of Shared Leadership

There is an abundance of popular leadership definitions and models. From bestsellers by Stephen Covey,[3] Simon Sinek,[4] Brené Brown,[5] Jim Collins,[6] John Maxwell,[7] Ray Dalio,[8] Dale Carnegie,[9] Angie Morgan,[10] Peter Senge,[11] Ronald Heifetz,[12] and the plethora of motivational and self-help literature that focuses on developing one's own capacity to lead well. What so much of the literature stresses is individual leadership. Texts promising to help you lead your teams or organizations are so commonplace, if we told you *How to Lead Others* was a bestseller, you would nod your head in agreement, not caring that it is a completely made-up title. The problem with so much of the literature is that it focuses on the individual leader. When leadership is defined or examples lifted up, it is

3. Covey, *The 7 Habits of Highly Effective People.*

4. Sinek, *Start with Why: How Great Leaders Inspire Everyone to Take Action.*

5. Brown, *Dare to Lead: Brave Work. Tough Conversations. Whole Hearts.*

6. Collins, *Good to Great: Why Some Companies Make the Leap and Others Don't.*

7. Maxwell has written a number of books on leadership.

8. Dalio, *Principles: Life and Work.*

9. Carnegie, *How to Win Friends & Influence People.*

10. Morgan et al., *Spark: How to Lead Yourself and Others to Greater Success.*

11. Senge, *The Fifth Discipline: The Art & Practice of The Learning Organization.*

12. Heifetz, *Leadership Without Easy Answers.*

never a community or team. It is always the one stand-out, or the helpful insights for how to lead more effectively.

What we are interested in is that working in teams is always preferable to leading alone. We have committed to rethinking leadership, driven by insights from the literature and the experience of our communities. We are not suggesting that the literature or individual leadership is necessarily or always a bad thing. The world needs leaders! Margaret Wheatley notes that "It is possible to find a path of contribution and meaning if we turn our attention away from issues beyond our control and focus on the people around us who are yearning for good leadership and engage them in work that is within reach. It is possible to use our influence and power to create *islands of sanity* in the midst of a raging destructive sea."[13] We were more interested in how to lead together. How do we define leadership that is not about me? Around the office, Patrick often says, "this is we work, not me work."

Matthew Wesley Williams, former Vice President at the Forum for Theological Exploration and Interdenominational Theological Seminary President, writes against what he calls a "warrior-hero" model of leadership. In that model, leadership is inevitably bound up in notions of the strong man.[14] We borrow this term, "strong man," from Ched Meyers. The evil version of the warrior-hero, the strong man is the hyper-male, who leads by dominating other human bodies. In Patrick's Latino context, machismo is not a strong enough term for the strong man. The strong man is the colonial power, exerting power over for his own benefit. The strong man often calls upon leadership questions to say that the only way to combat the strong man is to create an equally strong leader, who believes in doing right by the people. Think Goliath, Nebuchadnezzar, or Pharaoh. And for every one of them, there is a David, Daniel, Miriam, and Moses. In the present day, for every white male leader that seeks to do harm, there is another white male leader that seeks to do good.

The strong man's benevolent counterpart is Williams's warrior-hero. This is the alpha male, who seeks to do justice. Superman. This is the sort of male-dominated leadership that plagues so many of our justice-seeking and "helping industries," institutions, and organizations. The danger in the warrior-hero is that even at their best, they are seen as the only leaders with the solution. Williams claims a paradigm shift is needed.

13. Wheatley, *Who Do We Choose To Be?: Facing Reality, Claiming Leadership, Restoring Sanity*, 4.

14. Myers, *Binding the Strong Man: A Political Reading of Mark's Story of Jesus*.

He says, "Heroes rescue folks in danger and fix what's broken; healers help living systems reconnect to their wholeness."[15] The warrior-healer, he suggests, is a better way to liberate leadership. He goes on to write that liberating leadership "shifts the focus from an out-front warrior-hero who leads the charge to a warrior-healer who co-creates the conditions for the community to discover its power and address its complex challenges."[16] Williams gestures at the idea that the leader should lead with the community.

The quest to be seen as a leader, to be seen as the warrior-hero, as opposed to doing any real healing, is one of the greatest temptations we saw during the pandemic. Because pulpits and theological classrooms were shut down in 2020, the dial was turned all the way up on the noise coming from the church and academy of people who wanted to lead communities without any prior connection to or shared struggle with them. From the communities and young people we serve, people wanted to be seen for leading, often equated with who was streaming live or offering the latest spiritual vaccine to the racial and viral pandemics plaguing society: warrior-heroes. Because of our work being closely aligned to the church's and the faith community's role in supporting a new generation of healers, prophets, troublemakers, organizers, and educators, many sought leadership roles to be in proximity to the work, to gain notoriety for leading in this moment of crisis, and, more disturbingly, to be seen for leading through crisis.

Writing about her experience organizing in communities of color and the movement for Black lives, Alicia Garza notes, the quest to be seen as leading the work in a moment of crisis became a flash point in the moments of racial awakening and civil unrest. Garza, speaking specifically about organizing and Black liberation in San Francisco and the broader Bay Area, offers advice from more than two decades of organizing. She recalls asking the question, "Do you want to be part of an organization that is fighting to make sure all of the changes that happen in this community are for the benefit of this community?"[17] The challenge we faced as an organization was asking those who sought our platform and ourselves this very question. *How do we re-orient ourselves as a community that*

---

15. Lewis, Williams, and Baker, *Another Way: Living and Leading Change on Purpose*, 128.

16. Lewis, Williams, and Baker, *Another Way*, 129.

17. Garza, *The Purpose of Power*, 62.

seeks to heal as opposed to building platforms for people to be seen? How do we hold ourselves accountable to this moment and to the community?

We have been charged as responsible for leading teams and managing work in a moment of crisis. We wanted to lead together when society, our institution, and certainly our job descriptions did not say, "you are warrior-healers together." We had to learn how to lead in new ways in this moment.

Stephen Preskill and Stephen Brookfield reflect on this leadership challenge. Their solution is to be learners. Leaders need to develop the capacity to learn from those they serve. They write that "as teachers and as members of communities, we have tried to keep the focus on others, to give people control over their own learning. We have done so by keeping our own participation to a minimum, by encouraging people to interact with each other, by using questions to deepen these interactions, and by trying to create a space for participants to tell their stories."[18] This focus on others provides the baseline for what they call collective leadership. Collective leadership is found not in theoretical definitions for them, but in practice. They note:

> When collective leadership is being authentically practiced, all group members are committed to creating and implementing a shared vision. All assume some leadership responsibility. All have an opportunity to play a leadership role. All are willing to subordinate themselves to the group's goals and interests. When Collective leadership prevails, there is no one person everyone else depends on. Rather, work is done interdependently so that everyone is seen as being necessary to the group's success.[19]

This is not easy. Not only is this notion of collective leadership difficult, counter-cultural, and not how we are trained as leaders, but it is near impossible. It is near impossible because the problems are so complex. The vision and strategy are not always clear about how to solve problems. And more important, people are complex individuals with various levels of energy, time, and love to dedicate to shared projects. It is damn near impossible when teasing out the nuance between a difference of opinion and the ways that systems of racism and patriarchy emerge in collective leadership. In a success-driven economy, our leadership, often tethered

18. Preskill and Brookfield, *Learning as a Way of Leading: Lessons from the Struggle for Social Justice*, 69.

19. Preskill and Brookfield, *Learning as a Way of Leading*, 85.

to our livelihoods and occupations, can drive our individual leadership aspirations. And what made us the leaders we are, the experiences and educations we attained over a lifetime. Christina overcame patriarchal systems to create an organization that brought justice to the world prior to coming to FTE. She did so while constantly navigating gender discrimination and oppression in our broader field that continue to delegitimize women in leadership. There are traditions that we work with that still do not recognize women in leadership! In the words of Patrick, "Christina inspires me for her resilience, brilliance, and ability to break glass ceilings and create structures for the next generation of young women to dream big dreams as they gaze out windows built by the shards of shattered glass. Windows that provide safety from a violent world. Windows giving visions of better futures."

At the same time, Patrick overcame poverty, abuse, and white supremacy in work and education systems where he was often the first Chicano, Latinx, or person of color in leadership. Even when he attained the degrees and experience necessary for leadership, he is still challenged by the field and broader society as "just another brown man," where white opinions are often equated with his expertise and experience. He represents less than .01% from his community having any graduate education, who still has to answer the question of his children, "Will they lock us up? Will they kill us?" as his children witness children who look like them locked in cages on the news and learn they are the realization of generations of survival. He is a leader who says, "I have met death. We know each other by name. I refuse to let him erase us."

These larger systems are always at work, trying to drive leadership as a single-cause and single-experience model. It creates conditions where deep solidarity and relationship is near impossible to create. It forced both of us to overcome different obstacles, both committed to making a difference in the world. The white, hetero-patriarchal, colonial, normative leadership structure treats this moment where two leaders, forged in the fire of adversity, to not embrace difference and enact change together. Those systems promote a leadership Darwinism, Machiavellian ambition, Voldemort power thirst, and Vader-like power and capitulation to empire.

Crisis exacerbates this drive to divide among leaders. When resources are scarce, leaders often attempt to hold onto what power they perceive to have earned. For those in leadership, this grasping to maintain power is what is termed as the power paradox. Dacher Keltner writes: "This is the heart of the power paradox: the seductions of power induce us to lose the very skills that enabled us to gain power in the first place."[20] The seduction of a singular leadership model is reflected in idea that *If only I were in charge, things would be different.* This is all too resonant in the spaces we work—the church, the academy, non-profit change-making institutions, and social justice movements. In the very attempt to change unjust systems or address complex and systemic problems like racism, sexism, climate change, incarceration, etc., too many leaders aspire to or mirror dominating forms of leadership. We simply needed a different way of leading.

Returning to Keltner, he notes that power—defined as the ability to make a difference in the world—is given to us by others. It is given by others through "acting in ways that improve the lives of other people in our social networks. Our power is granted to us by others."[21] Not only is power given to us by others, Keltner's research found that power cannot be taken by force. Instead, Keltner and his team at the Greater Good Science Center at Berkley found that enduring power comes from empathy, giving, expressing gratitude, and telling stories that unite.[22] This leadership is found in the principles described by adrienne marie brown, who writes that her community would be led by:

> Impacted leadership (the leadership of communities directly impacted by economic and environmental injustice); Privileged support (the intentional support for impacted leadership from communities/people that can identify their privilege and want to see a rebalancing of power); Feminine leadership (not just women leaders, but leaders who shift our understanding of how power can be held).[23]

If we were going to lead together in a moment of complexity and crises, we too wanted to lead by similar principles. At times, our locations formed in different systems of privilege would necessitate us to lean on the other for wisdom, guidance, and care. At other times, it relied deeply on beliefs of trust and mutual admiration of the gifts, skills, experiences, and expertise the other brought to addressing crisis. With the full weight of oppressive systems encouraging us to behave as individual leaders who assumed authority and status to be ours alone, or to assume that

20. Keltner, *The Power Paradox: How We Gain and Lose Influence*, 9.

21. Keltner, *The Power Paradox*, 5.

22. Keltner, *The Power Paradox*, 72.

23. brown, *Emergent Strategy: Shaping Change, Changing Worlds*, 66.

our differences were too great to overcome, committing to shared leadership was about leading from the heart and the greater good. Described below are the principles, but more importantly, the practices that guide our shared leadership.

Principles of Shared Leadership

The four principles of shared leadership that we reflect on draw on the wisdom of our traditions. The principles reflect a valuing of the insight of the community over the insight of any individual. These practices have a way of asking the question who benefits and who suffers in any given circumstance. They include those with the most to gain or lose in the discernment process. They help us to understand power through a collective experience and which is measured against the community's well-being. These leadership practices favor intergenerational, intercultural modes of being which honor our ancestors as much as the present moment.

As we share about our leadership practices, we begin each practice with an invitation for contemplation, reflection, and grounding. These questions for reflection can be approached as a meditation for the reader to reflect on their own practices of leadership.

Stories

Our work begins with story; the stories of ourselves, our family, our communities, and our society. Sharing and receiving another's story is a gift of love and mutuality; stories invite us into the deeper lives with whom we toil. So, what is your life story? Your biography? Memoir? What is your genesis? Starting place? Who is part of your life? Who are the characters in your story, the wise sages, the supporting friend, the co-sojourner? Where have you traveled? What is the setting of your story? Where did you come most alive? Where have you been moved to tears? To laughter? What stories are unique to your family or to you? The stories that exist only in the space between your heart and your soul? What stories do you tell only your closest friends and loved ones? What are the stories you share, in embodied experience, with only your closest friends and family? What are the stories that have been passed down for generations, lived and spoken by your ancestors that rest directly on your heart? What is the story you are writing right now? Who is helping you author your story? Who is making enough space for you to author the story that will save your own life and the life of the community? What is the story that can only be told by you and lived by you? Who is listening to that story? Who loves that story? Who holds that story with the care and love it deserves?

For us, knowing each other's stories as well as the story of the people who came before us in the work we do, is a crucial part of shared leadership. Returning to Keltner's research, he writes that "good storytelling makes for enduring power for now-familiar reasons: it enhances the interests of others and reduces the stresses of group living. It promotes the greater good, generating shared mirth, levity, and joy—all dopamine-rich experiences that build strong ties within social networks."[24] Knowing each other's stories, we build our own story as colleagues, leaders and friends. Even the practice of remembering and telling our own story as human beings in relationship to each other helps to strengthen our trust and accountability and reminds us of the strong foundation we stand on even when we find ourselves in moments of tension or conflict. When we first met, we shared stories of our lives and our work. We asked about each other's families and longer ancestral histories. We asked each other questions about our leadership in the work we were each doing at that time, questions that were insightful in ways that not everyone is. We quickly saw that though we had different approaches, experiences, and backgrounds, yet we shared similar values.

When I, Christina, was discerning whether to leave my other job and come to work for FTE, and with Patrick, the job I held at the time was one that had come out of over a decade of work. I had gone through a discernment process with my community, which had resulted in the decision that I would not accept the offer from FTE. When I told Patrick that I had decided the answer was *no, it wasn't the right time,* his response to me was "I don't think your discernment process went the right way."

It is funny thinking about that because now that I know him even better I really appreciate his ability to cut through all the noise, and just to call it like he sees it. Naming it and speaking that kind of truth to me in ways that a lot of people do not. And he was right. It wasn't about the job. It was not a question of if I should do this job or that job, but really it was about seeing where my life was calling me at that moment and where to put my gifts and my skills to use in my leadership. It was a result of sharing stories and understanding more about me than that particular

24. Keltner, *The Power Paradox*, 94.

moment. He was really clear in saying this is the right move for me. And I am so grateful for that insightfulness and speaking into my life in a way that was really where my heart was anyway. It was what I was being called to do, but I felt like I had to say no for lots of other reasons. So even in the very beginning of our work together in shared leadership, we had shared stories and shared stakes in a way that had a deep impact. Patrick was seeing what was really true for me in that moment and naming it and calling it out.

Having a shared mission, shared goals, shared vision is all something we deeply value. Understanding this shared vision came out of sharing our stories. Part of storytelling is an act of cultural repair. With the many crises facing our world, there are painful legacies of violence and colonization. It is only through meeting each other's ancestors can we truly be connected in the present. In getting to know each other as friends, having each other share deeply about family and life outside of work, built the foundation for our trust. For example, Christina shared about her dad, who had recently passed away, and his spirituality of being in the woods. This is such a deep part of her. In every moment that we shared stories about what really mattered to us, the less we could distance ourselves from a shared vision for the world our ancestors wanted for us. Like those tender moments with Christina's father, Patrick recognized the quiet moments he had with his grandma in her back garden with her roses. These shared stories were lessons in how to care for people, how to care for self and be present to the earth and to the next generation. Hearing, listening, and receiving each other's story helped us go deeper, build trust, and commitment to shared work. The work we are doing is not just ours. It was never just ours in the first place. Shared leadership includes the leadership of our ancestors passed down in our blood and in our bones. When you start sharing like that, an Italian to a Chicano, despite our vastly different life experiences, we cannot help but imagine that our ancestors are celebrating as their love and story are extended.

Stakes

What is at stake for you in the work you do? When you are clear on your life's story and all the characters in it, and how you got to where you are, you are clearer about what is important to you. What is worth your life's energy? Why do you do what you do? Why does it matter? Who or what in your

life's story or what circumstances of your life story helped to shape what is
at stake for you? Where is the line in the sand about which you would not
compromise? How do you know where that is? How do you act on behalf of
what is at stake?

Patrick often remarks that Christina raises the stakes on him all the
time! "I didn't think that was possible. I have a million things going on
outside of work because I am trying to create the conditions for people to
thrive, not just our young adults and doctoral students but for children at
the school I am on the board of, students in higher education that I serve
through board leadership, what I write, in the work I do at the Children's
Defense Fund; I am out there in the world trying to make it happen. Then
when I meet someone like Christina who is matching it and next leveling
it, the stakes are clear. We realize the work that we are up to isn't just a
fluff program for young adults to come and have a great experience on
a retreat where they discern life's meaning and purpose, but it is life and
death work." For both of us, this is life and death work. The thriving of
future generations of all backgrounds, but especially the most marginalized, is how we thrive. As Audre Lorde said, "without community, there
is no liberation . . . but community must not mean a shedding of our differences, nor the pathetic pretense that these differences do not exist."[25]
Lorde states these famous lines in her speech, "The Master's Tools Will
Never Dismantle the Master's House." In that speech speaking of the differences between women, specifically white women and women of color.
She reminds all gathered:

> Within the interdependence of mutual (nondominant) differ-
> ences lies that security which enables us to descend into chaos
> of knowledge and return with true visions of our future, along
> with the concomitant power to effect those changes which can
> bring that future into being. Difference is that raw and powerful
> connection from which our personal power is forged.[26]

When you are doing life and death work, you need to find people with a
similar sense of the stakes. The stakes do not have to be exactly the same.
We do not have to share the same identity, but we have to acknowledge
that at times the stakes will be much higher for each other. We have to
acknowledge that the stakes are even higher for the people that we serve.

---

25. Lorde, "The Master's Tools Will Never Dismantle the Master's House," 110–14.
26. Lorde, "The Master's Tools."

We can only go so far on our own. Committed to the freedom and liberation of the people and this planet, we want to create the conditions for thriving. And when we do that work in a system, like theological education, or the church, systems that are very static, and resistant to our leadership, we need each other. In Patrick's words, "I have a strong sense that I will only witness so many sunrises and sunsets, who and how we spend our time matters. For so many BIPOC young people, survivors like myself, tomorrow is not guaranteed, so the *who* is equally as important as the *what* of my life." We are not going to do it the way it has always been done. We are going with the young people who have the vision to build something new, like the beginnings of our organization when C. Shelby Rooks and Benjamin E. Mays getting the Fellowship started in 1968, if they had not, we would not be here. Had our ancestors not committed to surviving their histories, thought different and under different social structures, we both would not be here. We are carrying on that legacy to not just win the game, not just to develop exceptions from our respective communities who can succeed in this current system, (more women and Latinx and Indigenous leaders, for example), but we are going to change the rules, design new systems, and create the conditions so all people can thrive. This is more than just caring for the work; this is soul care.

Support

Support is more than just affirmation or encouragement. Can you hold the full weight of the people you work with? Who can you turn to, to pick you up off the floor when you are down, and who can hold you when you are floating away like a Macy's Day balloon? Who do you turn to for support? Who sees something in you that you might not see in yourself? Who calls you beloved? Who loves you for who you are, but not for what you can do for them? Who has given something to you, not because of what they could get out of you, but who has held the weight of your pain, grief, joy, happiness, as a gift, a tender glance of mutual healing? Who supports you because seeing you thrive is the only outcome they are after? What communities send and support you in your vocation? Who calls you into being? What community welcomes you to the table every time you walk through the door? Who supported you for walking over that threshold? For simply breathing, for being you.

Support is not self-serving; support does not extract or mine gifts. Support is what Father Greg Boyle of Homeboy Industries says exists when we are gracious with our most tender parts: He says:

> Locating our wounds leads us to a gracious place of fragility, a contact point with another human being. When we share these shards . . . with each other, we move into the intimacy of healing. Awe softens us for the tender glance of God, then enables us to glance in just the same way.[27]

Support looks like more than just a comforting message, an empathetic conversation, or consolation in moments of grief and pain. It is more than celebrating wins and mourning losses together. Support of the kind we are talking about is being able to draw on that well-spring of love that we received from our ancestors and extending it to those with whom we share leadership. Support, as Father Boyle mentions above, is about the intimacy of healing. This is not surface level healing. This is healing the wounds of traumas and wounds that existed long before either of us entered this plane and will exist long after we are gone. Support of this kind is seeing each other's deepest wounds in those moments of leadership challenges and realize that while we may be addressing the crisis of this moment, our wounds extend further back and cast a long shadow into the future. The wounds are historical. The wounds are relational. The wounds are personal. It is only the practice of healing support that we can see each other into better life.

Patrick remembers his grandma greeted every person that walked through the door with "I am so glad you are here, sit down and let me get you something to eat." Every person who walked through her door was a distinguished guest, as if it were a planned occasion for them to be present in her home. Support of the healing Father Boyle speaks of means inviting and believing that Christina is fully welcome in Patrick's grandma's home. It is imagining the healing potential for her cooking, her patience, her love, is also extended to Christina. *It helps Christina's Spanish is better than Patrick's, which will make Grandma Carmen happy.* Likewise, when Patrick needs support and guidance that he can take comfort in the image of seeking Christina's dad while they walk in the woods. *It helps that Patrick and Bob, Christina's dad, are similarly stubborn and committed to calling it like they see it.* While both Patrick's grandma and Christina's dad are no longer on this plane, support in a shared leadership model means

27. Boyle, *Barking to the Choir: The Power of Radical Kinship*, 56.

that when we meet, so do our ancestors. We bring them fully to the here and now, to be fully present, to support the other when they need healing, knowing that we benefit from an expanded vision and trust that healing can be extended.

Practically speaking, support looks like pushing the other person to be better, to grow, to change. As colleagues, we show up very differently in our work life, and that can be hard and cause stress and conflicts sometimes. Support can look like trusting each other through disagreement and conflict and holding the space for the other person to mention issues. When FTE was restructuring a colleague noted that "this all seems to rely on Patrick and Christina getting along." At that time it seemed like a silly comment, of course we would get along. But as we have lived into this shared leadership model more, we have learned more about each other's ways of communicating and leading. We have also uncovered the ways that we can trigger each other in how we work together.

This support does not mean agreeing on one mode of working, one way of communicating, one leadership style, or agreeing that we will always honor the many assessments we have taken. Does it help to know what the Meyers-Briggs type, number on the Enneagram, or strengths are? Sure. But do our ancestors rely on these assessments and numbers? Do these assessments take in the stories and stakes? Just as our stories are different and the particularities of our stakes are different, we have vastly different leadership styles. We have different ways of leading our teams, different ways of communicating, and different ways of showing our care for each other. As a result, we have had our conflicts. Sometimes that has been a result of Patrick's "name the world for what it is," direct, and urgent style of communication, which is remarkably different from Christina's. As Christina says:

> One of the things I have learned and that I continue to learn from our relationship is that when we are in a shared leadership model, when we have shared our stories, when we have been that vulnerable together, when we know what our stakes are, there is a level of trust that we have established where I know that Patrick supports me. I know he trusts me. I know he is showing up for me. And that isn't always easy. We have called each other out. We have offended each other. We have hurt each other's feelings. Ultimately though, we have stayed in it because we are committed to this work and to each other. Patrick has made me a better leader because he has encouraged me to be more direct, to call it like I see it and not worry about everyone's feelings all

the time which is where my tendencies are. And when we can approach conflicts as potentially generative instead of scary or divisive, even when it is hard, then we can learn from each other and grow in our leadership, even when we have really different styles. This, for us, is a form of support.

Other ways that we support each other include knowing what is going on outside of work. Asking for prayers when something is happening in our family life, sending resources and silly notes at the end of the day, and checking in over the weekend. This kind of support can help pick the other up off the floor, can help ground us, keep us focused, and remind each other that this is about more than a job, it is about our children, our children's children, and the world we are trying to build, together.

Showing Up

Sometimes as leaders, we are just the people who keep showing up. We are the ones who slog through and make things happen, even when we are tired. Or uninspired, or when we don't think we know what to do. We keep showing up. How do you continue to show up for yourself, your community, the people you work with, the people you love, the people you don't love . . . How do you keep showing up, even when it is hard? Can you remember a time in your own leadership when simply showing up, even if you didn't have the answers, was enough? Who has shown up for you? How and for whom do you show up?

When Christina was in her early 20s, she interned for the Beloved Community Center in Greensboro, North Carolina, for Nelson and Joyce Johnson, some of the most wise and faithful elders on this planet. She writes of her experience:

> As I look back on that time, I had a lot of responsibility for someone a few years out of college with little experience. I did all kinds of things I didn't know how to do. I knocked on doors throughout the community, I talked to people about tenant rights, I organized meetings and facilitated conversations in a newly forming faith and labor coalition for the state. Recently, I had the opportunity to ask Joyce why they trusted me to do this important work. Why did they trust this young, inexperienced white woman to go with them into African American neighborhoods and churches to help them organize? What they told me was, "you showed up. You were there. We needed someone to do

it, and you were there. We put you to work. We needed someone and you were there."

Joyce shared that in her experience it was a kind of privilege to think that we cannot get to work on important issues until you have had all the proper training and study to "qualify" you for the work. Sometimes, just showing up is what is needed. Christina continues:

> Years after that experience I, along with a small group of others, started a national nonprofit. I knew nothing about how to write and file a 501(c)3 application, or how to file articles of incorporation, get the right kind of insurance, raise money, supervise staff, and many more things I had to learn how to do. Years into that work, I often said that if I had known all the things I would have had to learn how to do, I would have been too overwhelmed to do anything and it never would have happened. Instead, what I did was to keep showing up, day after day, to move the work forward because I was deeply sure that it was what I was called to do. I stuck with it, and kept showing up, and ended up building an organization that was remarkably successful, grew quickly, and is still going without me.

Showing up is a directive and non-negotiable. It is a practical, everyday activity. Shared leadership, like any relationship, means that being present is not an option. Showing up for shared leadership is creating models, practices, or rhythms for working together. Showing up is more than agreeing to be good colleagues at the same place of employment and keep each informed of each other's and our team's work. That is what is in our job description. Showing up means taking the time to deeply listen to the other for what their profound needs are; what deep wounds keep them up; what challenges they cannot overcome. Showing up is not saying to the other, "this is what I will do for you." Showing up in this way follows that warrior-hero model mentioned earlier.

We are not here to fix each other.

We are not showing up to fix the flaws in each other's leadership. In fact, we know, acknowledge, and work through all of those differences. It is knowing all of those idiosyncrasies and know how to dance in and among the ways they show up at moments of crisis. Showing up in shared leadership means fundamentally reorienting how we see our leadership. It requires that we release the notion that "this is the type of leader that I am." It requires that we release our ideas of our gifts, talents, skills, accomplishments, hopes, problems, and challenges. It does not mean these things do not exist. It means that we fundamentally change the way we approach the other. Instead of saying, "this is what I can do to fix your problem," we adjust our approach:

What can I do to help? What do you need?

We may have none of the skills, answers, capacity, and energy to address the questions. In shared leadership, having the answer to another's questions, problems, and challenges are not as important to being present to the questions, problems, and challenges. Showing up is not about complimenting the other's deficiencies. It goes back to Patrick's grandma's table or entering the woods with Christina's dad. It is in the sharing of time and space and feeling completely heard, seen, and welcomed.

In moments of crisis, it is challenging not to show up to fix. Because the problems can be overwhelming and the communities we serve are asking for solutions in these moments of crisis, showing up means precisely resisting the temptation to think we have the answer to someone else's troubles. It does not matter what the crisis or problem is. Our presence to the overwhelming crisis and the small moments of despair and pain we each experience is what showing up is about. It does not require special skills or training, as Christina learned from the Johnson's. It is about giving the other sacred presence, to see each other into greater being.

Shared leadership means extending how long you can be present to another's pain. It means giving the gift of time. It means getting to work when asked to get to work. At other times, showing up means slowing down enough to allow the gift of quiet presence to emerge among the many demands of the world. How long can you hold the silence and delight in the other? Showing up is being completely present to the other.

This is a challenging moment to talk about showing up. As a former organizer working for the freedom of his people, farmworkers, and laborers (the essential workers of this moment) and gang-affiliated youth who did not have the same access to opportunities and resources he did, Patrick used to view showing up as getting into the streets, being active, or in his words, "doing the work." That can still be true. And at the same time, we are writing and leading in a time of global health pandemic. We are learning to lead together when the tools and practices to honor and preserve the sacred wisdom of our elders and creating conditions for the next generation are challenged by the global health pandemic. The practices of showing up and being present in the flesh is greatly strained, especially across communities. We are challenged by what showing up looks like when future generations are going to be facing grave environmental challenges. We are trying to find a new way of relating to each other in a moment when Black, Brown, Indigenous, and broader peoples of color are being slain in our streets. How do we reframe what this moment means for our community in a current and future crisis?

Showing up means not just showing up for each other, but for each other's descendants sharing the sacred wisdom of our ancestors. Deuteronomy 6:11–12 reminds us that we live in "houses filled with all sorts of goods that you did not fill, hewn cisterns that you did not hew, vineyards and olive groves that you did not plant–and when you have eaten your fill, take care that you do not forget the Lord, who brought you out of the land of Egypt, out of the house of slavery." People have quoted Rev. Raible's adaptation of this passage, reflecting that we are the beneficiaries of our ancestor's love. However, showing up flips the chronology of this wisdom. Showing up is recognizing that we are elders in practice and ancestors in training. Showing up means planting trees, so that our children's children may find shade, shelter, and sustenance. Showing up means digging wells for future generations to drink from. Showing up means us committing to lighting ancestral fires that will burn across our communities. Showing up is not just about the here and now, but about laying the foundations from which freedom for future generations will build.

It is not easy to show up for each other in this moment of crisis. We wrote at the same time we mourned the loss of family and community members. The kaleidoscope of pain and trauma continued to warp what felt normal. Showing up for shared leadership meant showing up to be present as both of our worlds were upended. Showing up every day did not just help us lead in times of crisis but allowed us to survive and thrive in the inner and outer turmoil it meant to live in this time. Showing up in this moment meant bringing the seeds of generations past and planting together and digging deep wells from our diverse ancestral springs. It meant carrying our sacred fire into the future, together, so that future generations may sit by its warmth.

Conclusion

We want to be clear that we do not think we are creating some novel model of leadership. These are things all humans long for. To have our stories heard, to know our stories and our ancestor's stories. We long to be in relationships where we can name and live our stakes. We want to be supported and give support. We want to show up for each other and have others show up for us. These are not just leadership needs. What we have described are human needs, to be seen, to be loved.

In our work as shared leaders, today, we are focused on leading our teams to support young adults to discern their purpose, passion, and call to be change agents in the world. Vocational discernment of this nature is a lifetime pursuit that we are all engaged in all the time. As leaders, particularly in times of crisis, we know that our own vocational stories are full of people who supported us, showed up for us, and helped to shape who we are and what our stakes are.

Living the joys and challenges of how to discern vocation, discern how to live, lead, and love is the heart of our work. We are accompanying young adults and scholars of color in their own leadership journeys. We are hoping to model a different way of leading that is counter-cultural, but what we all long for. It is a model of leadership that recuperates our stories, doing the repair work from the legacies of colonization and slavery and violence against our communities. We are building a collective narrative of liberation and freedom. We are trying not to build the story of the individual leaders who are called to the hero's journey story. We are not supporting characters in each other's movies. Rather, this is the story of the community building a collective narrative where everyone can thrive. This is a moment where so many traumas have come together. These circumstances have challenged us in our leadership practices and called us to refocus on our purpose of building up and resourcing the next generation of leaders who we need for the long journey ahead. We want to prepare leaders who understand the stakes, who understand that they are called not just to save their own lives but the lives of those with whom they are in relationship with. This includes both in their community and those beyond. Shared leadership in times of crisis is to recognize difference and celebrate a mutual desire for love and freedom. We simply cannot tell that story alone. We know that where two or three are gathered sharing stories, recognizing the stakes for each other, supporting one another, and continuing to show up for the other, there is the divine.

Bibliography

Boyle, Gregory. *Barking to the Choir: The Power of Radical Kinship*. New York: Simon & Schuster, 2018.

brown, adrienne maree. *Emergent Strategy: Shaping Change, Changing Worlds*. Chico, CA: AK, 2017.

Brown, Brené. *Dare to Lead: Brave Work. Tough Conversations. Whole Hearts*. New York: Random House, 2018.

Carnegie, Dale. *How to Win Friends & Influence People*. New York: Pocket, 1998.

Collins, Jim. *Good to Great: Why Some Companies Make the Leap and Others Don't*. New York: Harper Business, 2001.

Cone, James H., and Cornel West. *Black Theology and Black Power*. Anniversary edition. Maryknoll, NY: Orbis, 2019.

Covey, Stephen R. *The 7 Habits of Highly Effective People*. 4th edition. Simon & Schuster, 1920.

Dalio, Ray. *Principles: Life and Work*. New York: Simon & Schuster, 2017.

Garza, Alicia. *The Purpose of Power: How We Come Together When We Fall Apart*. New York: One World, 2020.

Heifetz, Ronald. *Leadership Without Easy Answers*. Cambridge, Mass: Harvard University Press, 1998.

Deloria Jr., Vine, Leslie Silko, and George E. Tinker. *God Is Red: A Native View of Religion, 30th Anniversary Edition*. Golden, CO: Fulcrum, 2003.

Keltner, Dacher. *The Power Paradox: How We Gain and Lose Influence*. Reprint edition. Penguin, 2017.

Lewis, Stephen, Matthew Wesley Williams, and Dori Baker. *Another Way: Living and Leading Change on Purpose*. St. Louis: Chalice, 2020.

Morgan, Angie, Courtney Lynch, Sean Lynch, and Frederick W. Smith. *Spark: How to Lead Yourself and Others to Greater Success*. Reprint edition. Boston: Mariner, 2018.

Myers, Ched. *Binding the Strong Man: A Political Reading of Mark's Story of Jesus*. Anniversary edition. Maryknoll, NY: Orbis, 2008.

Preskill, Stephen, and Stephen D. Brookfield. *Learning as a Way of Leading: Lessons from the Struggle for Social Justice*. San Francisco: Jossey-Bass, 2008.

Senge, Peter M. *The Fifth Discipline: The Art & Practice of The Learning Organization*. New York: Doubleday, 2006.

Sinek, Simon. *Start with Why: How Great Leaders Inspire Everyone to Take Action*. New York: Portfolio, 2011.

Wheatley, Margaret J. *Who Do We Choose To Be?: Facing Reality, Claiming Leadership, Restoring Sanity*. Oakland: Berrett-Koehler, 2017.

9

Religious, Spiritual, and Moral Stress of Religious Leaders in Pandemics

Spiritual Self-care

Carrie Doehring

Introduction

How do religious leaders cope when overwhelmed by the anxiety of coronavirus and its related work, family, and financial struggles? What helps when people feel morally betrayed by politicians who cannot respond to catastrophic crises because they are entangled in bipartisan conflicts? How do religious leaders collectively use outrage as energy for change when Black people are killed by law enforcement officers entrusted with protecting life? How do religious leaders join protests against access to guns in the US, which increase violent death by those who are armed and politically enraged, as well as those whose hopelessness makes suicide the only way out of despair? How do religious leaders lead their communities in searching for meanings during national traumas? What awaits on the horizon, with so many deepening political, health, and climate crises? How can religious leaders come together to preserve life—for humanity and our planet—when people refute the scientific basis for understanding and responding to both our climate crisis and the pandemic?[1] While these intersecting crises are unique to 2020 and 2021, their underlying causes—our interconnected vulnerability to pandemics, systemic racism and enduring colonialism, the climate crisis, ignorance of science, and authoritarian tribalism—shape both present and future survival.

In the deepening gloom of these crises, what helps religious leaders take care of themselves in order to care for world?[2] The acute stressors of living with a pandemic, political betrayal, police violence, and climate crises all carry a sense of life threat. Enduring life threat without relief or support can intensify anxiety, depression, post traumatic symptoms, as well as religious, spiritual, and moral struggles.[3] In this chapter I describe how calming spiritual practices may help religious leaders re-experience a sense of trust connecting them to others and transcendent dimensions of life named through their religious and spiritual practices, beliefs, and values. Spiritual practices and conversations with trusted others may help religious leaders clarify values that enhance spiritual integration.

Why Calming Practices as the Foundation for Spiritual Self-Care?

Human beings, like many species, respond in complex ways to situations perceived as challenging, threatening, and/or beyond their control. The body's response to stress is immediate and pervasive, as detailed on the American Psychological Association's webpage on the physiology of stress.[4] Our autonomic nervous system (ANS) is the physiological 'switchboard' for our responses to stress. Its sympathetic nervous system (SNS) sets off our 'arousal' response when threat or challenge is perceived. The SNS quickly signals the adrenal glands to release hormones—adrenalin (epinephrine) and cortisol—energizing a 'fight or flight' response.

---

1. Bonnie Miller-McLemore raises "a critical question for pastoral theologians: Is hierarchy of 'man over nature' the deadliest binary of all, even a linchpin binary? The planet's imminent demise is not our only woe to be sure. Many issues demand attention today—white supremacy, immigration, women's body rights among the most perverse and pressing. The harm perpetuated by exploitation of the nonhuman world reflects the intersecting consequences of these other challenges and presses upon us with a unique urgency" Miller-McLemore, "Epilogue," 202.

2. I am echoing the title of pastoral theologian Larry Kent Graham, *Care of persons, care of worlds*. Religious leaders today play a key role in sharing lament arising from moral stress (see Graham, *Moral Injury*).

3. Pomerleau et al., "Religious and Spiritual Struggles as a Mediator."

4. https://www.apa.org/helpcenter/stress.

Blood vessels dilate, pumping blood to our large muscles, especially our hearts. Our heart rate increases. Our blood pressure may rise. We may experience rapid breathing and shortness of breath, as the airway between our nose and lungs constricts. Our 'gut' (the gastrointestinal system) may react with feelings of 'butterflies' in our stomach, and sometimes with pain, bloating, and other kinds of gut dysregulation affecting our moods.

The counterpart to the SNS is the parasympathetic nervous system (PNS) that signals a 'stand-at ease' return to pre-crisis functioning for our stress hormones, heartbeat, blood pressure, and breathing. This is the relaxation response that we can activate ourselves with slow, deep breathing or other kinds of relaxation practices. Slow deep breathing calms us by shifting our brains and bodies from a stress response into relaxation. Try this calming practice of slow deep breathing, while focusing on the sensation of air entering your nostrils, your throat, and into the full capacity of your lungs. Feel the sensations of holding the fullness of this breath, then slowing exhaling through your mouth. Next, try adding the pressure and warmth of touch to slow, deep breathing. Place your hand somewhere on your body where you tend to feel your body's stress response. You might place you hand on your chest, cup your hand around your jaw, or place your hand on your shoulder. When you slowly exhale, focus on the warmth and pressure of touch as a way to tangibly feel compassion toward yourself, and others' compassion for you.

Another variation of deep slow breathing is a "box" breath that combines a four-part breathing practice (inhale-hold-exhale-hold) with visualizing drawing four sides of a box. Here is how it works. With your eyes closed, inhale through your nostrils to the count of four while visualizing drawing one side of a square. Hold for four seconds while drawing the second side. Exhale to the count of four, expelling all of the air in your lungs, while visualizing drawing the third side of the square. Rest without breathing to the count of four, while visualizing drawing the fourth side of the square. When I first started using this practice, I found it helpful to "draw" the box with head movements. I lifted my head up in increments while counting to four, then moved my head horizontally, then down to the count of four, and so on. The practice concentrates attention on the sensation of breathing. I sometimes do box breathing while listening to music that is personally meaningful. I adjust the timing of my box breathing to the tempo of the music, taking in the beauty of music with the goodness of breath.

A calming practice such as slow deep breathing interrupts our body's stress response and helps us hold with compassion the emotions that often accompany stress like fear, anger, shame, guilt, or blame.[5] These emotions have a stealth-like quality and can easily overpower us, changing our mood or attitude without our awareness. These stress-generated emotions often propel people into automatic avoidant ways of coping such as snacking, shopping, using addictive substances, or turning to social mediation. The more we use calming practices such as slow deep breathing, the more likely we will notice when something triggers a stress response, its stealth emotions, and automatic ways of coping shaped by consumer culture. With enough practice, we may find that stress prompts us to take a slow deep breath that interrupts stress-based emotions and ways of coping. Space opens up for us to make choices about how to cope. Our compassionate self is now in the driver's seat, instead of the self who feels judged, guilty, angry, or shamed.[6] When we feel the impulse to cope with stress in habitual ways (through consumption and/or avoidance), we are able to surf the impulse until it dissipates.[7]

Making Calming Practices Spiritual

Calming practices may be incorporated into a variety of spiritual self-care practices, helping religious leaders more tangibly experience compassion. What do I mean by spiritual? Spiritual practices making calming

5. These emotions are called negative moral emotions by Jonathan Haidt and others using Moral Foundations Theory. See Haidt, "The Moral Emotions." Rita Nakashima Brock and Zachary Moon note the need for moral emotions like guilt to prompt remorse and justice seeking: "To build a just society, we must understand that the fierce energy of moral injury is grounded in love and empathy that fuel outrage and that cannot make sense of gross moral failure. Psychology has pathologized moral emotions such as guilt, shame, and fury as individual neuroses; however, such feelings can be appropriate, pro-social, collective responses to immorally destructive social and economic systems that deny people the possibility of decent lives and moral choices." Brock and Moon, "Activism Is Moral Injury Gone Viral."

6. "Higher shame, both in ministry situations and in secular situations, was associated with higher negative affect among seminarians and less satisfaction and more emotional exhaustion in ministry among clergy" Crosskey et al., "Role Transgressions, Shame, and Guilt Among Clergy."

7. "Urge surfing is a technique that can be used to avoid acting on any behavior that you want to reduce or stop. Some examples of behaviors may be smoking, overeating, substance use, spending, lashing out at someone, etc." https://med.dartmouth-hitchcock.org/documents/Urge-Surfing.pdf.

practices *relationally life-giving* by connecting people with goodness, beauty, and/or love felt deep within and/or all around them, through relational webs that include transcendence. Spirituality describes "the way individuals seek and express meaning and purpose and the way they experience their connectedness to the moment, to self, to others, to nature and to the significant or sacred."[8] In teaching students how to experiment with intrinsically meaningful calming practices, I echo Lartey and Moon's wisdom of looking beyond what are traditionally considered spiritual and religious practices:

> We *do not* think for a practice to be pastoral and/or spiritual, it must also be corporate or linked to and rooted in a faith community and its traditions. We understand that "religious traditions" are socially constructed or invented European categories, which are constantly changing. "Spiritual" or "pastoral" care should not be circumscribed to "faith" traditions. Such a mindset limits what is considered spiritual or even religious. If by "faith" or belief system, one refers to a broadly understood faith meaning as it was understood in medieval times, then "faith" refers to a concept of trust in someone, not belief in an epistemological sense of higher beings . . . When we limit what is "spiritual" to "faith" traditions, it reinforces Christian hubris: a combination of white Christian superiority as normative, with racism intertwined in those standards of the norm.[9]

Another reason to encourage experimentation in spiritual practices is the risk of feeling judged in simplistic, harsh ways when using traditional or childhood religious and spiritual practices, like reading sacred texts, prayer, and/or participating in communal rituals. Religious struggles with a judging God often include simplistic moral beliefs that we cause our own suffering because we are bad. Feeling bad can be life-giving when there is a collective sense of shared responsibility for wrongdoing.[10] Pandemics, systemic racism, and our environmental crisis are

8. Hirschmann et al., "Spiritual Care of Transgender Persons," 358.

9. Lartey and Moon, "Introduction," 5–6.

10. "When people err, they may respond either with shame (they judge themselves) or with guilt (they judge their action or inaction) (Tangney 1990). Research indicates these reactions are associated with different outcomes. For example, shame is positively associated with depression (Webb et al. 2007), alcohol and drug abuse (Dearing et al. 2005), burnout (Barnard and Curry 2011), and self-rumination (Joireman 2004), whereas guilt is positively associated with social connectedness, hope, and empathic concern (Joireman 2004)." Crosskey et al., "Role Transgressions, Shame, and Guilt Among Clergy," 783–84.

global problems that can only be addressed through shared actions. To what extent does guilt, shame, and blame connect us with compassionate others, with whom we can work for change? This question helps us discern when our emotional response to stress connects us to others or isolates and immobilizes us.

Returning to our "spirituality test," we need to assess whether a practice that we identify as spiritual makes us feel harshly judged or helps us trust in a benevolence.[11] For example, my particular childhood experience of Catholicism makes me often experience God as a harsh, distant, and unloving judge. Personal prayer easily evokes this false god. Collective prayer, on the other hand, invokes a loving God that connects me across centuries with communities of faith who share creedal statements, liturgies, and sacred music. Since childhood, sacred choral music has connected me with a profound sense of spiritual beauty.[12] The test for me of a spiritual practice is whether it connects me with beauty holistically in the ways that sacred choral music does, especially when I sing along with a familiar choral work. By holistic, I mean that I experience that deep and/or transcendent goodness in my very bones and breath, not simply as a cognitive affirmation of what I am "supposed" to believe.

I invite you to find ways to "test" whether a spiritual practice is life-giving. You may want to start from scratch and consider what moments in your daily routine invoke a sense of peacefulness, hope, and/or goodness, perhaps through the beauty of nature or the arts, and a profound sense of feeling at home or at one with others. What happens when you add a slow deep breath to this moment as a way of "anchoring" it in your body? Later in the day if you become aware that you are experiencing a stress response, might a slow deep breath return you to that memory of goodness or beauty?

Spiritually Calming Practices for Chronic Relational Stress

If stress continues over time or becomes chronic, then our body's arousal response is easily triggered and extenuated. It becomes increasingly

11. In a study of COVID-19 and religious coping among American orthodox Jews, Pirutinsky et al. found that "positive religious coping, intrinsic religiosity, and trust in God strongly correlated with less stress and more positive impact, while negative religious coping and mistrust in God correlated with the inverse." Pirutinsky et al., "Covid-19, Mental Health, and Religious Coping among American Orthodox Jews."

12. Doehring, "Searching for Wholeness amidst Traumatic Grief."

difficult to experience relief from stress. Chronic stress causes physiological, emotional, and relational problems. For example, relational conflicts generating chronic stress make people ruminate on arguments and power struggles with their partners, children, or work colleagues. The outburst of relational conflict continues to burn underground. Rumination revs up those fight and flight stress hormones that keep an argument going on within us, long past its initial outbreak, the research of marital conflict demonstrate.[13] Any sort of neutral or even positive interaction with this "problematic" person is likely to be perceived as negative.[14] The conflict that has continued to burn in our ruminations easily ignites above ground. Like chronic stress, chronic relational negativity becomes automatic. For example, faith communities often have members with intense complex needs. They expect their faith communities to be the family they never had. When a community faith leader does meet their expectations, they blame their faith leader for any sort of organizational struggle, such as financial stress, youth group programs not holding onto young adult members, religious education program not attracting enough families with children, etc. Now, this faith leader anticipates that every encounter will be negative. What helps when chronic stress pervades relationships with intimate partners, or members of our families, faith, or work communities?

Insights from marriage counseling are helpful here. Like a wildfire that continues underground, this negativity is difficult to douse, especially when either party has negative childhood experiences reactivated in relational conflicts infused with negativity. Willfully ignoring skyrocketing stress responses is physically and emotionally harmful. Also, ignoring these bodily responses to conflict may well replay other harmful relationships where everyone acted "nice" while conflict raged in various ways, sometimes consuming the "identified patient" designated as the scapegoat.

Often therapy is needed in order to gradually douse fiery negativity. If therapy is not readily available, self-care strategies based on marital interventions could be helpful.[15] The specific strategy I have in mind begins with some slow deep breaths, followed by visualizing your adult self that comes alongside a younger self. Perhaps your adult self has a hand on the shoulder of the younger self. Next, imagine facing off with your adversary. The adult self takes a slow deep breath, prompting the

---

13. Gottman and Gottman, "The Science of Togetherness."

14. Gottman, *What predicts divorce?*

15. Gottman et al., "Negative Sentiment Override in Couples and Families."

younger self to do the same. You might visualize your younger self giving your adult self their pain to hold. This bundle of pain might be like sticks of dry wood, ready to ignite when the adversary sparks a conflict. This image of handing over pain is especially helpful if there is not yet time, energy, or a trusted other available to unpack what makes this adversarial relationship so painful. You might add a spiritual dimension to this image, imagining your pain being held by a loving community and/or by a loving God.

Spiritually Settling Practices for Body Memories of Trauma

A key dynamic of calming practices is a *felt* sense of connection within relational webs of life. Trauma research and therapy uses neuroscience research on responses to life threat to demonstrate the importance of experiencing a felt sense of safety.[16] Fear easily disrupts this sense of trust. People who have experienced overwhelming life events that threaten their lives or their core sense of self may easily re-experience fears from past trauma. Much is now understood about how life-threatening events overwhelm people psychologically and may lead to posttraumatic symptoms when they do not get enough support to integrate the acute stress of life threat into their ongoing lives in healthy emotional and spiritual ways. Spiritually oriented approaches to trauma therapies can help community faith leaders re-experiencing past trauma during a pandemic, civil unrest, or racist violence. Using calming spiritual practices is a key component of trauma spiritual self-care.

Ongoing family and cultural dynamics can pose a pervasive sense of threat and danger that may not stand out as singular memories of trauma. The dynamics of domestic terrorism fueled by toxic masculinity and white supremacy may trigger memories of ongoing family dynamics that, over time, resulted in neglect and/or emotional abuse that was never acknowledged. It is not uncommon for those in caring vocations to have childhood and family roles of feeling/being solely responsible for the wellbeing of others.[17] They may have childhood memories of being

16. In her book *Through Dangerous Terrain: A Guide for Trauma-Sensitive Pastoral Leadership in Times of Threat* Jennifer Baldwin draws upon neuroscience and trauma care therapies (Internal Family Systems, Somatic Experiencing, and Polyvagal Theory) to help community faith leaders practice trauma-informed spiritual care, especially during a pandemic. See also Menakem, *My Grandmother's Hands*.

17. In developing a questionnaire measuring ministry-specific stress and job

overwhelmed by a sense of danger and imminent threat to themselves or others. When parents were neglectful or abusive, children may have felt like they had to pay attention to danger and protect themselves and others. These ongoing family dynamics may result in children developing traumatic responses to any sense of threat to their family's well-being. Children in caregiving roles who become community faith leaders may be attuned to the potential for danger in partner, family, and church family relationships. Their childhood memories of caregiving, easily triggered in their spiritual caregiving roles, may make them helpless, and angry. Often aspects of one's social identity, such as one's gender, sexual and/ or racial identity shape these childhood experiences, and these aspects of self are implicated in adult caregiving roles. For example, one's gender identity as girls or young women may make women feel responsible for their community of faith's well-being. Or a boy's conflicts about how toxic masculinity energizes family neglect or abuse may make boys and young men conflicted about their gender identities and potential to cause harm. Children experiencing struggles with gender and sexual orientations that don't fit family and religious expectations may experience a sense of life threat and despair about feeling "at home" in their bodies, families, and communities of faith. When past family dynamics seem vividly real in the present, religious leaders may experience their childhood orientations to/theologies of family stress (values, beliefs, and ways of coping) as more compelling than their intentional values and beliefs about spiritual care and leadership.

Similar to childhood family dynamics, cultural dynamics of systemic oppression can instill bodily memories of fear that become easily triggered in moments of stress arising from COVID-19, civil unrest, and systemic racism. Resmaa Menakem draws on research in trauma to describe how memories of systemic racism are "stored in our bodies as wordless stories about what is safe and what is dangerous."[18] He describes the skill of "settling one's body" as essential for the work of socially just care:

> If you're white, you may discover that you when you can settle . . . your own body . . . you'll . . . be better able to manage, challenge, and disrupt white-body supremacy. If you're Black . . . you'll be

---

satisfaction, Malcolm et al. noted that some aspects of ministry like preaching and pastoral care are both a source of stress and satisfaction. See Malcolm et al., "Measuring Ministry-Specific Stress and Satisfaction."

18. Menakem, *My Grandmother's Hands*, 5.

better equipped to not internalize the standards of white-body supremacy. You'll also be better able to challenge it through organized and sustained resistance.[19]

Menakem describes a simple settling practice of slowly looking over each shoulder and surveying your surroundings while paying attention to your breathing and how you experience stress in your body. This practice helps community faith leaders become aware of their own bodily memories of overwhelming stress and deepens their awareness of life threat arising from systemic oppressions. Those who have experienced sexual harassment, abuse, or assault may find that settling practices raise awareness of how body memories may be re-awakened to create a sense of pervasive threat and danger. For example, symbols used by the mob who violated the Capitol may remind people of how sexism, racism, and heterosexism justified through religious doctrine or texts was part of past trauma for them. Settling practices invoke a calming adult self who can reassure the childhood self who is hyper aware of danger in their surroundings. When settling practices are combined with calming spiritual practices, community faith leaders will be able to use a momentary settling practice of surveying their surroundings. Regular use of such practices when they begin their day will help them pay attention how they experience stress. While they will not be able to go through the bodily movements of settling during a meeting or spiritual care conversation, they may be able to retrieve a body memory of settling. For example, they may associate settling practices with the sensation of their strong core muscles against the back of a chair, or the flow of energy through a body posture that combines the power of self-agency with receptive power that takes in the mystery of oneself and another.[20]

Settling practices may make community faith leaders more aware of the lasting impact of past experiences of trauma involving ongoing family and cultural dynamics. With such awareness may come grief and rage about innocence lost, and the "holiness" or sanctity of self and/or homes that were violated. Awareness of how adults did not/were not able to protect them may contribute to a sense of betrayal.[21] They may need to

19. Menakem, *My Grandmother's Hands*, 152–53.

20. Doehring uses process theologies to define and describe agential and receptive power in spiritual care relationships. See Chapter 2 in Doehring, *The Practice of Pastoral Care*, 45.

21. Moral injury occurs when people with legitimate power and authority violate what is right in high stakes situations resulting in harm. It is more likely to afflict

seek out trusted others with whom to share lament and process complex grief. Using settling and calming spiritual practices will help them return over and over again to a safe space that holds their lament.

Once people have settling and calming spiritual practices that ground or anchor them in a felt sense of trust, they are less likely to be swept off their feet by stress. Spiritual practices may become a tether to the inherent goodness of one's body, trustworthy others, lament for social injustice, and transcendent interconnections. They help people give voice to the emotional and spiritual pain of suffering without becoming isolated in lament. Trust opens up relational spaces for collaboratively searching for values and meanings that support accountability and foster justice.

Calming and settling practices will help community faith leaders trust the process of lament,[22] and find trusted others who can help them integrate trauma into their ongoing sense of self and vocations as community faith leaders. When community faith leaders find practices for holding stress in self-compassionate and self-transcendent ways, they can then enter into an ongoing integrative process of aligning spiritual beliefs, values, practices, and experiences. For example, community faith leaders can track how they experience stress in their bodies to become aware of stress-based values and beliefs, like being/feeling solely responsible for another's wellbeing. In group sharing and supervision, they can name and explore the familial and cultural origins of these values and beliefs and their inherent moral stress with compassionate support rather than self-judgment, shame, or guilt. They can integrate their intentional values and beliefs about spiritual caregiving (such as interconnected responsibility for protecting life) into calming practices, in order to embody these values and beliefs in the practice of spiritual care. What would this process of spiritual integration look like in practice? Imagine how a religious leader might experience stress at the prospect of talking to a member of their faith community whose strong needs for family cause them to expect their faith community leader to become like a parent to them. The community faith leader takes a deep slow breath and realizes with self-compassion their re-experiencing of the moral stress of being solely responsible for this member's spiritual and emotional wellbeing. Another slow deep

---

people who are idealistic, empathetic, and compassionate and who expect moral behavior of themselves, their societies, and their leaders. Brock and Moon, "Activism Is Moral Injury Gone Viral," 2.

22. In *Moral Injury*, Graham describes a three-part process of sharing anguish, interrogating causes, and reinvesting hope.

breath using words or images with spiritual meanings helps this faith leader embody their intentional values and beliefs about spiritual care. The faith leader is now ready to trust the process of spiritual care, bringing the mystery of who they are to meet the mystery of who the other is. The process of integration is what grounds community faith leaders in their own religious and/or spiritual heritage, identities, and communities, in ways that enhance spiritual differentiation, a core interpersonal competency for community faith leadership and spiritual care.

Spiritual Self-Differentiation

When community faith leaders are attuned to how stress triggers bodily memories, they can use calming spiritual practices to hold their childhood experiences of danger in self-compassion. They may then be able to care for self by separating past memories from present circumstances in a process of spiritual self-differentiation. *Self-differentiation* helps community faith leaders manage relational boundaries in the emotional intensity of intimate, family, and community of faith relationships. Family therapist Murray Bowen [23] describes how families may cope with the stress of power struggles by blurring boundaries between self and others.[24] When self and other become fused, people cannot discern where their "self" ends and the other's self begins. One way of coping with fusion is emotional disengagement or cutoff which, as Schnarch and Regas emphasize, is not the opposite of fusion but an attempt to regulate one's emotions and sense of self.[25] Self-differentiation in intimate/high investment relationships is both an interpersonal process of managing relational boundaries and a psychological process of managing emotions, thoughts, and behaviors. Those in professional helping relationships learn how to *psychologically* self-differentiate in order to maintain healthy boundaries. Community faith leaders draw upon their knowledge of faith traditions in order to be *spiritually* self-differentiated.[26] They are able to separate their beliefs and values about suffering from another's beliefs and values, in order practice

23. Bowen, *Family Therapy in Clinical Practice.*

24. In "The Crucible Differentiation Scale" Schnarch and Regas trace this history of how self-differentiation was first described by Bowen.

25. Schnarch and Regas, "The Crucible Differentiation Scale," 642.

26. In "Practicing Socially Just, Interreligious, and Evidence-Based Spiritual Care" Doehring and Kestenbaum describe self-differentiation as one of three interpersonal competencies for spiritual caregivers.

spiritual empathy—an interpersonal capacity to imagine how another experiences stress and stress-related emotions that generate their orientation to suffering.[27]

How to Have Spiritual Self-Care Conversations about Moral Stress

I have developed steps for having spiritual care conversations about COVID-19 stress in spiritual care courses and workshops for community faith leaders and frontline health care professionals. As a prelude to such conversations, I lead people in a simple mindfulness practice of slow deep breathing that (1) focuses on the sensations of air entering our bodies, being held, and then exhaled, (2) adds the sensation of touch by placing our hands on our chest or over our heart, and then (3) adds words (e.g., from a sacred text), or an image or memory that connects us with a sense of transcendent goodness. I describe the steps below for having a spiritual care conversation that focuses on a source of COVID-19 stress for one of us. Students/participants will use these steps in spiritual care conversations with each other.

1. Identify a source of COVID-19 stress. How do you experience stress in your body?

2. Let's try using a calming practice of deep slow breathing, while placing a hand over our chest or heart. Close your eyes if you wish or look down. Breath in slowly, hold for a few seconds, exhale slowly and rest for a few seconds. Let's do that again and pay attention to the warmth of touch. How does your body feel now?

3. Looking back at your experience of COVID-19 stress, what emotions go with that stress? Let's take another slow deep breath and hold those COVID-19 emotions in compassion.

4. Is there a value that gives you a sense of purpose when you experience your particular COVID-19 stress (e.g., caring for self in order to care for others; protecting life; do no harm)?

5. Concluding with words of thanks for their sharing.

27. Doehring has used the term theological empathy to describe imagining another's lived theology or theological orientation to a particular stressor. See Doehring, "Teaching Theological Empathy." Doehring and Kestenbaum use the term spiritual self-differentiation in similar ways, in "Practicing Socially Just, Interreligious, and Evidence-Based Spiritual Care."

Before beginning the conversation, those in the spiritual caregiver role can be reminded of their two roles of (1) guiding the conversation and (2) listening without interruptions. In their guiding role, they will need to have the conversational guide available for easy reference. After each conversational invitation, they will shift into their listening role, using their own calming practices to simply follow the care receiver, and resist urges to share aspects of their own story or give advice in order to solve problems.

An Illustration

When invited to talk about a source of coronavirus stress, I describe how fearful I was early on in the pandemic that my 93-year-old mother living alone in Montreal would die of COVID-19. I panicked when I saw a photo of two ambulance attendants in full protective gear pushing a stretcher with someone encased in what seemed to be a plastic bubble. I could easily imagine my mother struggling for breath in a bubble that isolated her. With my heart pounding, I'd email my sisters and confer about how to protect our mother. After many family Zoom calls, we devised ways to help her stay in her own place without being too isolated.

Taking slow deep breaths when I felt overwhelmed with fear about protecting my mother didn't lessen what felt like the grim inevitability that she would become sick.[28] Over time, slow deep breathing helped me name my anxiety as love. Instead of judging myself for "over-reacting" or my mother for being "oppositional" to our efforts to protect her, I valued the love that made me want to protect my mother and reach out to my siblings. Slow deep breathing also helped me not script COVID-19 conflicts in terms of my age-old conflicts with my mother. New ways of being in relationship with our mother opened up for me and my sisters and brother. We learned how to hold our anxiety together and to appreciate the various talents we each brought to the challenges of caring from afar, especially when the border to Canada closed for me and my brother living in the US. Taking slow deep breaths helped me focus on many sources of thanksgiving and the goodness of caring together.

---

28. "Fear experiences during the COVID-19 pandemic are organized on the psychological level around four interrelated dialectical domains, namely (1) fear of the body/fear for the body, (2) fear of significant others/fear for significant others, (3) fear of not knowing/fear of knowing, and (4) fear of taking action/fear of inaction. These domains represent the bodily, interpersonal, cognitive, and behavioral features of fear, respectively." Schimmenti et al., "The Four Horsemen of Fear."

I have been experimenting with using slow deep breathing while I listen to sacred choral music, which has always been the most tangible and transcendent way I experience goodness. Listening to music in early morning hours of writing, and watching the sun rise on the mountains and downtown Denver buildings ground me in goodness. Sometimes when I meditate, I visualize aspen trees golden against an early snowfall in the mountains. Aspen trees have a root system that makes them a single organism.

> A grove of quaking aspens in Utah is the largest known living thing on Earth. Nearly 50,000 stems protrude from a single root system. The entire organism covers over 100 acres and weighs 6,000 tons! When trees that are a part of these large clones die, they are eventually replaced with new growth. Therefore, while one stem has a relatively short lifespan, the entire clone can live for tens of thousands of years! Quaking aspen clones are virtually impossible to kill. Individual stems can be destroyed by humans, wildlife, and disease, but the below ground root system is resistant to almost all of these factors![29]

Visualizing myself as an aspen clone makes me imagine that my deep breathing connects me with the living breathing organism of the human race, bearing the suffering of this pandemic together. I sometimes use the phrase, "I am because we are"[30] when I visualize an aspen grove.

This spiritual practice reveals an interconnected sense of responsibility for protecting life. This complex value illumines the childhood experience of feeling solely responsible for protecting life—that it was all up to me. I can see how that the panic set off by COVID-19 stress is tied to this childhood experience. I realize that I can easily get stuck in "old" conflicts generating negativity.

The value of interconnected responsibility for protecting life emerges when I use spiritual practices and talk about this source of coronavirus stress. This generative value extends beyond family care. I realize that protecting life means confronting white supremacy and systemic racism, and the destruction wrought from climate crises. I also can appreciate more complex beliefs about tragedies, like COVID deaths, as well as tragic deaths of family members for which I felt responsible, even though

29. https://www.nwf.org/Wildlife/Wildlife-Library/Plants/Quaking-Aspen.aspx.

30. Larry Kent Graham uses this aphorism from African philosophy and religion to explore how African and Native American perspectives challenge the individualism of the West. Graham, *Moral injury*, 20–24.

I know "in my head" that the causes of death were complex. Sharing interconnected responsibility for protecting life in a pandemic has helped me reframe my past tragic experiences of death. I can know in my heart this more complex sense of tragedy. I also see how daily ways of protecting life, like wearing a mask, getting tested when I might have been exposed, and participating in a vaccine trial are all part of this collective protection of life. I can also see how much my social privileges of a job and an affordable home, working from home, being a citizen, and having health care have made it so much easier for me to protect life than for those without these privileges.

How Spiritual Care Helps

If our participants are learning how to practice spiritual care in academic courses or clinical settings, I highlight the ways that these spiritual care conversations are different from psychological care. Students often have a hard time understanding these differences because they so rarely see examples of spiritual care conversations[31] and often have not experienced for themselves the differences between receiving spiritual and psychological help. I highlight two major differences between spiritual and psychological care. One has to do with trust, the other with contracts of care. Making these distinctions before embarking on spiritual care conversations about COVID-19 stress helps people understand their role as listeners.

Research on how psychotherapy helps people demonstrates that the quality of the relationship between therapist and client is a big factor. The stronger the 'alliance' between therapist and client, the more likely clients will experience positive outcomes from therapy (e.g., symptom reduction). The therapeutic alliance is called the "working relationship," which describes how much therapists and clients are able to collaborate.[32] A related factor in how therapy helps is the contract of care which guides the process of therapy. At the very outset, a basic contract of care outlines

31. There are few portrayals of community faith leaders having spiritual care conversations in movies or fiction. I have found examples of white male Protestant pastors in these films: *You can count on me, Italian for Beginners, First Reformed.* The Chaplaincy Innovation Lab is creating teaching modules with videos of spiritual care conversations that can be used for teaching.

32. Baier et al. evaluated 37 research studies examining the alliance as a potential mediator of symptom change and found that "alliance mediated therapeutic outcomes in 70.3% of the studies." Baier et al., "Therapeutic Alliance as a Mediator of Change."

the limits of confidentiality, length of sessions, cancellation policies and fees, and the therapist's availability between sessions. During the initial session/s of therapy, therapists explore with clients what their "presenting" problem is: why they are seeking help. Therapists then describe how therapy could help, with details about what kinds of therapeutic models/strategies they use. They may add details about research on their therapeutic approach (for example, cognitive behavioral therapy). Clients at this stage often are assessing the extent to which they trust (1) this therapist, and (2) the process of change offered by the therapist. The working alliance depends upon whether clients trust their therapist and the process of change: "The alliance [is] a collaborative relationship between therapist and patient that is influenced by the extent to which there is agreement on treatment goals, a defined set of therapeutic tasks or processes to achieve the stated goals, and the formation of a positive emotional bond."[33]

How are spiritual care alliances the same as/different from psychotherapy? One way to describe these similarities and differences in trust is the added dimension of spiritual trust in spiritual care relationships, a term described by Doehring and Kestenbaum:

> Spiritual care, then, helps people experience *spiritual trust* that goes beyond the caregiving relationship to include spiritual dimensions of relationality. Spiritual trust is named in many ways: for example, as an immanent ground of being and a transcendent oneness with creation. What is common across diverse ways of experiencing and describing spiritual trust is a felt sense of spiritual interconnectedness beyond oneself. Spiritual trust helps people collaborate with community faith leaders, chaplains, and spiritual mentors in searching for values and beliefs.[34]

The second major difference between psychotherapy and spiritual care is that the contract of care is usually implicit. There is no initial contract detailing limits of confidentiality, length and frequency of spiritual care conversations, and the faith leader/chaplain's availability. There is no negotiated contract of how spiritual care could help. The community faith leader and the care receiver each have their own often unstated or unexamined values and beliefs about whether/how spiritual care might help. Here is the most common implicit understanding of how spiritual

---

33. Baier et al., "Therapeutic Alliance as a Mediator of Change," 101920.

34. Doehring and Kestenbaum, "Introduction to Interpersonal Competencies."

care helps: spiritual care helps people search for meanings—beliefs about suffering and values that make life purposeful, especially when people are overwhelmed by stress or suffering. Spiritual care within their own traditions/communities of faith helps people draw upon shared beliefs, values, and spiritual practices in this meaning-making process.[35] Many community faith leaders do their graduate theological studies in seminary degree programs within their faith traditions. They often learn to use a guiding style of spiritual care that helps people understand their suffering through the beliefs and rituals of their traditions. A common often unaddressed problem is that many people, and indeed faith community leaders, experience religious, spiritual, and moral struggles when overwhelmed by suffering. Struggles may arise from experiencing God and/or faith community leaders as judging them, and/or questioning beliefs about suffering or conflicts in values that heighten moral stress about causing harm. When people can share such struggles within their communities of faith without being judged or shunned, then transitory struggles will often deepen spiritual trust in their communities of faith. They will trust an ongoing collaborative process of spiritually integrating their struggles while co-creating a coherent orientation to suffering that includes trust in the goodness/benevolence of God and/or humanity and differentiated meanings that are flexible and integrated.[36] When spiritual struggles elicit shame and fear of judgment, struggles may become chronic, with negative spiritual, psychological, and relational outcomes.[37]

I describe spiritual care as a two-part process.[38] Spiritual care begins with exploring calming spiritual practices, helping people experience spiritual trust. When spiritual practices help people feel held within compassionate and trustworthy relationships, they will be ready to explore what their suffering means, which is the second way that spiritual care helps. Returning to the conversational steps outlined above, readers can see how the first phase of spiritual care is represented in questions about calming practices. The second phase begins when people reflect

---

35. Community faith leaders need to be cautious about making assumptions that members of their communities share core beliefs. More and more of the younger generation describe themselves as religious multiple or spiritually fluid, terms described by Bidwell, *When one religion isn't enough*.

36. Hart et al., "Predictors of Self-Reported Growth Following Religious and Spiritual Struggles."

37. Pomerleau et al., "Religious and Spiritual Struggles as a Mediator."

38. Doehring, *The Practice of Pastoral Care*.

on how core values about COVID-19 stress are clarified when they use calming practices; that is, when they are no longer fear-driven by COVID-19 stress responses. I focus the conversation on core values rather than beliefs because values are usually more immediately relevant in acute crises that generate moral stress because of conflicting values (e.g., care of self/family vs. care of patients/community faith members). Research on moral psychology demonstrates that stress-based emotions generate moral intuitions that shape the ways people respond to stress. Jonathan Haidt uses the metaphor of riding an elephant to describe how emotions (the elephant) carry our cognitive selves, generating moral intutions about acute stress grounded in five or six moral foundations shared across cultures.[39] Using calming practices helps people slow down a runaway emotional, morally intuitive response to stress, opening up space for understanding how stress-generated values may be life giving or life limiting in their current circumstances. Clarifying values helps people navigate a crisis. In contrast, sorting out beliefs about suffering is more often part of the long-term process of meaning-making that unfolds when people are able to cope with stress. Often when people state beliefs in moments of stress, they are describing how their emotional response to stress shapes their relational experience of God, humanity, and creation. For example, if they experience shame or guilt, God may be experienced as judge. Anxiety may generate anxious attachments to God or others. If they are angry, they may blame God/others. If they are simply overwhelmed and helpless they may express a fatalism and/or surrender/deferring to God (e.g., the 12-step adage to "Let go and let God") and "the Fates" (e.g., "So be it"). During a crisis, community faith leaders will want to pay attention to what these beliefs say about a care receiver's sense of spiritual trust. It is often premature to focus on how beliefs fit together into a coherent whole.

When students/spiritual care practitioners understand this two-phase process of spiritual care they will be able to experience how spiritual trust provides the relational foundation for spiritual care. They may be able to somatically and relationally experience a felt sense of spiritual trust as they move through the first steps in the spiritual care conversation, and how this trust opens up an intersubjective space for exploring values. When students understand the phases of spiritual care, they will

39. Haidt, *The Righteous Mind.*

be able to use the steps in spiritual care conversations about COVID-19 to experience the process of care somatically, emotionally, and relationally.

How Spiritual Practices and Conversations are Spiritually Integrative

Finding calming spiritual practices that connect us with others and with God, or however we name transcendent realities, helps us identify and unpack sources of COVID-19 stress. Often when I participate in spiritual care conversations focused on me, I feel as though I have found my way back onto a path of spiritual integration that has unfolded throughout my life. Spiritual integration is a collaborative and relational process of using spiritual practices for holding stress compassionately, finding purpose through values, and understanding and being appropriately accountable for suffering in a variety of ways unique to persons, families, and communities. Spiritual integration is "the extent to which spiritual beliefs, practices, and experiences are organized into a coherent whole."[40] Spiritual integration necessarily includes a reckoning with one's participation in social oppression and suffering because all relationships and interactions are embedded in intersecting social systems that enhance or undermine justice, compassion, and healing of persons, families, communities, and organizations.

Practicing spiritual care conversations about COVID-19 stress may help community faith leaders re-experience covenantal promises to be faithful made along the way of their formational process of becoming ordained or endorsed. Faith community leaders continually *practice with others*. They are not solo virtuosos. Spiritual care conversations about COVID-19 stress are like being in a musical ensemble or acting troupe. Each person integrates knowledge with interpersonal skills and capacities (e.g., to improvise and attune with others) into the ensemble/drama. Often this commitment to practicing spiritual care imbues many aspects of one's life with a sense of purpose, ongoing lament for suffering, and longing for hope. Many faith community leaders listen for the "music" of spiritual care in ordinary conversations and the drama of human life portrayed in media stories, literature, and the arts. They move back and forth between receptive and agential power[41] in interactions where they may in one

---

40. Pargament et al., "Spirituality: A Pathway to Posttraumatic Growth or Decline?"

41. This process philosophical/theological way of describing power has been elaborated by Larry Kent Graham, James Poling, Carrie Doehring, and others.

moment receive spiritual care and in the next initiate spiritual care interactions with others. This commitment to the formational, covenantal process of spiritual care may at times feel like one is always "on duty," which can become overwhelming when the moral stress of bearing witness to suffering feels like a lonely vigil. Spiritual self-care helps community faith leaders feel held in their covenantal relationships. Sharing moral stress helps us bear it together, as Larry Kent Graham wisely counseled.[42]

Bibliography

Baldwin, Jennifer. *Sensing Sacred: Exploring the Human Senses in Practical Theology and Pastoral Care*. Lanham, MD: Lexington, 2016.

Bidwell, Duane R. *When One Religion Isn't Enough: The Lives of Spiritually Fluid People*. Boston: Beacon, 2018.

Brok, Rita Nakashima and Zachary Moon. "Activism Is Moral Injury Gone Viral." 2020, https://medium.com/@rita_brockVOA/when-moral-injury-goes-viral-5f22b983e726.

Crosskey, Laura Barnard, John F. Curry, and Mark R. Leary. "Role Transgressions, Shame, and Guilt among Clergy." *Pastoral Psychology* 64, no. 6 (2015): 783–801.

Doehring, Carrie. *The Practice of Pastoral Care: A Postmodern Approach*. Revised and expanded ed. Louisville: Westminster John Knox, 2015.

———. "Searching for Wholeness Amidst Traumatic Grief: The Role of Spiritual Practices That Reveal Compassion in Embodied, Relational, and Transcendent Ways." *Pastoral Psychology* 68, no. 3 (2019): 241–59.

Doehring, Carrie, and Allison Kestenbaum. "Introduction to Interpersonal Competencies." In *Introduction to Chaplaincy and Spiritual Care*, edited by Shelly Rambo and Wendy Cadge. Chapel Hill: University of North Carolina Press, in press.

———. "Practicing Socially Just, Interreligious, and Evidence-Based Spiritual Care." In *Introduction to Chaplaincy and Spiritual Care*, edited by Shelly Rambo and Wendy Cadge. Chapel Hill: University of North Carolina Press, In press.

Ettman, Catherine K., Salma M. Abdalla, Gregory H. Cohen, Laura Sampson, Patrick M. Vivier, and Sandro Galea. "Prevalence of Depression Symptoms in US Adults before and During the Covid-19 Pandemic." *JAMA Network Open* 3, no. 9 (2020): 2019686–2019686.

Gottman, John M. *What Predicts Divorce? The Relationship between Marital Processes and Marital Outcomes*. Hillsdale: Lawrence Erlbaum Associates, 1994.

Gottman, John M., Carrie Cole, and Donald L. Cole. "Negative Sentiment Override in Couples and Families." In *Encyclopedia of Couple and Family Therapy*, edited by Jay Lebow, Anthony L. Chambers and Douglas C. Breunlin, 2019–2022. Cham, Switzerland: Springer International, 2019.

Gottman, John M., and Julie Gottman. "The Science of Togetherness." *Psychotherapy Networker* 41, no. 5 (2017): 43–59.

---

42. Graham, *Moral Injury*.

Graham, Larry Kent. *Care of Persons, Care of Worlds: A Psychosystems Approach to Pastoral Care and Counseling*. Nashville: Abingdon, 1992.

———. *Moral Injury: Restoring Wounded Souls*. Nashville: Abingdon, 2017.

Haidt, Jonathan. "The Moral Emotions." In *Handbook of Affective Sciences*, edited by Richard J. Davidson, Klaus R. Scherer and H. Hill Goldsmith. Series in Affective Science, 852–70. New York: Oxford University Press, 2003.

———. *The Righteous Mind: Why Good People Are Divided by Politics and Religion*. New York: Pantheon/Random House, 2012.

Hart, Allison C., Kenneth I. Pargament, Joshua B. Grubbs, Julie J. Exline, and Joshua A. Wilt. "Predictors of Self-Reported Growth Following Religious and Spiritual Struggles: Exploring the Role of Wholeness." *Religions* 11, no. 9 (2020): 445.

Hirschmann, Jo, Emilee Walker-Cornetta, and Susan Jelinek. "Spiritual Care of Transgender Persons." In *Transgender Medicine: A Multidisciplinary Approach*, edited by Leonid Poretsky and Wylie C. Hembree, 357–76. Cham, Switzerland: Springer International, 2019.

Kwok, Pui-lan, and Stephen Burns. *Postcolonial Practice of Ministry, Leadership, Liturgy, and Interfaith Engagement*. Lanham: Lexington, 2016.

Lartey, Emmanuel, and Hellena Moon. "Introduction." In *Postcolonial Images of Spiritual Care: Challenges of Care in a Neoliberal Age*, edited by Emmanuel Lartey and Hellena Moon, 1–14. 1–14. Eugene: Wipf and Stock, 2020.

Malcolm, Wanda M., Karen L. Coetzee, and Elizabeth Fisher. "Measuring Ministry-Specific Stress and Satisfaction: The Psychometric Properties of the Positive and Negative Aspects Inventories." *Journal of Psychology & Theology* 47, no. 4 (2019): 312–27.

Miller-McLemore, Bonnie. "Epilogue: Beyond 'Classic Readings' in Pastoral Theology." In *Postcolonial Images of Spiritual Care: Challenges of Care in a Neoliberal Age*, edited by Emmanuel Lartey and Hellena Moon, 190–202. Eugene: Wipf and Stock, 2020.

Pirutinsky, Steven, Aaron D. Cherniak, and David H. Rosmarin. "Covid-19, Mental Health, and Religious Coping among American Orthodox Jews." *Journal of Religion and Health* (2020).

Pomerleau, Julie M., Kenneth I. Pargament, Neal Krause, Gail Ironson, and Peter Hill. "Religious and Spiritual Struggles as a Mediator of the Link between Stressful Life Events and Psychological Adjustment in a Nationwide Sample." *Psychology of Religion and Spirituality* 12, no. 4 (2020): 451–59.

Schimmenti, Adriano, Joël Billieux, and Vladan Starcevic. "The Four Horsemen of Fear: An Integrated Model of Understanding Fear Experiences during the Covid-19 Pandemic." *Clinical Neuropsychiatry: Journal of Treatment Evaluation* 17, no. 2 (2020): 41–45.

Schnarch, David, and Susan Regas. "The Crucible Differentiation Scale: Assessing Differentiation in Human Relationships." *Journal of Marital and Family Therapy* 38, no. 4 (2012): 639–52.

CPSIA information can be obtained
at www.ICGtesting.com
Printed in the USA
LVHW081424300922
729611LV00003B/339